'OUT OF EGYPT'
THE EXODUS MOTIF IN THE BIBLICAL TRADITION

'OUT OF EGYPT'
THE EXODUS MOTIF
IN THE BIBLICAL TRADITION

FAITH ELIZABETH LUND

CHEROHALA PRESS
CLEVELAND, TENNESSEE USA

'Out of Egypt'
The Exodus Motif in the Biblical Tradition

Published by Cherohala Press
An Imprint of CPT Press
900 Walker ST NE
Cleveland, TN 37311
USA
email: cptpress@pentecostaltheology.org
website: www.cptpress.com

ISBN-13: 9781953358028

Original cover art, 'Let My People Go', ink on papyrus, by Lee Roy Martin

To my parents, my inspiration;
and Danny, my support

CONTENTS

PREFACE

Several years ago, I was in a doctoral class on biblical theology with Dr Dale Brueggemann at the Assemblies of God Theological Seminary. He asked each student to write a paper tracing the development of a biblical motif, and my Exodus journey began! I was captivated by the rich tapestry of Exodus themes and imagery throughout the Bible. The more I investigated, the more I realized that forty pages could never do justice to the topic. I went on to use it as the focus for my dissertation, of which this is a revision.

Further down the road, I began to grasp the massive scope of the project I had undertaken. The volume of texts that echo the Exodus, along with the existing literature pertaining to them, imposed constraints on how thoroughly I could cover each section. This was not my only challenge. Any attempt at biblical theology must grapple with the issues of organization, unity and diversity, and the relationship between the Testaments. In what order should I treat books? Should I appropriate the same outline for each chapter? Exactly how forward and backward looking were the biblical authors? More pressingly, how would I not project my agenda onto the text? (After all, if you put on Exodus-colored glasses, you will find the Exodus!)

As I forged my less-than-perfect path, I decided not to force a template onto every section. The OT books varied considerably in their approaches, and the Gospel writers' typological hermeneutics were distinct from both one another and from the other NT writers. The length of the Gospels also presented a challenge, so I opted to analyze their Introductions and select parts and summarize broader narrative trends. Throughout, I attempted to respect the diversity of the authors' hermeneutics and still showcase how their complementary perspectives added progressive complexity and depth to an overall unifying plot.[1] Like individual pieces of a stained-glass window, the

---

[1] William J. Dumbrell, *The End of the Beginning: Revelation 21-22 and the Old Testament* (Eugene, OR: Wipf & Stock, 2001), p. i. Dumbrell comments that the Bible moves and grows 'according to a common purpose and towards a common goal'. The successive development includes both historical and canonical progression. This study will mostly treat books in canonical order, examining canonical theological

variegated viewpoints and emphases more fully express their artistry in panorama.

Originally, I did not intend to devote so much attention to the development of the motif in the OT. I had underestimated its frequency and diversity, and the OT is not my area of expertise. However, as I delved into the different parts of the canon, I found the study both indispensable and enriching. I was more than happy to make room for more conversation partners, although my trek through the OT more resembles a sketch than a completed drawing. Looking back, I believe that my NT research would have been shallow and one-dimensional without this first section.

With regard to the relationship between the Testaments, I defer to Richard Hays, who argues compellingly for a spiral of reading *forwards* and reading *backwards*.[2] Our post-resurrection eyes must inform our reading of the OT, and we must go back to the OT in order to interpret the New. The Exodus is no exception. From early in Israel's history, the Exodus offered God's people words and symbols to describe new situations (as a motif), provided a framework by which to understand other acts of deliverance or judgment (as a paradigm), and was itself invested by God with eschatological expectation and forward-looking elements (as a type). It had forward momentum, but its transcendent significance can only be fully appreciated in retrospect. We who view events in the OT in light of their fulfillment are like the audience of a drama who knows how the play will end. Understanding the plot, we are able to 'recognize and appreciate the subtlety of the dramatic irony by which the divine dramatist had made every stage of the action prefigure ... the final *denouement*'.[3]

Finally, I am further indebted to Hays for his seven tests for hearing echoes of Scripture: availability, volume, recurrence, thematic coherence, historical plausibility, history of interpretation, and satis-

---

development, while attempting to maintain an awareness of the historical chronology of events and the order in which books may have been written. Moreover, the primary object of study will be the final canonical form of the books, and I will assume traditional conservative views of authorship.

[2] Richard Hays, *Reading Backwards: Figural Christology and the Fourfold Gospel Witness* (Waco, TX: Baylor University Press, Kindle edn, 2014).

[3] G.W.H. Lampe, 'The Reasonableness of Typology', in by G.W.H. Lampe and K.J. Woollcombe, *Essays on Typology* (SBT; London, 1957), p. 10.

faction.[4] These offered some guidance in the inevitably subjective and imprecise enterprise of discerning intertextuality. Naturally, each reader will find some occurrences compelling and others a stretch of the imagination.

> Now the God of peace, who brought up from the dead the great Shepherd of the sheep through the blood of the eternal covenant, even Jesus our Lord, equip you in every good thing to do His will, working in us that which is pleasing in His sight, through Jesus Christ, to whom be the glory forever and ever. Amen (Heb. 13.20-21).

Faith Elizabeth Lund
Xi'an, China
August 2019

---

[4] Richard B. Hays, *Echoes of Scripture in the Letters of Paul* (New Haven, CT: Yale University Press, 1989), pp. 29-32.

ACKNOWLEDGMENTS

My work is indebted to the support and sacrifice of many others. Above all, I am grateful to God, who 'daily bears our burdens' (Ps. 68.19). His grace is sufficient, and His power is perfected in my weakness (2 Cor. 12.9). In addition, my parents, Quentin and Elizabeth McGhee, instilled in me the value of education and piqued my interest in theology. Danny, my husband, listened tirelessly to my musings as I wrote. He planned countless outings with the kids so that I could have quiet study time. He went grocery shopping and washed dishes with a servant's heart. He and our kids, Caleb and Viola, were content with many less-than-gourmet dinners and with 3-person games. I would also like to thank Dr James Hernando, my dissertation advisor, whose thoughtful comments added focus, depth, and clarity to my writing. Rick Oliver and the library staff at AGTS helped track down all kinds of resources to which I had no access in Asia. I appreciate the assistance of Dr Lee Roy Martin, with whom I have previously collaborated (*A Future for Holiness: Pentecostal Explorations* [Cleveland, TN: CPT Press, 2014]). Finally, I am grateful to Cherohala Press for undertaking the publication of my work.

LIST OF TABLES

ABBREVIATIONS

ABD	David N. Freedman (ed.), *The Anchor Bible Dictionary* (6 vols.; New York, Doubleday, 1992).
AUSS	*Andrews University Seminary Studies*
BAGD	Walter Bauer, W.F. Arndt, F.W. Gingrich, and Frederick W. Danker, *A Greek–English Lexicon of the New Testament and Other Early Christian Literature* (Chicago: University of Chicago Press, 2nd edn, 1958).
Bib	*Biblica*
BK	*Bibel und Kirche*
BSac	*Bibliotheca Sacra*
BZ	*Biblische Zeitschrift*
CBQ	*Catholic Biblical Quarterly*
CBR	*Currents in Biblical Research*
CTM	*Concordia Theological Monthly*
ExpTim	*Expository Times*
EvQ	*Evangelical Quarterly*
HBT	*Horizons in Biblical Theology*
HZ	*Historische Zeitschrift*
ICC	International Critical Commentary
IDB	*The Interpreter's Dictionary of the Bible*
Int	*Interpretation*
JBL	*Journal of Biblical Literature*
JETS	*Journal of the Evangelical Theological Society*
JPT	*Journal of Pentecostal Theology*
JR	*Journal of Religion*
JSNT	*Journal for the Study of the New Testament*
JSOT	*Journal for the Study of the Old Testament*
JSNTSup	Journal for the Study of the New Testament Supplement Series
JSS	*Journal of Semitic Studies*
NASB	New American Standard Bible
NICNT	New International Commentary on the New Testament

NICOT	New International Commentary on the Old Testament
NIGTC	The New International Greek Testament Commentary
NIV	New International Version
NovT	*Novum Testamentum*
NovTSup	*Novum Testamentum,* Supplements
OTL	Old Testament Library
RB	*Revue Biblique*
RevExp	*Review and Expositor*
RevScRel	*Revue des sciences religieuses*
RTL	*Revue théologique de Louvain*
SBL	*Society of Biblical Literature*
SBLASP	SBL Abstracts and Seminar Papers
SBLDS	SBL Dissertation Series
SBLMS	SBL Monograph Series
SBT	*Studies in Biblical Theology*
SJT	*Scottish Journal of Theology*
SNTSMS	Society for New Testament Studies Monograph Series
STDJ	*Studies on the Texts of the Desert of Judah*
Str–B	[Hermann L. Strack and] Paul Billerbeck, *Kommentar zum Neuen Testament aus Talmud und Midrasch* (7 vols.; Munich: Beck, 1922–1961).
TS	*Theological Studies*
TynBul	*Tyndale Bulletin*
UNT	Untersuchungen zum Neuen Testament
VT	*Vetus Testamentum*
VTSup	Supplements to Vetus Testamentum
WBC	Word Biblical Commentary
WTJ	Westminster Theological Journal
WUNT	Wissenschaftliche Untersuchungen zum Neuen Testament
ZAW	*Zeitschrift für die alttestamentliche Wissenschaft*

1

INTRODUCTION

> Who is like You among the gods, O YHWH? Who is like You, majestic in holiness, awesome in praises, working wonders? In Your lovingkindness You have led the people whom You have redeemed; in Your strength You have guided them to Your holy habitation.[1]
>
> – Exod. 15.11, 13

The Exodus stands out as the definitive act of redemption in Israel's early history. Just as NT theology looks back to the cross, OT theology looks back to the crossing of the Red Sea.[2] The Bible mentions and alludes to this signal event in diverse genres and contexts, and its influence spans both historical and theological domains. The Exodus serves as a vehicle of God's self-revelation that exercises decisive and lasting influence on the way God's covenant people conceived of him; it is a paradigm[3] that embodies lasting truth about God's plans and

---

[1] Unless otherwise noted, all Scripture is taken from the New American Standard Bible (NASB) Copyright © 1995, The Lockman Foundation. In some texts, 'LORD' will be replaced with 'YHWH', and uppercase letters in the middle of sentences may be replaced with lowercase ones.

[2] Lit., 'Sea of Reeds'. Yair Hoffman observes that the Exodus is mentioned about 120 times in 'stories, laws, poems, psalms, historiographical writings and prophecies'. Yair Hoffman, 'A North Israelite Typological Myth and a Judaean Historical Tradition: The Exodus in Hosea and Amos', *VT* 39.2 (April 1989), pp. 169-82 (170).

[3] In this monologue, *paradigm* will refer to a pattern, model, framework, or lens used to analyze, understand, or classify another event or idea. Throughout biblical history, 'prophets and historians, sages and psalmists' looked at what God had done in the past and 'insisted that it could be and was repeated' (Francis Foulkes, *The Acts of God* [London: Tyndale Press, 1966], p. 345). The Exodus was one example of this phenomenon: the narrative itself became a mold or prototype for describing other moments (Walter Brueggemann, *Reverberations of Faith: A Theological Handbook of Old*

activities and a type[4] that looks forward by divine intention to a greater event in redemptive history; and it is a fundamental and fruitful lens for biblical theology. It is a bright and recurrent thread woven into the Scriptures, and its events are never far from the minds of biblical authors and readers.[5]

Study of the Exodus as a *motif* includes all references and allusions to it in the Bible, aside from straightforward historical reiterations.[6] This approach emphasizes the motif's repetition and development as well as its effects on the audience, since 'such symbolism and imagery powerfully convey a sense of evocative and emotive force'.[7] Israel had a strong tradition of remembering and retracing her history; thus a small allusion – a word, a symbol, or a metaphor – could function synechdochically to evoke implicitly an entire narrative.[8] Being deeply 'embedded as a fundamental structure of the biblical historical imagination', the Exodus contained a tremendous capacity simultaneously to 'elicit memory and expectation, recollection and anticipation'.[9] With the Exodus motif, authors imparted hope by transferring the power of emotion from the original Exodus to the similar situation in history

---

Testament Themes [Louisville, KY: Westminster / John Knox Press, 2002], p. 72). No other story is taken up by the biblical authors and recast as the framework for salvation and judgment with the frequency or to the extent of the Exodus.

[4] I will use the word *type* to designate a person, institution, or event in Scripture that prefigures and corresponds historically to a subsequent and greater complement (an *antitype*). See Daniel J. Treier, 'Typology', in Kevin J. Vanhoozer (ed.), *Dictionary for Theological Interpretation of the Bible* (Grand Rapids: Baker Academic, 2005), pp. 823-27; E.E. Ellis, *The Old Testament in Early Christianity* (Grand Rapids: Baker Academic, 1991), p. 106.

[5] Richard D. Patterson and Michael Travers, 'Contours of the Exodus Motif in Jesus' Earthly Ministry', *WTJ* 66.1 (Spring 2004), pp. 25-47 (47).

[6] In this study, *motif* refers to a recurring image or verbal pattern within a piece of literature. Motifs support thematic development, contain symbolic value, and connect disparate events or moments. Authors creatively weave in motifs to 'evoke psychological or emotional resonance with the audience' through the associative power of metaphor' (Emmanuel Yun-wing Hung, 'Relationship and Rebirth: A Literary Study of the Exodus Motif in Jeremiah' [PhD dissertation, Westminster Theological Seminary, 2001], pp. 20, 38-39, 224).

[7] Jan A. du Rand and Young M. Song, 'The Story of the Red Sea as a Theological Framework of Interpretation', *Verbum et Ecclesia* 30.2 (2009), pp. 94-98 (98).

[8] N.T. Wright, *Paul: In Fresh Perspective* (Philadelphia: Fortress Press, 2009), p. 9. Closely related to this is *metalepsis* or *transumption*, whereby an author uses literary echo to link a text with an earlier text to amplify their implicit resonance. Richard Hays notes that metalepsis 'places the reader within a field of whispered or unstated correspondences'. Hays, *Echoes of Scripture in the Letters of Paul*, p. 20.

[9] Michael Fishbane, *Biblical Text and Texture: A Literary Reading of Selected Texts* (Oxford: Oneworld Publications, 1998), p. 140.

from which people needed salvation.[10] As with a fugue, different voices interpreted the theme 'at different pitch, with a different timbre and at a different volume', maintaining an underlying unity while offering unique variations.[11]

Relevance of the Study

Scholars have devoted much research to examining the development and importance of the Exodus motif throughout Scripture. [12] Regarding the motif as a whole, there are dissertations and scholarly articles specifically analyzing its presence throughout the OT, especially in Judges, 1 Kings, Isaiah, Jeremiah, and Ezekiel. Likewise, significant research on the Exodus motif in the NT attests to its consequence and appeal. There is focused scholarly research on the Exodus motif in Mark, Luke-Acts, and John; Romans, First Corinthians, and Galatians; Hebrews and First Peter; and most prominently, Revelation. In addition to these studies on specific biblical books, there are broader investigations that explore the paradigmatic significance of the Exodus [13] and its influence on

---

[10] Leland Ryken, James C. Wilhoit, and Tremper Longman III (eds.), 'Exodus, Second Exodus', *Dictionary of Biblical Imagery* (Downers Grove, IL: InterVarsity Press, 1998), p. 253.

[11] Bas van Iersel, Antonius Weiler, and Marcus Lefébure (eds.), *Exodus–A Lasting Paradigm* (Concilium, Religion in the Eighties 189; Edinburgh: T. & T. Clark, 1987), p. xvi.

[12] As the Exodus was understood in a paradigmatic way and the motif expanded, it became intertwined with expectations of similar activity, sometimes referred to as the 'Second Exodus' or 'New Exodus'. This is broadly included in the phrase 'Exodus motif'.

[13] Iersel, Weiler, and Lefébure (eds.), *Exodus–A Lasting Paradigm*; David Daube, *The Exodus Pattern in the Bible* (All Souls Studies 2; London: Faber & Faber, 1963); Friedbert Ninow, *Indicators of Typology Within the Old Testament: The Exodus Motif* (Friedensauer Schriftenreihe; Bern: Peter Lang, 2001). Two more recent monographs partially cover the motif. The first is *Echoes of Exodus: Tracing Themes of Redemption through Scripture*, by Alastair Roberts and Andrew Wilson (Wheaton, IL: Crossway, 2018). This brief book is written more for a pastoral than an academic audience and assumes more of a systematic/thematic approach than a biblical theology approach. (For example, the authors treat all of the Gospels together and have a chapter called 'Paul's Gospel' that covers everything from Romans to Jude.) The second is *Echoes of Exodus: Tracing a Biblical Motif*, by Bryan D. Estelle (Downers Grove, IL: IVP Academic, 2018). This book is scholarly and methodologically sound. However, although the book is close to 600 pages long, the author still presents an incomplete survey of the Exodus motif. For example, he skips from Genesis to Psalms, only examines Isaiah 40–55 (and no minor prophets), and completely neglects books such

hermeneutics and theology.[14] The works of prominent biblical scholars such as N.T. Wright, G.K. Beale, Brevard Childs, Ben Ollenburger, Elmer Martens, and William Dumbrell demonstrate how Exodus themes are central to the Bible's storyline and serve as important intra-biblical bridges.[15]

However, the narrow scope or limited depth of these studies has resulted in an assortment of rich but fragmented analyses of the Exodus motif that fails to convey its enduring prominence, consistent development, and profound significance for biblical theology. It is important for research to be done that unites the existing studies into one expansive canonical framework that explores the common motifs that are prevalent in them. Moreover, many of these studies examine the motif in secondary or partial ways (e.g. the New Exodus motif of Isaiah 40–55 in John 5–10) and dichotomize the original Exodus and later New Exodus developments.[16] The diverse agendas and perspectives of the authors do not engender a swift or readily apparent unity; the relevant data need to be woven together within a cohesive structure. Finally, while scholars have carefully considered the Exodus background of some books or passages of the Bible, the unmistakable Exodus allusions that are embedded in others have gone largely unnoticed or are mentioned only in passing. These gaps make it

---

as John and Hebrews that are replete with Exodus typology and literary allusions. In addition, Estelle does not cover the prominence of the Exodus as an ironic paradigm of judgment in both Testaments. He seems more focused on soteriology than on laying out a biblical theology.

[14] Patterson and Travers, 'Contours of the Exodus Motif'; Richard J. Clifford, 'The Exodus in the Christian Bible: The Case for "Figural" Reading', *TS* 63 (2002), pp. 345-61; Otto Alfred Piper, 'Unchanging Promises: Exodus in the New Testament', *Int* 11.1 (January 1957), pp. 3-22. Countless others chronicle the development of separate themes from the Exodus through the Bible or touch on the Exodus in relation to a larger theological agenda.

[15] N.T. Wright, *Jesus and the Victory of God*, vol. 2, Christian Origins and the Question of God (Philadelphia: Fortress Press, 1997); N.T. Wright, 'The Lord's Prayer as a Paradigm of Christian Prayer', http://ntwrightpage.com/Wright_Christian_Prayer.htm, accessed 29 January 2014; G.K. Beale, *A New Testament Biblical Theology: The Unfolding of the Old Testament in the New* (Grand Rapids: Baker Academic, Kindle edn, 2011); Brevard S. Childs, *The Book of Exodus: A Critical, Theological Commentary* (OTL; Louisville, KY: Westminster/John Knox Press, Kindle edn, 2004); Ben C. Ollenburger, *Old Testament Theology: Flowering and Future* (Winona Lake, IN: Eisenbrauns, 2004); Elmer A. Martens, *Plot and Purpose in the Old Testament* (Leicester: Inter-Varsity Press, 1981); Dumbrell, *The End of the Beginning*.

[16] Paul S. Coxon, *Exploring the New Exodus in John: A Biblical Theological Investigation of John Chapters 5–10* (Eugene, OR: Resource Publications, 2015).

difficult to grasp the full extent and consequence of the Exodus in Scripture. All of these factors demonstrate the need for a more integrated analysis of the Exodus motif.

Other developments point to the timeliness and exigency of studying the progression and theological implications of the Exodus motif in Scripture. In the recent past, it would have met with currents that produced an inhospitable academic environment: a rigid division of the testaments, strict historical inquiry and a rejection of theological presuppositions, reductionism via the imposition of one overarching theme or *Mitte* ('center'), a hermeneutical tendency toward atomization, a polarized stance on unity and diversity (even an assumed theological discontinuity), inattentiveness to literary concerns, and the denial of canonical coherence.[17] However, there has been a resurgence of biblical theology that embraces whole-Bible and intentionally canonical context, diachronic development, chastised typology, explicitly theological interpretation, increased literary sensitivity, multi-thematic richness within an overarching storyline, and dialectical tension between unity and diversity.[18] A comprehensive, canonical study of the Exodus motif will showcase the confluence of these positive trends.

Focus

In light of these factors, this book aims to provide a panoramic view of how the Exodus motif is recapitulated and consummated in the NT. It will primarily address the question, 'How do the authors of the

---

[17] See James Barr, *The Concept of Biblical Theology: An Old Testament Perspective* (Minneapolis: Augsburg–Fortress, 1999); Krister Stendahl, 'Contemporary Biblical Theology', in George A. Buttrick (ed.), *IDB* (Nashville: Abingdon Press, 1962); see also John Sandys-Wunsch and Laurence Eldredge, 'J.P. Gabler and the Distinction between Biblical and Dogmatic Theology: Translation, Commentary, and Discussion of His Originality', *SJT* 33.2 (1980), pp. 133-58.

[18] See Gerhard Hasel, *Old Testament Theology: Basic Issues in the Current Debate* (Grand Rapids: Eerdmans, 4th edn, 1991); Brevard S. Childs, *Biblical Theology of the Old and New Testaments: Theological Reflection on the Christian Bible* (Minneapolis: Augsburg–Fortress, 2011); Francis Watson, *Text and Truth: Redefining Biblical Theology* (Grand Rapids: Eerdmans, 2009); Geerhardus Vos, *Biblical Theology: Old and New Testaments* (Edinburgh: Banner of Truth, rev. edn, 1975); Brian S. Rosner *et al.* (eds.), *New Dictionary of Biblical Theology: Exploring the Unity & Diversity of Scripture* (Downers Grove, IL: InterVarsity Press, 2000); Kevin J. Vanhoozer (ed.), *Dictionary for Theological Interpretation of the Bible* (Grand Rapids: Baker Academic, 2005).

NT individually and corporately appropriate Exodus/New Exodus
components in literary and typological ways to communicate truth
about God's redemptive plan for His creation through Christ?'

Components of the Exodus Motif and Method
of Inquiry

In order to identify the Exodus motif in later passages, it is first
necessary to define its core components and its conceptual and
linguistic markers. Broadly, it includes all of the events from the
oppression of the people of Israel to their instruction when they
were about to enter the promised land (the interplay among God,
Moses and Aaron, and Pharaoh; the ritual of the Passover; the
departure from Egypt; the crossing of the Red Sea/Sea of Reeds; the
defeat of the Egyptians; the giving of the Law at Mt. Sinai; and the
wilderness wanderings) as well as numerous discrete, forward-
looking elements (e.g. the provision of manna, water from the rock,
the bronze serpent, rest or inheritance, the tabernacle, and the figure
of Moses).[19] Its main storyline is the deliverance of Israel from
bondage to be God's special people. Israel is not only set free from
slavery, but ransomed by YHWH from the destroying angel by the
blood of the Passover lamb to be his own possession.[20] As it makes
its way through the OT, the motif becomes intertwined with
additional New Exodus expectations, such as the coming of the
Servant of YHWH and the Branch of David.

The following table identifies important linguistic and conceptual
markers of this motif:

---

[19] For a concise theological discussion of the components of the Exodus, see
Rita Burns, 'The Book of Exodus', in *Exodus – a Lasting Paradigm* (Edinburgh: T. &
T. Clark, 1987), pp. 11-21; James T. Dennison Jr., 'The Exodus: Historical Narrative,
Prophetic Hope, Gospel Fulfillment', *Presbyterion* 8.2 (September 1982), pp. 1-12 (1-
5). Arlis Ehlen notes three key 'theological consequences' related to the Exodus:
Israel's special relationship with God, the gift of the land, and the covenant
obligations. Arlis John Ehlen, 'Deliverance at the Sea: Diversity and Unity in a Biblical
Theme', *CTM* 44.3 (May 1973), pp. 168-91 (168-69).
[20] Daube, *Exodus Pattern*, pp. 42-46. Daube notes that redemption was the right
of possession and notes the use of גאל ('to redeem') in Exod. 6.6; YHWH is acting
as kinsman-redeemer. See also Dennison Jr., 'The Exodus', p. 2.

Verbs	Groan, labor, hear, lead, carry, shepherd, bring (up) out (of Egypt), smite, strike, go up, plunder, swallow, be king over, worship, deliver, ransom, redeem, pass over, serve, crave, rebel, wander, tempt/test, dwell, sojourn, intercede, stand before God, bring into the land, give rest
Names/titles	Moses, Aaron, Sinai, Horeb, Hebrews, sons of Israel, Egypt, Pharaoh, YHWH, YHWH your God, Red Sea/Sea of Reeds, Branch of David, Servant
Nouns & concepts	Oppression/bondage, bitter, affliction, groaning, yoke, deliverance, killing male children, son, sonship, plagues/judgments, miracles, signs, wonders, firstborn, death of firstborn, the Passover, lamb, blood, redemption, atonement, yeast, unleavened bread, bitter herbs, sea, the deep, horses, chariots, water, manna, rock, desert, wilderness, tabernacle/temple, altar, glory, (dark) cloud, pillar, fire, thunder, law, covenant, mediator, mercy, temptation, forty, rebellion, idolatry, murmuring, inheritance, rest, foreigner/alien, slave, few, numerous, fruitful, judge, victory, defeat
Phrases	Ten plagues, 'my people', mountain of God, mighty deeds, signs and wonders, mighty hand and outstretched arm, the glory of YHWH, water from the rock, streams in the desert, road/highway in the wilderness, golden calf, shining face, forty years, forty days/nights, dividing waters, mighty waters, being 'lifted up', 'flowing with milk and honey', 'be fruitful and multiply', 'fill the earth/land', 'I will dwell with/among you', 'You will be my people, and I will be your God', 'my own possession', kingdom of priests, holy nation, 'then you/they will know that I am YHWH'
Metaphors	Riding on eagle's wings (Exod. 19.4), God as a warrior (Exod. 15.3), being filled with God's bounty (Deut. 29.12), Egypt as an iron-smelting furnace (Deut. 4.20), Israel as God's son/firstborn (Exod. 4.22), manna as bread of heaven (Exod. 16.4)

Table 1: Linguistic/Conceptual Signals of the Exodus Motif

A cluster of these markers, or their use in certain (and especially parallel) contexts beyond straightforward historical reiteration, indicates to a competent and sensitive reader that the author intended to allude to or evoke the events of the Exodus for a theological purpose. Therefore, a careful and methodical analysis of the biblical authors' uses of these signals to link their writing with scriptural antecedents, both in discrete passages and in their works as a whole, will comprise the primary method of inquiry for the study. This will involve understanding the background, meaning and implications, and development of the motif in each significant context that contains terminological and/or conceptual parallels (including antitypes) as well as evaluating the appropriation of the motif in entire biblical books and groups of books.

The Exodus and Israel's Worldview

Finally, understanding the profound influence of the Exodus on Israel's worldview helps establish the basis for its use as a motif throughout Scripture. As David Tracy observes, 'The history of Jewish thought and Jewish existence as the people of the Covenant is the history of the memory and life of the event and texts of Exodus'.[21] The Exodus is not only fundamental to Israel's self-understanding, but is also the 'the cornerstone of the biblical perceptions of YHWH, Israel's God'[22] and is woven into the fabric of Israel's laws, liturgy, and social practices.

The Exodus and Israel's Self-Understanding

The Exodus and Israel are bound together inextricably. This great event provides more than deliverance and the hope of promises fulfilled; it gives birth to the nation of Israel and shapes her worldview.[23] First, Scripture shows that the Exodus is an integral part of Israel's national identity and occupies a prime place in her narrative. When Jacob entered Egypt, his family comprised about seventy direct (male) descendants (Gen. 46.26-27). They entered as sojourners, seeking refuge from a devastating famine. God had directed them to Egypt and promised to be with them (Gen. 46.3-4) but had also foretold that Abraham's descendants would certainly be strangers and slaves in a foreign land for four hundred years (Gen. 15.13). God had promised that after this time, he would judge the nation whom they were serving, and they would come out with many possessions (Gen. 15.14).

---

[21] David Tracy, 'Exodus: Theological Reflection', in Bas van Iersel, Anton Weiler, and Marcus Lefébure (eds.), *Exodus: A Lasting Paradigm* (Concilium: Religion in the Eighties 189; Edinburgh: T. & T. Clark, 1987), p. 118.

[22] Lee Roy Martin, 'Where Are All His Wonders?'': The Exodus Motif in the Book of Judges', *Journal of Biblical & Pneumatological Research* 2 (2010), pp. 87-109 (87).

[23] For a discussion about the historicity of the Exodus, see Appendix A: The Exodus as a Historical Event.

During their time in Egypt, the Israelites suffered and were oppressed, but in accordance with his promise, God made them into a great nation there (Gen. 46.3).[24] Moses brought the long-awaited word that God had seen the affliction of his people and given heed to their cry; he had come down to deliver them from the power of the Egyptians and bring them into the land of promise (Exod. 3.7-8). After a glorious display of YHWH's judgment on Israel's enemies, through plagues and later the defeat at the Red Sea, Israel emerged out of Egypt a nation of six hundred thousand men (Exod. 12.37).[25] She left as a victorious warrior, with the plunder of Egypt, flocks and herds, and a very large number of livestock (Exod. 12.36-38). She left with excitement and hope, amid public demonstrations of God's power and favor.[26]

This was a turning point in Israel's history. Before this time, God's people looked forward to the fulfillment of his promises – but this was 'the time of the promise' (Acts 7.17). They could see the actualization of their long-cherished hope. Now, they would look not only forward, but backward to this great deliverance, the subsequent constituting of

---

[24] John Howard Yoder offers a reminder, largely in response to Liberation Theology, that Israel's identity and relationship to God were already in formation during their stay in Goshen; 'peoplehood is the presupposition, not the product of Exodus'. John Howard Yoder, 'Exodus and Exile: The Two Faces of Liberation', *Cross Currents* 23.3 (Fall 1973), pp. 297-309 (342). Conversely, scholars like R.E. Nixon focus on the decisive and transformative nature of the event in Israel's history – calling it the true beginning of Israel's story and the founding of Israel as a self-conscious community. R.E. Nixon, *Exodus in the New Testament* (London: Tyndale Press, 1963), p. 5.

[25] For a compelling explanation of the plagues as humiliation of Egypt's gods, see R.E. Watts, 'Exodus', Brian S. Rosner *et al.* (eds.), *New Dictionary of Biblical Theology: Exploring the Unity & Diversity of Scripture* (Downers Grove, IL: IVP Academic, 2000), p. 479. For a discussion of how the language of the plagues foreshadows the defeat of the Egyptians at the Red Sea, see Terence E. Fretheim, 'The Plagues as Ecological Signs of Historical Disaster', *JBL* 110.3 (September 1991), pp. 385-96.

[26] The language here looks back to the creation mandate to be fruitful, fill the earth, and subdue it (Gen. 1.28). In addition, the language in the Red Sea crossing of darkness and light, divided waters, wind, and the appearance of dry land 'mark this as a moment of new creation'. Watts, 'Exodus', p. 480; Fretheim, 'The Plagues as Ecological Signs of Historical Disaster', p. 392; See also Blenkinsopp, 'Scope and Depth', pp. 47-48. For a discussion of the application of the creation motif to the crossing of the Red Sea in other biblical texts, see Ehlen, 'Deliverance at the Sea', pp. 175-80. For further study of how Israel's experience is cast in the pattern of and filled with echoes of the story of Adam and Eve in Eden, see David VanDrunen, 'Israel's Recapitulation of Adam's Probation under the Law of Moses', *The Westminster Theological Journal* 73.2 (September 2011), pp. 303-24.

the nation, and the confirmation of their unique covenant bond with
YHWH (Exod. 19.3-7; Deut. 7.7; 8.3, 12-18; 9.6).[27] They would have
the tabernacle among them as a symbol of God's royal presence.[28]
They would make known to each new generation the story of what
God had done at the Exodus (Exod. 12.8, 14; Deut. 6.20), and when
they recounted their story, they bore witness to the significance of this
event to their identity.[29]

The Exodus and Israel's Understanding of YHWH

In addition, God's self-revelation during the events surrounding the
Exodus exercised decisive and lasting influence on how God's people
conceived of him. God purposed that his people would associate his
name and his nature with this mighty act of deliverance. In Exodus 6,
God told Moses that God did not reveal himself by his name, YHWH,
to the fathers – they knew him as 'El Shaddai' – the God who promised
them a land when they were still sojourners.[30] But Moses was to deliver
this message from God to the people, bracketed at beginning and end
with the proclamation of his name:

---

[27] Ninow, *Indicators of Typology*, p. 98. Matthew Pearce also comments that
YHWH's salvation and judgment for Israel substantiate his self-revelation as the one
true God. Furthermore, Pearce sees the Exodus as '*the* event which establishes and
defines Israel's very existence and relationship before Yahweh'. Matthew Alan Pearce,
'The Redemptive Function and Theological Meaning of Matthew's Citation of
Hosea 11.1' (PhD dissertation, The Southern Baptist Theological Seminary, 2008),
pp. 99, 102.

[28] Scott Hahn notes how an intertextual reading of Genesis 1 and Exodus 25–40
sheds light on the 'close connection between sabbath, creation, covenant, and the
dwelling that Israel is instructed to build'. Hahn, 'Worship in the Word', p. 109. He
interprets Moses' time on the mountain in light of the creation motif (with parallels
such as the cloud of divine presence, divine blueprint for the dwelling, a series of
seven commands concluding with ordinances for the Sabbath in Exod. 31.12-17, the
making of the priestly vestments done in seven stages, and refrains such as blessing
the work and finishing work). Furthermore, he shows how the creation themes of
'man as made for worship in a covenant relationship as God's royal and priestly
firstborn' are made explicit in Exodus (Adam made in God's image/Israel as God's
own people; Adam made to worship/people liberated to worship; Israel as a
'kingdom of priests and a holy nation' [p. 110]). These ties strengthen as the Exodus
motif is developed and brought to fulfillment.

[29] This is evident in speeches and prayers as well as messages from God to the
people of Israel (e.g. Samuel's speech in 1 Sam. 1.8; David's prayer in 1 Chron. 17.21;
Stephen's speech in Acts 7.2-53; Paul's speech in Pisidian Antioch in Acts 13.16-41;
and God's accounting of his dealings with Israel throughout the prophetic books,
such as Ezek. 20.10-26; Amos 2.10; Mic. 6.4; and Hag. 2.5).

[30] Childs, *The Book of Exodus*, p. 115.

I am YHWH, and I will bring you out from under the burdens of the Egyptians, and I will deliver you from their bondage. I will also redeem you with an outstretched arm and with great judgments. Then I will take you for My people, and I will be your God; and you shall know that I am YHWH your God, who brought you out from under the burdens of the Egyptians (Exod. 6.6-7).[31]

Now God reveals himself as YHWH, who remembers his covenant and acts to fulfill his promises. From this point forward, his people would identify him by this name. Israel's God is the one who would deliver her from bondage, redeem her, take her for his own possession, and fulfill the promises he made to her patriarchs.[32] *This God* is YHWH.[33] After the Exodus, the answer to questions such as, 'Which God are you talking about?' or 'What is characteristic of this God?' naturally becomes 'YHWH, our God, who brought us out of the land

---

[31] The emphatic expression in v. 8, 'I YHWH', shows that 'the work of Israel's redemption resided in the power of the name'. Carl Friedrich Keil and Franz Julius Delitzsch, *Commentary on the Old Testament* (Grand Rapids, MI: Eerdmans, 1988), p. 468. As Childs contends, the content of this message is only an 'explication of the name itself and contains the essence of God's purpose with Israel' (promised deliverance, adoption as God's covenant people, and the gift of land). Childs, *The Book of Exodus*, p. 115.

[32] The language of the Pentateuch bears out this conceptual shift in God's self-disclosure and how his people identify him. In Genesis, for example, God is primarily described as אלהי אבותכם ('God of your fathers', used about twenty times). By contrast, in Exodus–Deuteronomy, we find אלהי העברים ('God of the Hebrews') or אלהי ישראל ('God of Israel', used ten times), יהוה אלהיכם ('YHWH your God', used more than one hundred times), and יהוה אלהיך אשר הוצאתיך מארץ מצרים ('YHWH your God, who brought you out of the land of Egypt', used about twenty times). Roland Beaudet also notes this: *'Dieu ne sera plus seulement le « Dieu d'Abraham, d'Isaac, et de Jacob » (Exod 3 15) mais bien Yahvé qui « nous a fait sortir du pays d'Égypt, de la maison de servitude » (Exod 13 14)',* ('God is now not only the "God of Abraham, of Isaac, and of Jacob," but *Yahweh* who "brought you up out of Egypt, out of the land of slavery"'). Roland Beaudet, 'La typologie de l'Exode dans le Second-Isaïe', *Etudes Théologiques: Tricentennaire du Seminaire de Quebec* (Quebec: Les Presses de l'Université Laval, 1963), p. 11.

[33] James Reynolds observes that to the Israelites, the meaning of the name *YHWH* was not found in its linguistic background or translation, but in the events of the Exodus. 'The Exodus gave content to the name of Yahweh and in turn determined the nature of Israel's response in faith and practice.' James Ellis Reynolds, 'A Comparative Study of the Exodus Motif in the Epistle to the Hebrews' (ThD dissertation, Southwestern Baptist Theological Seminary, 1976), pp. 15-16. Watts adds, from a slightly different perspective, that the Israelites' identity was not grounded in their independence and liberty but, as God's son, in YHWH's presence with them and their worship of and loyalty to him. Watts, 'Exodus', p. 479.

of Egypt'. YHWH is known by what he has done.[34] He is the God of deliverance and redemption; the God of covenant and lovingkindness. His name would henceforth be a prayer on their lips and a promise when spoken by YHWH. In the mind of Israel, YHWH and the Exodus go hand in hand.

The Exodus and Israel's Laws and Traditions

Finally, the Exodus was pivotal to Israel's laws and traditions. 'I am YHWH your God, who brought you out of Egypt' undergirded, for example, the giving of the Decalogue and Israel's covenant with YHWH (e.g. Exod. 19.4-6; 20.1-3; Deut. 5.6); it was the main historical warrant for their covenant bond.[35] Furthermore, the Exodus had far-reaching effects, from Israel's food laws to her social relationships.[36] In Lev. 11.45, it provided the justification for distinguishing clean from unclean foods: 'For I am YHWH who brought you up from the land of Egypt to be your God; thus you shall be holy, for I am holy.' In Lev. 19.33-36, it was the basis for loving foreigners, treating them with justice, and having ethical business practices (e.g. just weights). In Lev. 25.35-42, it regulated the treatment of poor Israelites (not exacting interest from them; providing food and housing; and not treating them as slaves). Here, it also explained the release of slaves during the year of Jubilee: they should return to their families and reclaim the land of

---

[34] Other Scriptures reinforce this integral link, e.g. Josh. 24.17: 'For YHWH our God is He who brought us and our fathers up out of the land of Egypt'; Ezek. 20.9: 'I made myself known to them by bringing them out of the land of Egypt'. See Craig Bartholomew *et al.*, *Out of Egypt: Biblical Theology and Biblical Interpretation* (Grand Rapids: Zondervan, 2006), p. 127.

[35] Hendel, 'The Exodus in Biblical Memory', p. 601. Kitchen shows that it also recurs in instances of covenant renewal (e.g. Josh. 24.5-7; Judg. 2.1-3; 1 Sam. 10.18-19; 1 Kgs 8.51-53; Hos. 12.9-10; Amos. 2.10-11). K.A. Kitchen, 'Exodus, The', in David Noel Freedman *et al.* (eds.), *ABD* (New York: Doubleday, 1992), p. 701. Christophe Dohmen observes that the Exodus ordered the Israelite's ethical and spiritual life and consisted of an outward movement as well as an inner orientation toward the commandments of God and a being-on-the-way mentality. Christoph Dohmen, 'Exodus: Einem zentralen biblischen Motiv auf der Spur', *BK* 62 (2007), pp. 206-209 (207). Watts notes that in accepting the covenant bond, God's son Israel renounces the autonomy that Adam and Eve sought in Eden. As the people of Israel keep the commandments, they will be recreated in the image of God their father. Watts, 'Exodus', pp. 480-81.

[36] Th. C. Vriezen comments that YHWH's reminder, 'I am YHWH your God, who brought you up out of the land of Egypt', undergirds the 'whole body of Israelite law, both cultic and moral'. Th. C. Vriezen, *An Outline of Old Testament Theology* (Oxford: Basil Blackwell, 2nd edn, 1970), p. 193. As cited in Pearce, 'Redemptive Function', p. 103.

their fathers, 'For they are My servants whom I brought out from the land of Egypt' (Lev. 25.42). The Israelites are not even to abhor the Egyptian (Deut. 23.7).[37]

The Exodus also pervaded Israel's liturgy and traditions. Her New Year, sabbath, and most of her yearly feasts commemorated the Exodus.[38] The calendar was re-ordered so that the month of deliverance would be the beginning of the year (Exod. 12.2). In Deuteronomy, YHWH exhorted Israel to observe the sabbath as a holy day, remembering, 'you were a slave in the land of Egypt, and YHWH your God brought you out of there by a mighty hand and by an outstretched arm; therefore YHWH your God commanded you to observe the sabbath day' (Deut. 5.15).[39] Every year, the Israelites celebrated the Passover and the Feast of Unleavened Bread as a 'permanent ordinance', continually remembering how God spared the Israelites from the death of the firstborn and delivered them from slavery Egypt (Exod. 12.1-20).[40] They were required to redeem the firstborn of their sons and of all of their animals (Num. 18.15-19), and God set apart the Levites for himself in place of the firstborn of Israel (Num. 3.11-13; 8.15-18). During the Feast of Tabernacles/Booths, all native-born Israelites were required to live in tents for 7 days 'so that your generations may know that I had the sons of Israel live in booths when I brought them out from the land of Egypt. I am YHWH your God' (Lev. 23.43). The Feast of Weeks, when the people rejoiced in the harvest of the land, likewise called to mind the fact that Israel was in slavery in Egypt: 'You shall remember that

---

[37] Watts, 'Exodus', p. 482.

[38] Reynolds, 'Comparative Study', p. 20.

[39] See Hui, 'The Purpose of Israel's Annual Feasts', p. 150; Foulkes, *The Acts of God*, p. 352.

[40] Interestingly, this provided an opportunity for each generation to 'relive common history'. Foulkes, *The Acts of God*, p. 352. The historical distance of the Exodus was continually drawn into the present, as fathers told their children, 'It is because of what Yahweh did *for me* when He brought me out of Egypt' (Exod. 13.8; cf. Deut. 6.20-25, ital. mine). In light of Exod. 13.8, the Mishnah says, 'In every generation a person is duty-bound to regard himself as if he has personally gone forth from Egypt'. Jacob Neusner, *The Mishnah: A New Translation* (New Haven: Yale University Press, 1988), p. 250. See also Pinchas Lapide, 'Exodus in the Jewish Tradition', in Bas van Iersel, Anton Weiler, and Marcus Lefébure (eds.), *Exodus: A Lasting Paradigm* (Concilium: Religion in the Eighties 189; Edinburgh: T. & T. Clark, 1987), p. 49.

you were a slave in Egypt, and you shall be careful to observe these statutes' (Deut. 16.12).[41]

All of these demonstrate the unparalleled importance of the Exodus to the people of Israel. The Exodus was prominently and permanently embedded in their history, their understanding of God, their laws, their ethics and social practices, their celebrations and holy days – practically every area of their lives. It is understandable, then, how it came to represent the foundation for their hope of future deliverance and gave shape to their expectations of how their God would act.

Overview of Chapter Contents

Chapter 2 will survey the OT journey of the Exodus motif through the Law, the Prophets, and the Writings. An analysis of the motif's continued presence throughout the OT, its paradigmatic character, its developmental contours, its theological purposes, and its eschatological expectation will provide a framework for understanding its expansion and consummation in the NT.

Chapters 3–6 will constitute the heart of the study, exploring the development of the Exodus motif in sections of NT books (the Gospels and Acts, Pauline Epistles, Hebrews and the General Epistles, and Revelation). This process will involve observing the selected verbal and conceptual indicators of the motif, examining the overarching emphases of each book, and analyzing current scholarly literature to determine where the motif is present in significant ways and how it contributes to each author's theological agenda. Finally, the Conclusion will provide an overview of the recapitulation and consummation of the Exodus motif in the NT and expound on its implications.

---

[41] According to Jewish tradition, this feast (Weeks/Pentecost) also commemorates the giving of the Law at Mt. Sinai, although this is not explicit in the biblical text. See J. Davis, 'Acts 2 and the Old Testament: The Pentecost Event in Light of Sinai, Babel and the Table of Nations', *Criswell Theological Review* 7.1 (2009), pp. 29-48; Moshe Weinfeld, 'Pentecost as Festival of the Giving of the Law', *Immanuel* 8 (1978), pp. 7-18.

2

THE EXODUS MOTIF IN THE OLD TESTAMENT

Introduction

The OT is replete with references and allusions to the Exodus, as God's people remembered their history, found comfort and hope in the past, prayed for God's continued deliverance and guidance, instructed a new generation, spoke words of prophetic warning and admonition, and praised God for his faithfulness and power.[1] Many of these instances are infused with typological anticipation. Even as writers recall the great works of God in the past, they do so to provide a platform for faith in God's future acts of salvation.[2] Moreover, 'the Prophets foretell events to come as the recovery as what has passed'.[3] As Fishbane notes, each generation 'looked to the first exodus as the archetypal expression of its own future hope'.[4] Thus OT authors often shaped their expectation of coming deliverance according to the pattern of the historical Exodus under

---

[1] Patterson and Travers, 'Contours of the Exodus Motif'.

[2] Jean Daniélou describes this movement as history's becoming 'at the same time both commemorative and prophetic'. Jean Daniélou, *From Shadows to Reality: Studies in the Biblical Typology of the Fathers* (trans. Wulstan Hibberd; Charleston, SC: CreateSpace Independent Publishing Platform, 2011), p. 12. Roland Beaudet also notes this double movement. Beaudet, 'La typologie de l'Exode', p. 12.

[3] Daniélou, *From Shadows to Reality*, p. 154.

[4] Fishbane, *Biblical Text and Texture*, p. 121. George Balantine concurs that from the time of the prophets and before, the Exodus had 'long been regarded as the *Vorbilt* or prototype of the messianic redemption'. George L. Balentine, 'Death of Jesus as a New Exodus', *RevExp* 59.1 (January 1962), pp. 27-41 (27). See also Str–B, pp. 85-88.

Moses.[5] As God's eschatological plan unfolds, the Exodus motif is repeated at key junctures.[6]

This chapter will first survey shadows and repetitions of the Exodus in the Pentateuch. It will then focus primarily on the cries of the prophets, who warned of judgment and exile but also offered glimpses of hope and homecoming in a future salvation that would be like, yet even greater than, its historical precedent. Finally, it will detail how the Writings, especially the Psalms, contain the expectation of continued and consummated salvation through the lens of the Exodus motif.

The Torah

Genesis

Given the presuppositions of typology, it should not be surprising to discern prototypes in Scripture of later typological elements. This is the case with the Exodus, of which we find shadows in the book of Genesis.[7] For example, just as the Lord saved Noah and his family through the water (Genesis 7–9), he would safely bring the Israelites through the Red Sea. Much as the Lord called Abram out of Ur on a paradigmatic journey and entered into covenant with him (Gen. 12.1-3; cf. Heb. 11.13-16), God would one day call his people out of Egypt

---

[5] Estelle, 'The Exodus Motif in Isaiah'.

[6] Michael Boulton remarks that for Israel, deliverance happens typologically, 'because God is a typological poet'. Correspondence with the Exodus is, in a sense, a signature of divine authority. Matthew Myer Boulton, 'Supersession or Subsession? Exodus Typology, the Christian Eucharist and the Jewish Passover Meal', *SJT* 66.1 (February 2013), pp. 18-29 (24).

[7] Several scholars have examined the stories of Hagar in the wilderness (Gen. 16, 19) in light of the Exodus motif, noting points of contact such as her oppression, being driven out and fleeing to the wilderness, being given God's provision, naming of God, and receiving promises about the formation of the Ishmaelite people (as well as parallels between Hagar and Moses. Ironically, in this story, 'Sarai does to a child of Egypt ... what the Egyptians would later do to Sarai's children'. M. Tsevat, 'Hagar and the Birth of Ishmael', *The Meaning of the Book of Job and Other Biblical Studies: Essays on the Literature and Religion of the Hebrew Bible* (New York: KTAV, 1980); Quoted in Thomas B. Dozeman, 'The Wilderness and Salvation History in the Hagar Story', *JBL* 117.1 (1998), pp. 23-43 (29); cf. David Daube, *The Exodus Pattern in the Bible* (All Souls Studies II; London, England: Faber and Faber Limited, 1963), pp. 23-38; Yair Zakovitch, *'And You Shall Tell Your Son ...': The Concept of the Exodus in the Bible* (Jerusalem: Magnes Press, 1991).

and make a covenant with them at Sinai.[8] In the same way that Abraham went up (עלה)[9] from Egypt with flocks and herds, silver and gold, into the desert and built an altar, the Israelites would later depart with their livestock and Egypt's spoils and enter the wilderness to worship God (Gen. 13.1-11; Exod. 12.31-35).[10] Just as God's presence passed through (עבר) the split animals as a flaming torch and smoking brazier to ratify his covenant with Abraham, he would journey with the Israelites as a pillar of fire by night and a cloud by day (Gen. 15.17; Exod. 13.21).[11] In the same way that God provided a sacrifice in Isaac's place, he would accept the blood of the Passover lamb to redeem his people (Gen. 22.1-18).[12] Even before Jacob went down to Egypt, God's plan of salvation had been put into motion – God had begun weaving together prophecies and promises that provided veiled silhouettes of his saving purposes (Gen. 3.15, 21; 15.15-21).

Numbers

Numbers 23–24 recounts the enigmatic story of the encounter of Balak, Balaam, and the people of Israel.[13] In the context of the

---

[8] Brueggemann, *Reverberations of Faith*, p. 72; F.F. Bruce, *New Testament Development of Old Testament Themes* (Eugene, OR: Wipf & Stock, 2004), p. 32; Dohmen, 'Exodus', p. 206. According to Bruce, this is undergirded by later biblical authors' repeatedly setting forth Abraham's departure as an example of faith as they recall the subsequent deliverance of Israel from Egypt (e.g. Isa. 51.2; Neh. 9.7-38). Umberto Cassuto further shows how the narrative of Abraham's sojourn in Egypt and interactions with Pharaoh in Genesis 12–13 foreshadow the history Israel, and texts are worded precisely to emphasize parallel aspects for instruction. See Umberto Cassuto, *A Commentary on the Book of Genesis* (trans. Israel Abrahams, vol. II; Jerusalem: Magnes Press, 1st English edn, 1964), pp. 334-37.

[9] For the sake of simplicity and continuity, Hebrew words will be presented in their lexical root.

[10] du Rand and Song, 'The Story of the Red Sea', p. 94. du Rand and Song also suggest that the Exodus theme is present in the story of Jacob, noting similarities such as the portrayal of Jacob's departure from Laban as the release of a slave; the use of verbs such as 'drive out' and 'send'; Jacob's return to Canaan with a wealth of possessions (cf. Exod. 12.30-36); the use of military terminology (Gen. 32.2; Exod. 12.41); a change of identity (Gen. 32.28); and an emphasis on serving God (Gen. 35.14-15; Exod. 8.1). Cf. Daube, *The Exodus Pattern in the Bible*, pp. 63-64.

[11] Watts, 'Exodus', pp. 478-79. Watts posits that God's passing between the split animals could also foreshadow Israel's passing through the split Red Sea.

[12] Patterson and Travers, 'Contours of the Exodus Motif', p. 41.

[13] John Sailhamer identifies the important function of this narrative in the developing plot of OT theology, specifically in relation to God's desire to bless people, his promises to Abraham and Abraham's seed (Gen. 12.1-3; cf. Gen. 3.15), and the prophecy of a messianic king who will come out of Judah (Gen. 49.8-12). John Sailhamer, *The Pentateuch As Narrative: A Biblical-Theological Commentary* (Grand Rapids: Zondervan, 1992), p. 405.

historical Exodus, Balaam issues one set of two oracles in Num. 23.7-10 and 18-24 and a set of three oracles in Num. 23.3-9, 15-19, and 20-24. It seems that the events and ideas of the Exodus lie behind the Balaam narratives as a *Vorbild* into which the story has been molded.[14] Sailhamer and Friedbert Ninow note parallels such as these:

- Pharaoh and Balak were kings of powerful nations who wanted to thwart Israel's entry into the promised land (and thus the fulfillment of God's blessing of fruitfulness on humankind and his promises to Abraham of land, seed, and blessing). They feared Israel because she had become numerous (רב, Exod. 1.7, 9; Num. 22.6) and powerful (עצום, Exod. 1.9; Num. 22.6).[15] Thus Ninow comments that 'the two major roadblocks between Egypt and Canaan, Pharaoh and Balak, are linked together structurally, thematically, and linguistically'.[16]

- Pharaoh made three attempts to curtail God's blessing on Israel (assigning slave masters to oppress them, commanding the midwives to kill male children, and ordering male children to be thrown into the Nile); however, YHWH intervened and continued to bless his people. Woven into the story of Pharaoh's third scheme is the announcement of Moses as God's appointed deliverer for Israel. Likewise, Balak tried three times to curse Israel, yet each curse was turned to blessing. After the third attempt, the author looks ahead to the birth of a star arising out of Jacob to deliver Israel (24.12-25).[17] Sailhamer notes further thematic parallels between the specific content of Pharaoh's attempts to oppress Israel and the content

---

[14] Ninow, *Indicators of Typology*, p. 137. See also Charles David Isbell, *The Function of Exodus Motifs in Biblical Narratives: Theological Didactic Drama* (Studies in the Bible and Early Christianity 52; Lewiston, NY: Edwin Mellen Press, 2002), pp. 75-96.

[15] Sailhamer, *The Pentateuch as Narrative*, p. 408.

[16] Ninow, *Indicators of Typology*, p. 143.

[17] Sailhamer notes that 'though Balaam gave more than three oracles, the writer has arranged the oracles into three attempts to curse Israel. Balak himself reflects the writer's interest when he says, "I summoned you to curse my enemies, but you have blessed them these three times" (24.10).' Sailhamer, *The Pentateuch As Narrative*, p. 406.

of Balaam's successive oracles and details similar verbal patterns, such as the use of כבד ('be honored').[18]

Balaam's last oracles are especially noteworthy for their messianic overtones and the typological application of the Exodus to Israel's future king.[19] The author distinguishes these oracles by their introduction.[20] Balaam's outward senses were closed, his spiritual eyes were opened, he fell prostrate, and the Spirit of YHWH came upon him.[21] The oracles in chs. 23 and 24 contain many parallels, but with subtle shifts that are obscured by some English translations.[22] (Compare Num. 23.22, 'God brings *them* out of Egypt, He is for them like the horns of the wild ox' with Num. 24.8a, 'God brings *him* out of Egypt, He is for him like the horns of the wild ox'.) The first expression refers to the Israelites' Exodus from Egypt, but the second refers to the future king of Israel mentioned in the preceding verse.[23]

---

[18] Sailhamer, *The Pentateuch As Narrative*, p. 407. For example, the growth of God's people, deception, and an ironic reversal of intended evil for Israel's 'seed' in relation to water (Pharaoh's attempting to harm the 'seed' in the water vis-à-vis the image of the 'seed' in abundant waters, Exod. 1.22; Num. 24.7). Pharaoh's heart being hardened (as in Exod. 8.15), God's receiving glory, and Balaam's being honored share the same root (כבד or כבוד).

[19] For other interpretive options of this passage that are not messianic, see Pearce, 'Redemptive Function', p. 75.

[20] Compare Num. 23.7, 18 'Then he took up his discourse and said …' with additional statements in 24.3-4, 15-16. 'The oracle of the man whose eye is opened; the oracle of him who hears the words of God, who sees the vision of the Almighty, falling down, yet having his eyes uncovered' … 'The oracle of the man whose eye is opened, the oracle of him who hears the words of God, and knows the knowledge of the Most High, who sees the vision of the Almighty, falling down, yet having his eyes uncovered'.

[21] Franz Julius Delitzsch and Carl Friedrich Keil, *Commentary on the Old Testament* (trans. James Martin; Digital Library Series; Hendrickson Publishers, 2006), Num. 24.3-4.

[22] Ninow details how versions such as *The New International Version* and *The Berkeley Version in Modern English* render the Hebrew 3rd personal masculine singular pronominal (מוֹצִיאוֹ) as a plural ('brings them' instead of 'brings him') in Num. 24.8. This maintains parallelism with Num. 23.22 (מוֹצִיאָם), but changes the meaning. Ninow, *Indicators of Typology*, p. 139. *NET Bible* also does this.

[23] 'And his seed shall be by many waters, and his king shall be higher than Agag, and his kingdom shall be exalted' (Num. 24.7). Balaam expounds further on the dominion of this future king in his fourth oracle: 'I see him, but not now; I behold him, but not near; a star shall come forth from Jacob, and a scepter shall rise from Israel', Num. 24.17. There is much debate concerning whether the king in 24.7 and the star/scepter in 24.17 are general statements; references to David, through whom Israel realized partial victory over the Edomites; prophecies about the Messiah; or some combination of these. Ashley points out that the

Thus the writer's intent appears to be to typecast the experience of Israel's future king in terms gleaned from God's great acts of salvation in the past: 'this future king will have an Exodus like that of the people'.[24] Moreover, the author anticipates that the deliverance brought about by this king will conform to God's deliverance of Israel in the past. 'What God did for Israel in the past is seen as a type of what he will do for them in the future when he sends his promised king.'[25] Finally, these past and future acts share the goal of restoring the blessing that was lost in Eden and had been promised to Adam and Eve and later to Abraham.[26]

Deuteronomy

The last book of Moses adds to a growing understanding of the Exodus as paradigmatic and forward-looking by portraying Moses as a typical prophet and applying the Exodus to new situations in the future in a symbolic way (as a motif).

Moses was one of Israel's greatest leaders – the recipient of God's self-revelation (Exod. 6.1-8), the instrument of deliverance for the people of Israel from Egypt, the first (and perhaps greatest) of the prophets, the mediator of the covenant at Sinai, and the author of the Pentateuch.[27] Moses was faithful in all God's household

---

Targumim read 'the Messiah' for 'a scepter', and the LXX personifies 'scepter' as ἄνθρωπος ('a man'). He acknowledges that at a minimum, the ultimate reference of the passage gives some of the first glints of messianic hope (even if in an indirect way) and shows something of God's future victory. Timothy R. Ashley, *The Book of Numbers* (NICOT; Grand Rapids: Eerdmans, 1993), p. 496. Keil & Delitzsch consider the reference in 24.7 to be 'not one particular king ... not the Messiah exclusively, nor the earthly kingdom without the Messiah, but the kingdom of Israel that was established by David, and was exalted in the Messiah into an everlasting kingdom'. In 24.17, they comment that 'In the "star out of Jacob," Balaam beholds not David as the one king of Israel, but the Messiah, in whom the royalty of Israel promised to the patriarchs ... attains its fullest realization'. Delitzsch and Keil, *Commentary on the Old Testament*, Num. 24.7; 24.17.

[24] Ninow, *Indicators of Typology*, p. 140. Here, one thinks of Mt. 2.15, 'Out of Egypt I called my Son', applied directly to the life of Jesus.

[25] Sailhamer, *The Pentateuch As Narrative*, p. 408. Sailhamer also examines allusions in this passage to Jacob's prophecy of a king from Judah (Gen. 49.9), the blessing of Abraham's seed (Gen. 12.2), and God's promise that Adam's seed would one day crush the head of the serpent (Gen. 3.15).

[26] Ninow, *Indicators of Typology*, p. 144.

[27] Craigie notes that although Abraham is called a prophet (Gen. 20.7), Moses is the first in relation to the nation of Israel. Peter C. Craigie, *The Book of Deuteronomy* (NICOT; Grand Rapids: Eerdmans, 1976), p. 38. For a discussion on authorship and unity of the Pentateuch, see pp. 20-35. Within the biblical text,

(Num. 12.6-8; Heb. 3.5); God spoke to him face to face (or 'mouth to mouth', Num. 12.8; Deut. 34.10); and Moses beheld God's form or glory (Num. 12.8; Exod. 33.18–34.8). Although many genuine prophets followed in the footsteps of Moses throughout Israel's history, 'none was comparable to him in terms of [the] significance of his work under God's direction'.[28]

When Moses talked to the people about keeping the covenant after he died, he told them, 'YHWH your God will raise up for you a prophet like me from among you, from your countrymen, you shall listen to him' (Deut. 18.15).[29] Rather than consulting pagan fortune-tellers or soothsayers, the people should listen to God's prophet when they need counsel. On the one hand, some interpret these verses as referring to the *office* of the prophet and thus the many prophets whom God would raise up to speak his words and his will to the people after Moses.[30] Joshua was the first of these, and the end of Deuteronomy affirms that he was a capable leader, 'filled with the spirit of wisdom' because Moses had laid his hands on him (Deut. 34.9). As did Moses, Joshua received a commission from YHWH and helped lead the people to the land God had promised them: 'Be strong and courageous, for you shall bring the sons of Israel into the land which I swore to them, and I will be with you' (Deut. 31.23).

On the other hand, many scholars believe that these verses point forward to a specific prophet and were understood this way from early on. Sailhamer, for example, contends that 'even within the OT

---

the Pentateuch is unequivocally attributed to Moses (Exod. 24.4, 34.27; Num. 33.2; Deut. 1.1; 31.9; Josh. 8.32; 2 Chron. 34.14; Mk 7.10, 10.3-5, 12.19; Lk. 16.29; Jn 1.17, 45; 5.46-47; Rom. 10.5; 2 Cor. 3.15).

[28] Craigie, *The Book of Deuteronomy*, p. 263.

[29] The Lord also says in vv. 18-19, 'I will raise up a prophet from among their countrymen like you, and I will put My words in his mouth, and he shall speak to them all that I command him. And it shall come about that whoever will not listen to My words which he shall speak in My name, I Myself will require it of him' (Deut. 18.18-19). Ninow comments that this passage is 'one of the most widely recognized Pentateuchal passages in regard to the typological view of the Exodus in general and Moses in particular'. Ninow, *Indicators of Typology*, p. 144.

[30] Dale Allison discusses two interpretive options for those who see this as exclusively related to the prophetic office (the second is more nuanced, a succession of prophetic *rulers*, including Moses, Joshua, Samuel, David, and perhaps other prophets like Jeremiah). See Dale Allison, *The New Moses: A Matthean Typology* (Eugene, OR: Wipf & Stock, 2013), pp. 74-75. For a further list of scholars who interpret this solely in light of the prophetic office, see Ninow, *Indicators of Typology*, p. 146 n. 483.

itself this passage was taken to refer to a specific individual and not merely to the succession of prophets who were to arise after Moses'.[31] Old Testament authors seem to have deliberately portrayed later leaders such as Joshua, Gideon, Samuel, Elijah, Ezekiel, and Jeremiah in ways that resemble Moses, perhaps echoing this expectation.[32] By the last few centuries prior to the time of Jesus, later Judaism, the Samaritans, and the Qumran community were expecting the advent of *the* prophet like Moses in connection with these verses.[33] Verses such as Acts 3.17-26 show that the early Christian community likewise believed that Moses and all of the prophets told of the coming of One to whom Israel must listen or be destroyed (Deut. 18.19).

Finally, the last chapter of Deuteronomy lends support to the expectation that not just any great leader would fulfill the promise of the 'prophet like Moses'.[34] Even as the last chapter of Deuteronomy

---

[31] Sailhamer, *The Pentateuch As Narrative*, p. 456. (Unfortunately, Sailhamer does not substantiate his claim.) Ninow concurs: 'Deut. 18:15 and 18 seem to have an individual in view who transcends the level of an "ordinary" prophet'. Ninow, *Indicators of Typology*, p. 147. These scholars and others allow for these verses to refer to the succession of prophets as well as point forward to an ultimate fulfillment.

[32] Fishbane, *Biblical Text and Texture*, p. 123; Isbell, *The Function of Exodus Motifs in Biblical Narratives: Theological Didactic Drama*; Watts, 'Exodus', p. 473; Daube, *Exodus Pattern*; Gregory T.K. Wong, 'Gideon: A New Moses?', in Robert Rezetko, Timothy L. Lim, and W. Brian Auker (eds.), *Reflection and Refraction: Studies in Biblical Historiography in Honour of A. Graeme Auld* (VTSup 113; Leiden: Brill, 2007); Henry McKeating, 'Ezekiel the "Prophet Like Moses"', *JSOT* 19.61 (March 1994), pp. 97-109; Jack R. Lundbom, *Jeremiah: Prophet Like Moses* (Eugene, OR: Cascade Companions, 2015); Tawny Holm, 'Moses in the Prophets and Writings of the Hebrew Bible', *Illuminating Moses: A History of Reception from Exodus to the Renaissance* (Boston: Brill, 2014); Allison, *The New Moses*.

[33] Allison clarifies that some expected one prophet; some expected the Messiah (cf. Jn 1.19-23); some thought the coming prophet and Messiah were the same person; and some expected Moses himself to return. Allison, *The New Moses*, pp. 74-75. He refers to 1QSa, 1QSb, and 4QTestim. For further discussion, see Craigie, *The Book of Deuteronomy*, p. 263; Howard Merle Teeple, *The Mosaic Eschatological Prophet* (Philadelphia: Society of Biblical Literature, 1957); John M. Allegro, 'Further Messianic References in Qumran Literature', *JBL* 75.3 (September 1956), pp. 174-87; Hannah S. An, 'The Prophet Like Moses (Deut. 18:15-18) and the Woman at the Well (John 4:7-30) in Light of the Dead Sea Scrolls', *ExpTim* 127.10 (July 2016), pp. 469-78; Holm, 'Moses in the Prophets and Writings of the Hebrew Bible'; Ferdinand Dexinger, 'Reflections on the Relationship between Qumran and Samaritan Messianology', in J.H. Charlesworth, H. Lichtenberger, and G.S. Oegema (eds.), *Qumran-Messianism: Studies on the Messianic Expectations in the Dead Sea Scrolls* (Tübingen: Mohr Siebeck, 1998).

[34] Sailhamer ventures to say that perhaps even by the closing of the Pentateuch, these verses in Deuteronomy 18 'were already being understood eschatologically and messianically'. Sailhamer, *The Pentateuch As Narrative*, p. 456.

is affirming that Joshua had fulfilled his role well as Moses' successor, the author adds, 'No prophet has risen in Israel like Moses, whom YHWH knew face to face, for all the signs and wonders which YHWH sent him to perform in the land of Egypt against Pharaoh, all his servants, and all his land, and for all the mighty power and for all the great terror which Moses performed in the sight of all Israel' (Deut. 34.10-12). The author, with unmistakably specific wording, expresses that while other leaders spoke God's words to the people, the 'prophet like Moses' was yet to come.[35]

In addition to this typological depiction of Moses, Deuteronomy also contains hints of later New Exodus activity and applies extensive Exodus language to new future situations as a pattern or model (chs. 28–30).[36] The people of Israel have spent 40 years wandering in the desert because of their disobedience. Moses is about to make Joshua their new leader and is explaining the covenant blessings and curses to them. He proclaims that if the people are faithful to YHWH, YHWH will grant them honor, make them numerous and fruitful, strike down their enemies, give them prosperity in the land of promise, and establish them as a holy people to himself, as he swore to them. Then all the peoples of the earth will see that they are called by the name of YHWH (Deut. 29.1-14). These recall the purposes for which he brought the people of Israel out of Egypt.

The warnings of covenant curses likewise evoke the Exodus, and in a symbolic way.[37] The curses are portrayed as the plagues of Egypt,

---

[35] See Chapter 3 on the Gospels for more discussion of Moses as a type.

[36] Although earlier passages in Deuteronomy likewise indicate that the Exodus provides the model for YHWH's continued salvation on Israel's behalf and for judgment on those who oppose him, chs. 28–30 contain the clearest and most extensive appropriation of the motif. Deuteronomy 7, for example, urges the people to remember their deliverance in Egypt and God's judgment on Pharaoh. Then it says, 'So shall YHWH your God do to all the peoples of whom you are afraid' (Deut. 7.19). In Deuteronomy 4–5, Moses tells the people that if they do not follow the covenant, 'YHWH will scatter you among the peoples, and you will be left few in number among the nations where YHWH drives you. There you will serve gods, the work of man's hands, wood and stone, which neither see nor hear nor eat nor smell' (Deut. 4.27-28; cf. 11.22-33). As in chs. 28–29, this speaks of an undoing of the Exodus.

[37] Ninow, *Indicators of Typology*, p. 139. There is a parallel passage in Leviticus 26 that also affirms that the purposes of the Exodus will come to pass if Israel obeys the covenant ('I will also walk among you and be your God, and you shall be My people. I am YHWH your God, who brought you out of the land of Egypt so that you would not be their slaves, and I broke the bars of your yoke and made you walk

effectively depicting a *reversal* of the Exodus (italics mine):[38]

- 'YHWH will smite you with the *boils of Egypt*' (Deut. 28.27).

- 'You will never be anything but *oppressed and crushed* continually' (Deut. 28.33).

- YHWH will bring you and your *king* 'to a nation which neither you nor your fathers have known' (Deut. 28.36).[39]

- '[The plagues] shall become *a sign* (אות) and a *wonder* (מופת) on you ... forever' (Deut. 28.46).

- 'You shall *serve* (עבד) your enemies whom YHWH will send against you' and 'He will put an *iron yoke* on your neck until He has destroyed you' (Deut. 28.48).[40]

- If you are not careful 'to *fear this honored and awesome name, YHWH* your God, then YHWH will bring extraordinary *plagues* (מכות) on you and your descendants'; 'He will bring back on you all the *diseases of Egypt* of which you were afraid, and they will cling to you' (Deut. 28.58-60).[41]

- 'Then you shall be left *few in number*, whereas you were as numerous as the stars of heaven ... It shall come about that as the Lord delighted over you to prosper you, and multiply you, so YHWH will delight over you to make you perish and destroy you; and you will be *torn from the land* where you are entering to possess it' (Deut. 28.62-63).

- 'YHWH will bring you *back to Egypt* in ships, by the way about which I spoke to you, "You will never see it again!" And there you will *offer yourselves for sale* to your enemies as male and female slaves, but there will be no buyer' (Deut. 28.68).

---

erect' Lev. 26.11-13). However, 26.14-39 warns that if the people turn against YHWH, they will be the objects of his plagues and judgment.

[38] Pearce, 'Redemptive Function', p. 117; Ninow, *Indicators of Typology*, p. 148.

[39] Here, note the contrast between YHWH as Israel's King in the Exodus event (Exod. 6.7; 1 Sam. 12.10; Ezek. 20.33) and YHWH's sending Israel with her corrupt king into captivity.

[40] In vv. 49-52, eagle imagery is used, as in the Exodus (Exod. 19.4, 'You yourselves have seen what I did to the Egyptians, and how I bore you on eagles' wings, and brought you to Myself'). Ironically, the eagle here represents the nation that would devour Israel and destroy her offspring.

[41] Peter Craigie observes that this is presumably the disease with which God afflicted the Egyptians before the Exodus. Craigie, *The Book of Deuteronomy*, p. 344.

- You stand today before *YHWH, your God* 'in order that He may establish you today as *His people* and that *He may be your God*, just as He spoke to you and as He swore to your fathers, to Abraham, Isaac, and Jacob' (Deut. 29.10-13).

If the Israelites were not faithful to YHWH, the outcomes of the Exodus – freedom from oppression, serving and worshiping YHWH, being fruitful, and possessing the land promised to the patriarchs – would be reversed. The people would go into exile back to 'Egypt'. They would sink lower and lower, while in an ironic twist, the foreigner in their midst would be exempted from God's judgment – just as the Israelites had been from the plagues of Egypt (Deut. 28.43).[42]

Chapter 30, which presents the return from exile as a New Exodus, further distinguishes the use of Exodus allusions in this passage. The author layers historical reiteration, motif (using symbolic language, connecting disparate events, and evoking an emotional response), and paradigm (like the later prophets, depicting YHWH'S saving activity in the first Exodus as a pattern for his future restoration of Israel).[43] If the people are in exile and return to YHWH, he will *once again* lead them out of captivity, gather them from where they have been scattered, bring them back to the land that he promised to their fathers, make them be fruitful and multiply, bless their work, rejoice over them as he did over their fathers, and inflict the plagues on their enemies (30.1-10).

This description of repeated Exodus salvation and judgment is programmatic for the history of Israel in the remainder of the OT. It aligns with the tension between the covenant expectations and Israel's continually re-emerging inability to live up to them. As the OT story unfolds, this leads to a dual emphasis on the punishment and the

---

[42] Delitzsch and Keil, *Commentary on the Old Testament*, Deut. 28.43.

[43] Craigie also notes the forward-looking orientation of the sections that bracket specific covenant regulations in Deuteronomy (11.26-32 and 27.1-26), which both anticipate renewal of the covenant in the future. This shows how the people of Israel 'believed that there was a close relationship between the present moment, the events leading up to that moment, and those events still lying in the future, when the essence of God's ancient promise to the patriarchs would be fulfilled'. Craigie, *The Book of Deuteronomy*, p. 327.

longsuffering of YHWH as well as a growing contrast between Israel's disloyalty and YHWH's חסד (covenant faithfulness).[44]

The Prophets

Of the books in the OT, those grouped as 'the Prophets' stand out as a theological repository of New Exodus language and imagery. As David Tracy observes, 'Exodus is the story which the great prophets retell and develop in and for later times'.[45] Not only do they employ the Exodus as a 'starting point in their consideration of God's dealings with Israel',[46] but also as a paradigm of YHWH's judgment and salvation for the present and the future.

Joshua

The first 6 chapters of Joshua continue the fusion of the Exodus and conquest themes found in the 'Song of the Sea' (Exod. 15.1-18).[47] The narrative surrounding the crossing of the Jordan is pregnant with elements designed to recollect the crossing of the Red Sea under the leadership of Moses.[48] In addition to depicting the continued fulfillment of the telos of the Exodus (i.e. Israel's enjoying rest in the land that God had promised her fathers, having a special relationship with YHWH as his covenant people, and being a means of light and blessing to the nations), this text includes comparisons between Moses and Joshua as well as structural similarities, close verbal correspondences, and overt references and parallels to the Exodus

---

[44] Rolf Rendtorff, *The Canonical Hebrew Bible: A Theology of the Old Testament* (trans. David E. Orton; Tools for Biblical Study 7; Leiden: Deo, 2005), p. 73.

[45] David Tracy, 'Exodus: Theological Reflection', in Iersel, Weiler, and Lefébure, *Exodus–A Lasting Paradigm*, p. 118.

[46] Haugen, 'Consummation of the Exodus', p. 5. See also Josh. 24.5-9, 17; Judg. 2.1; 6.8, 13; 1 Sam. 2.27; 8.8; 10.18; 12.6-8; 2 Sam. 7.6, 23; 1 Kgs 8.51, 53; 9.9; 2 Kgs 17.7, 36.

[47] The first half of the Song of the Sea refers to the Exodus (1b-12) and the second half to the conquest (vv. 13-18). Watts, 'Exodus', p. 482; Ehlen, 'Deliverance at the Sea', p. 173. Fishbane points out how the fusion of these two redemptive events achieved liturgical expression in Ps. 114.3: 'The sea looked and fled; the Jordan turned back'. Fishbane, *Biblical Text and Texture*, p. 123.

[48] Daube, *The Exodus Pattern in the Bible*, p. 11. Peter Leithart has even suggested that the author of Joshua binds the events of these chapters as an inclusio to Exodus 14–15. Peter Leithart, 'Passover and the Structure of Joshua 2', *Biblical Horizons* 99 (November 1997), n.p. [cited 25 October 2012]. Online: http://www.biblicalhorizons.com/biblical-horizons/no-99-passover-and-the-structure-of-joshua-2/.

narrative.[49] Together, these constitute the crossing of the Jordan in Joshua as a 'paradigmatic replication' of the Exodus event.[50]

First, the passage contains several explicit comparisons between Joshua and Moses, leading some scholars to comment that here, the author is seeking to establish Joshua as a second Moses figure.[51] This provides continuity with the end of Deuteronomy, in which Joshua is designated as Moses' successor – Moses lays his hands on Joshua and Joshua is filled with the Spirit of wisdom (Deut. 34.9). Joshua 1–6 also emphasizes how Joshua's calling, mission, and reception were like those of Moses (1.3, 5, 14, 17). Joshua 3.1-8 recapitulates Joshua's divine commission, in which YHWH specifically tells Joshua that YHWH will exalt Joshua in the sight of the people so that they will know that YHWH is with him just as YHWH was with Moses (Exod. 14.31). This is reiterated in 4.14.[52] In addition to these details, both Moses and Joshua have a holy encounter and receive instructions for their quests (Exod. 3.5; Josh. 5.15; 6.1-5). Fishbane speculates that the command for circumcision in 5.2-3 may be intended to parallel Moses' experience in Exod. 4.24-26, and Watts comments that Joshua's actions at Ai (Josh. 8.18-19, 26) reflect Moses' actions against Amalek (Exod. 17.8-11).[53]

---

[49] The theme of God's promised 'rest' is introduced in Genesis and becomes intertwined with the Exodus motif through the OT. In Eden, Adam and Eve lived in fellowship with God, shared his sabbath rest, and dwelled in the land he had provided for them. Their work was not portrayed as laborious. Sin, however, broke this fellowship, resulting in exile and heavy labor (Gen. 3.16-19). From that time on, people sought rest; this longing for rest is expressed by Noah's father: 'Now he called his name Noah, saying, "This one shall give us rest from our work and from the toil of our hands arising from the ground which YHWH has cursed"' (Gen. 5.29). Through the Exodus, God offered partial restoration of what had been lost: fellowship, rest, and a homeland. Although Joshua led the people into the land, he was ultimately unable to offer them this rest (as indicated by David in Psalm 95, interpreted by the author of Hebrews). Along with the salvation of the Exodus, Joshua and the partial rest of Canaan become types that the NT presents as fulfilled in Christ.

[50] Brueggemann, *Reverberations of Faith*, p. 72.

[51] Watts comments that 'Joshua is presented as a new Moses'. Watts, 'Exodus', p. 482. Fishbane sees a 'typological link' between Moses and Joshua. Fishbane, *Biblical Text and Texture*, p. 123. Woudstra speaks of 'striking parallels' and an 'intimate connection'. Marten H. Woudstra, *The Book of Joshua* (NICOT; Grand Rapids: Eerdmans, 1981), p. 86. See also Isbell, *The Function of Exodus Motifs in Biblical Narratives: Theological Didactic Drama*, pp. 102-10.

[52] Woudstra notes additional related phrases in 7.23; 8.21, 24; 18.1; 22.2, 14, 18; 23.2; and 24.1. Woudstra, *The Book of Joshua*, p. 82.

[53] Fishbane, *Biblical Text and Texture*, p. 123; Watts, 'Exodus', p. 482.

Second, the narratives bear structural similarities. In both instances, the people crossed on dry land, during the spring harvest season, and with similar miraculous divine intervention. Leithart points out that the Exodus followed the pattern of destruction of Egypt, Passover, and water crossing, and the entry into Canaan chiastically reverses the sequence to water crossing, Passover, then destruction of Jericho.[54] Woudstra and Fishbane focus on the significant temporal coincidence. Joshua 4.19 states that 'the people came up from the Jordan on the tenth of the first month', the day on which Passover preparations began (Exod. 12.15-20). The Passover meal was eaten on the fourteenth day of the first month (Josh. 5.10). Thus, the entry into the promised land coincided with the commemoration of the first Passover. The people of Israel laid aside manna, the bread of wandering, and ate again the unleavened bread of redemption.[55]

Third, the Exodus narrative and the first six chapters of Joshua include several close verbal correspondences. Especially prominent is the use of the mighty 'hand of YHWH' in Josh. 4.24, which was evident in the wonders of the Exodus (cf. Exod. 3.19; 6.1; 9.3; 13.9; 32.11; Deut. 4.34 in ref. to the Exodus).[56] Also, Josh. 3.13 and 16 state that the waters of the Jordan stood up in a 'heap'. The Hebrew word נֵד ('heap') is used only five times in the OT: twice here in Joshua of the Jordan crossing, in Exod. 15.8 and Ps. 78.13 of the crossing of the Red Sea ('And at the blast of Thy nostrils the waters were piled up, the flowing waters stood up like a heap'; 'He divided the sea, and caused them to pass through; and He made the waters stand up like a heap'), and once in Job (unrelated).[57] In addition, as in the parting of the Red Sea, God parted the Jordan so that Israel and other peoples would see his wonders and know and fear his name (Josh. 4.24; Exod. 14.4, 17; 15.14-16).[58] Other parallels include allusions to the diseases and reproach of Egypt (Exod. 15.22-27; Josh. 5.2-9), the inauguration and ceasing of the manna (Exod. 16.1-36; Josh. 5.10),

---

[54] Leithart, 'Passover and the Structure of Joshua 2'.

[55] Fishbane, *Biblical Text and Texture*, p. 123. He comments, 'The homology with the first Passover, also celebrated on the eve of the fourteenth day of the first month, could not be more precise or pointed'. See also Woudstra, *The Book of Joshua*, p. 94.

[56] את־יד יהוה כי חזקה, 'the hand of YHWH is mighty'.

[57] Both Ehlen and Woudstra note this connection. Ehlen, 'Deliverance at the Sea', p. 174; Woudstra, *The Book of Joshua*, p. 86.

[58] Hung, 'Relationship and Rebirth', p. 73; Woudstra, *The Book of Joshua*, p. 96; Ehlen, 'Deliverance at the Sea', p. 174.

and the consecration of the people in preparation for YHWH's action (Exod. 19.10; Josh. 3.5).[59]

Ultimately, Joshua explicitly declares to the people that their crossing of the Jordan is on par with their fathers' crossing of the Red Sea: 'For YHWH your God dried up the waters of the Jordan before you until you had crossed, just as YHWH your God had done to the Red Sea, which He dried up before us until we had crossed' (Josh. 4.23). This, viewed in tandem with the other parallels, suggests deliberate and meaningful correspondence in order to emphasize the great name of YHWH, his faithfulness and power, his special covenantal relationship with Israel, and his larger purposes. The author seems to view the crossing of the Jordan as the fulfillment or continuation of God's earlier deliverance in the same way that later biblical writers would envision New Exodus activity. The verbal and structural parallels are indicators of a deeper theological conviction about the continuity of the past and the future, the consistent action of YHWH on Israel's behalf, and the growing expectation of the Exodus as a fundamental and typological event.

Judges

Several narratives set during the times of the judges and kings of Israel exhibit striking intertextual connection with the Exodus tradition. As in Joshua, these are extensions of the expectation established in Deuteronomy that YHWH would raise up a prophet like Moses (who was also a judge and deliverer) and that the Exodus event would be repeated or reversed as the people kept or broke the covenant.

Judges introduces what Ryken terms a 'motific use of the Exodus at a structural level'.[60] The people of Israel are continuing the process of possessing the land and learning to live as God's special people. In this context, themes from the Exodus occur in a cyclical manner: the people are crushed and oppressed by their enemies; they cry out for deliverance; God raises up a deliverer in their defense and performs mighty acts on their behalf; as in the wilderness, the people are continually and progressively unfaithful to the covenant; and once

---

[59] Keil and Delitzsch, *Commentary on the Old Testament*, II, p. 42; Hung, 'Relationship and Rebirth', p. 73.

[60] Ryken, Wilhoit, and Longman III, 'Exodus, Second Exodus', p. 254.

more, they fall into oppression.[61] In this cycle, the suffering, salvation, and judgment of the Exodus are paradigmatic.[62] The author of Judges reinforces the parallel situations of Israel in the past and present with frequent references to the Exodus (Judg. 2.1, 12; 6.8, 9, 13; 10.11; 11.13, 16; and 19.30) and with specific usage of words or phrases (such as זעק, 'to cry out', Exod. 2.23; Judg. 3.19, 15; 4.3; 6.6, 7; 10.10, 12; נאקה, 'groan', Exod. 2.24; 6.5; Judg. 2.18; נצל, 'to deliver', Exod. 3.8; 6.6; Judg. 6.9; אני יהוה אלהיכם, 'I am YHWH your God', Exod. 6.7; Judg. 6.10; פלאת, 'wonders', Exod. 3.20; Judg. 6.13) that signal the motif. As Martin points out, Judg. 6.9 ('I delivered you from the hands of the Egyptians and from the hands of all your oppressors') even juxtaposes the Exodus with subsequent acts of deliverance, thus implying that they represent a continuation of YHWH's earlier works.[63]

In addition, three specific pericopes in Judges show evidence of overlapping historical correspondence and deliberate narrative shaping to emphasize the connections between the Exodus and Israel's present history: the defeat of Sisera's army and the poetic account of the battle led by Deborah and Barak (Judg. 4.1–5.31); the call of Gideon (Judg. 6.11-21); and the encounter of Samson's parents with the angel of YHWH (Judg. 13.1-25). The first contains the use of corresponding vocabulary as well as an analogous plot.[64] The second introduces Gideon as a possible new Moses by emphasizing their similar

---

[61] Frederick Greenspahn asserts that YHWH's acts of deliverance in Judges are based on a theology of the Exodus (a cry for deliverance and a response of gracious salvation rather than a cry of repentance and an act of atonement). Greenspahn asserts, 'The framework thus perceives the period of the judges as continuing the process initiated by the exodus in which Israel's suffering is dealt with by divine salvation'. He also points out that this is consistent with God's relationship with Israel in the wilderness as well as the later times of the prophets. Frederick E. Greenspahn, 'The Theology of the Framework of Judges', *VT* 36 (1986), pp. 385-96 (395-96).

[62] Martin, 'Where Are All His Wonders?', p. 89. Martin builds on Greenspahn's argument.

[63] Martin, 'Where Are All His Wonders?', p. 94.

[64] The people cried out to YHWH, he sent a reluctant deliverer, YHWH routed Israel's enemy (המם, 'to throw into confusion', Exod. 14.24; Judg. 4.15), and water swept away the overwhelmingly superior enemy chariot force with water. Lewis Scott Hay, 'What Really Happened at the Sea of Reeds', *JBL* 83.4 (December 1964), pp. 397-403 (403); Ehlen, 'Deliverance at the Sea', p. 174 n11. The song of Deborah and Barak focuses on this element: 'The torrent of Kishon swept them away, the ancient torrent, the torrent Kishon' (Judg. 5.21).

circumstances and responses.[65] Finally, the story of Samson's birth announcement contains echoes of the call of Moses.[66] The parallel situations serve as a reminder to the people of their status as a nation founded by and dependent upon God's election;[67] provide an interpretive lens for the present and the future;[68] witness to the continuity of YHWH's past and present salvation; and contrast YHWH's covenant faithfulness with Israel's disloyalty and apostasy.[69] In framing Gideon and Samson vis-à-vis Moses, the author could be seeking to establish their divine authority (Martin), but he is more likely drawing attention to the personal reluctance of the characters (typical of the nation as a whole) to obey YHWH's instructions.[70]

---

[65] Their calls are presented as a response to Israel's distress by foreign oppression ('cried out', Exod. 2.23 and Judges 6.6); Moses and Gideon are met by the angel of YHWH; later in the narratives, there is a switch from the angel of YHWH to YHWH himself (Exod. 3.4a; Judg. 6.14); protagonists are in both cases tending to their father or father-in-law's business when the angel appeared (Exod. 3.1; Judg. 6.11); both father-figures seem to be connected to non-YHWHistic cults; certain verbs appear in both narratives (הלך, 'to go', and שלח, 'to send'); the commission is repeated in the objection of the protagonists (Exod. 3.10-11; Judg. 6.14-15); in both cases, YHWH counters the objections with an identical promise of his presence (כי אהיה עמך, 'For I will be with you', Judg. 6.16, sometimes considered a direct quote from Exod. 3.12); Gideon sees the angel of YHWH face to face (Exod. 33.11; Deut. 34.10; Judg. 6.22); and the Midianites are portrayed as a plague of locusts (Exod. 10.1-20; Judg. 7.12). Wong, 'Gideon: A New Moses?' See also Martin, 'Where Are All His Wonders?'; Larry D. Martens, 'The Echoes of Moses in Judges: A Study of the Echo Narrative Technique in Exodus 3:1-15, Judges 6:11-21, and Judges 13:1-25' (MA thesis, Providence College and Seminary [Canada], 1995); Childs, *The Book of Exodus*, Loc. 1498; Isbell, *The Function of Exodus Motifs in Biblical Narratives: Theological Didactic Drama*, pp. 111-14.

[66] This comparison is less compelling, but noteworthy. Martens notes the mention of Manoah as a 'man of God' (Deut. 33.1); the state of oppression of the Israelites; the weakness and inability of Samson's mother to understand YHWH; a recurring thematic use of ראה ('to see', Judg. 13.3, 10, 19, 20, 21, 22, 23); restrictions of imperatives to YHWH; cryptic divine answers; a progressive revelation of the messenger; the themes of fire, sacrifice, and altars; some kind of revelation of YHWH; and the announcement of the coming of a deliverer (pp. 95-100). He also discusses structural similarities (pp. 102-10). Martens, 'The Echoes of Moses in Judges'.

[67] Greenspahn, 'The Theology of the Framework of Judges', p. 396.

[68] Elaine Marie Prevallet, 'The Use of the Exodus in Interpreting History', *CTM*, 37.3 (1966), pp. 131-45 (144).

[69] Martin, 'Where Are All His Wonders?', pp. 94, 106; Martens, 'The Echoes of Moses in Judges', pp. 94-95.

[70] Wong, 'Gideon: A New Moses?', pp. 544-45. Wong mostly interprets the comparison as a strategy to build narrative suspense but fails to account for the author's theological motivation. He sees Gideon's idolatrous golden ephod (parallel to Aaron's golden calf) as the definitive answer to the question of whether Gideon

First Samuel

Several events in the first eight chapters of 1 Samuel contain interwoven strands of Exodus parallels: the judgment of Eli's household (1 Sam. 2.10, 27-35; 3.11-13),[71] the calling and ministry of Samuel as a priest and prophet of YHWH in the footsteps of Moses (interspersed throughout 1 Samuel 1–8),[72] the return of the ark of the covenant from the Philistines (1 Samuel 6),[73] and the defeat of the

---

could be the new Moses. Martens focuses on the characters' increasing lack of spiritual insight. Martens, 'The Echoes of Moses in Judges', pp. 111-15.

[71] This is framed in terms of the covenant curses of Deuteronomy 28, which present the undoing of the Exodus: YHWH will shatter Eli's sons and fight against them, dishonor them, break their strength, show them distress, cause them to die young, cut them off, and send a sign of their destruction (cf. Deut. 28.46). Hannah's song in 1 Sam. 2.10 foreshadows the destruction of Eli's sons as well as the Philistines in chapter 7 (note use of 'thunder' in 7.10).

[72] Parallels run through Samuel's special birth (ch. 1, when YHWH 'sees' and 'remembers' Hannah, 1 Sam. 1.11, 19; cf. Exod. 2.24-25); Hannah's song (2.35, YHWH will 'raise up' a faithful priest [קום, as in Deut. 18.15]); references to the Exodus (e.g. 2.27); Samuel's situation outside his parental home in a place from which he would exercise authority over God's people; Samuel's call (1 Sam. 3, which seems to have been patterned after the call of Moses in Exodus 3, e.g. failure to recognize divine presence; response of 'Here I am' in Exod. 3.4 and 1 Sam. 3.4); and his role as priest, prophet, and national leader. Isbell, *The Function of Exodus Motifs in Biblical Narratives: Theological Didactic Drama*, pp. 115-18; Martens, 'The Echoes of Moses in Judges', pp. 114-15. See Martens for more detailed comparison of the call narratives. Mark Leuchter points to other biblical traditions that establish the relationship between Moses and Samuel (Jer. 15.1; Ps. 99.6) and lays out parallels between their ministries. He notes how Samuel, like Moses, helped Israel transition through a key juncture in her history and reestablished the foundational importance of the Law. Mark Leuchter, 'Samuel: A Prophet like Moses or a Priest like Moses?', in Mignon R. Jacobs and Raymond F. Person Jr. (eds.), *Israelite Prophecy and the Deuteronomistic History: Portrait, Reality, and the Formation of History* (Ancient Israel and Its Literature 14; Atlanta: Society of Biblical Literature, 2013), pp. 147-56.

[73] Daube, Isbell, du Rand and Song, and Antony Campbell note Exodus parallels in this text, such as punishment on the gods of Egypt and Philistia (Exod. 12.12; 1 Sam. 5.3-4), the Philistines' being inflicted with tumors (Exod. 9.10; 1 Sam. 5.6), the theme of service to God (1 Sam. 7.3), and words such as 'hand of YHWH', 'heavy', 'smite', 'plague', 'confusion', and 'diviners' (Exod. 9.14-15; 1 Sam. 5.6-7, 11-12; 6.2, 4). Isbell argues that this represents a 're-creation and "update" of the experience of the exodus in the time of Samuel', and Campbell suggests that the narrative depicts the sovereign movement of YHWH as a second Exodus for the purpose of transitioning to the time of the kings and underscoring YHWH's freedom and self-initiative. Isbell, *The Function of Exodus Motifs in Biblical Narratives: Theological Didactic Drama*, pp. 118-23; Antony F. Campbell, *The Ark Narrative* (SBL Dissertation Series 16; Missoula, MT: Society of Biblical Literature, 1975), pp. 204-205; Daube, *Exodus Pattern*, pp. 73-74; du Rand and Song, 'The Story of the Red Sea', p. 94; see also Moshe Garsiel, *The First Book of Samuel: A Literary Study of Comparative Structures, Analogies and Parallels* (Ramat-Gan, Israel: Revivim, 1985), pp. 45-54. In

Philistines at Mizpah (1 Samuel 7–8).[74] As in Judges, the purposes for the use of the motif include drawing attention to the deteriorating spiritual state of Israel;[75] emphasizing the greatness of YHWH's salvation and the continuity of his actions (thus both references to the historical Exodus and prophecies about future salvation, such as 2.10, 2.35); and underscoring the similarities between the leadership of Moses and that of Samuel.[76]

First Kings

First Kings 1–14 and 18–19 contain further developments of the Exodus motif. In chs. 1–14, Amos Frisch analyzes the significance of explicit and more subtle Exodus allusions, drawing several

---

addition, 1 Sam. 6.6 seems to propose explicitly that the situation is similar in some respects (and contains additional Exodus vocabulary): 'Why then do you harden your hearts as the Egyptians and Pharaoh hardened their hearts? When He had severely dealt with them, did they not allow the people to go, and they departed?' These words precede the sending off of the ark on cows with 'articles of gold' (כלי הזהב, cf. Exod. 12.34). The thunder (קול) is reminiscent of the plague of hail, fire, flashing, and thunder in Exodus 9 (קול appears in Exod. 9.23, 28, and 33, and 34).

[74] J. Ernest Runions proposes an intertextual relationship between Exodus 17–18 and 1 Samuel 7–8. He notes the following parallels: Israel's rebellion, water poured out, judgment, an enemy attack, intercession, victory, and an altar. He suggests that the parallels helped legitimate Samuel's role in reconstituting Israel under a king. J. Ernest Runions, 'Exodus Motifs in First Samuel 7 and 8: A Brief Comment', *EvQ* 52 (July 1980), pp. 130-31. He fails to note other connections, such as the use in 1 Sam. 7.10 of המם, 'to throw into confusion' (Exod. 14.24) and נגף, 'to smite' (Exod. 8.2; 12.23).

[75] YHWH tells Samuel, 'Like all the deeds which they have done since the day that I brought them up from Egypt even to this day – in that they have forsaken Me and served other gods – so they are doing to you also' (1 Sam. 8.28). Later, Samuel emphasizes that the people of Israel are turning away from serving YHWH as their King ('When you saw that Nahash the king of the sons of Ammon came against you, you said to me, "No, but a king shall reign over us," although YHWH your God *was* your king' (1 Sam. 12.12).

[76] First Samuel 7.8, for example, frames Samuel in the role of covenant mediator, like Moses, and contains a cluster of words from the Exodus: צעק, 'to cry out'; יהוה, *YHWH*; ישׁע, 'to save' (Exod. 14.30); מיד, 'from the hand of' (Exod. 3.8; 14.30). Martens notes that Samuel was the last person to function as both prophet and national leader, like Moses. He sees the parallel as a way of affirming Samuel's identity as a messenger of YHWH and adding credibility to his message. Martens, 'The Echoes of Moses in Judges', pp. 114–15. Isbell and Walsh also discuss Elijah's being framed as a second Moses and point out similarities between their careers, their successors, and their deaths. Isbell, *The Function of Exodus Motifs in Biblical Narratives: Theological Didactic Drama*, pp. 160-62; Jerome T. Walsh, 'Elijah', in David Noel Freedman *et al.* (eds.), *ABD* (New York: Doubleday, 1992), pp. 464-65.

conclusions.[77] First, he proposes that the dating of the building of the temple (480 years after the Exodus, 1 Kgs 6.1) indicates that the temple represents the 'apex of the extended process that began with the Exodus from Egypt'.[78] Second, he comments that the Exodus provides the theological basis for the temple's later destruction and exile in 1 Kings (1 Kgs 9.6-9) as well as the precedent for hope that YHWH will act in a similar way in the future when the people cry out to him (1 Kgs 8.52-53).[79] Frisch also perceives purposeful analogies between various characters and Pharaoh or Moses (especially Solomon, Rehoboam, and Jeroboam) for the purpose of character and legacy evaluation.[80] First Kings ultimately offers a pointed contrast between Solomon, who erects the legitimate temple and carries on Moses' true legacy, and Jeroboam, who leads people astray through golden calf worship. This leads to Shishak's ascent from Egypt, which is tantamount to 'an abrogation of the telos of the Exodus'.[81]

In addition, a few scholars have noted the Exodus motif in the story of Elijah after his encounter with the prophets of Baal

---

[77] Watts echoes these observations. He adds that YHWH caused Rehoboam not to listen to the people (1 Kgs 12.15; cf. YHWH's hardening Pharaoh's heart). Throughout 1 Kings, Watts points to the continued themes of exile and return (1 Kgs 9.9), national hope founded on the election of the Exodus (8.51, 53), and the culmination of the Exodus signaled by the Shekinah's presence at the temple dedication (8.10). Watts, 'Exodus', p. 482.

[78] Amos Frisch, 'The Exodus Motif in 1 Kings 1–14', *JSOT* 87 (2000), pp. 3-5 (5).

[79] Frisch also finds in the Exodus the catalyst for proclaiming YHWH's name to the world (1 Kgs 8.41-43) and the basis of God's commitment to his people (8.50-51), their debt of loyalty to him, and the justification of their punishment for ascribing to the golden calves the work of YHWH in the Exodus (12.28).

[80] Solomon and Rehoboam, for example, are described in the language of the oppression in Egypt as imposing *hard service*, a *yoke*, and *servitude* on the people in building their *store cities* (1 Kgs 12.4, 7, 15; cf. Exod. 1.14; 6.9; Lev. 26.13; Deut. 26.6) and leading the people astray toward the loss of sovereignty – a reversal of the Exodus. Jeroboam resembles Moses: both had a close court relationship, committed a radical nationalistic deed and had to flee, then returned upon the king's death to confront the king with demands on the people's behalf. Jeroboam eventually joins in this through golden calf worship, and Solomon is seen as the legitimate successor of Moses. Frisch also examines Hadad the Edomite (1 Kgs 11.14-22) as a Moses-figure.

[81] Frisch, 'The Exodus Motif in 1 Kings 1–14', p. 19. Frisch concludes that the uses of the Exodus motif in these chapters as a unifying element in 1 Kings, which he believes is composed of various sources and bears the marks of several redactors.

(1 Kings 18–19).[82] Elaine Prevallet details how Elijah, after a contest between Baal and YHWH, journeys through the desert for 40 days and nights on the strength of a miraculous feeding (19.6-8). He goes up to Mt. Horeb (Sinai), where he sees a theophany (first the angel of YHWH comes to him, then the word of YHWH, and finally YWHW himself).[83] In this story (esp. 1 Kings 18), Elijah is cast as a covenant mediator and intercessor, like Moses. Later, the account of Elijah's departure and election of Elisha as his successor recollects the mysterious death of Moses and his commissioning of Joshua (Deut. 34.6; Elisha, like Joshua, parts the waters of the Jordan as he assumes leadership of the people).[84]

Prevallet ties this to the renewal of the Mosaic covenant and the affirmation of Elijah as a valid successor of Moses. [85] More intriguingly, she proposes that the use of the Exodus motif here served to guide Israel toward the increased spirituality of finding God not only in extraordinary demonstrations of his might (e.g. the Exodus events and the revelation of the covenant with thunder, lightning, fire, and earthquakes, Exodus 19), but in gentle whispers and ordinary blessings like rainfall (1 Kgs 18.41-46; 19.9-18).[86] She asserts that it was crucial to validate this development by identifying with Israel's founding events and Moses, her first mediator. 'Hence in this portrayal Elijah graphically catches up the experience of the original Mosaic revelation and adds to it a new depth and refinement, one which is relevant for contemporary Israel.'[87] In this way, the Exodus grounds Israel's deepening faith and becomes normative for a new generation.[88]

---

[82] George Savran, '1 and 2 Kings', in Robert Alter and Frank Kermode (eds.), *The Literary Guide to the Bible* (Cambridge, MA: The Belknap Press of Harvard University Press, 1987), pp. 162-63; Frisch, 'The Exodus Motif in 1 Kings 1–14', p. 4; Prevallet, 'The Use of the Exodus in Interpreting History'; Reynolds, 'A Comparative Study of the Exodus Motif in the Epistle to the Hebrews', pp. 39-40.

[83] She sees 19.8 as parallel with Exod. 24.18 and 34.28; 19.9 with Exod. 33.22; 19.11 with Exod. 33.22; 19.11-12 with Exod. 19.16-19; and 19.13 with Exod. 33.22. Prevallet, 'Use of the Exodus', p. 132.

[84] Savran, '1 and 2 Kings', pp. 162-63.

[85] Prevallet, 'Use of the Exodus', p. 133; Reynolds, 'Comparative Study', p. 40.

[86] Savran believes that this narrative is a repudiation of the god Baal, a storm god, who was thought to reveal himself in thunder and lightning. Savran, '1 and 2 Kings', p. 163.

[87] Prevallet, 'Use of the Exodus', p. 134.

[88] Paul Evans proposes that Evil-merodach's release of Jehoiachin (2 Kgs 25.27-30) presages New Exodus activity through structural parallels with the story of Joseph:

Isaiah[89]

The prophet who employs the Exodus motif 'most frequently and in [the] most poetic and creative way' is Isaiah.[90] As Isaiah depicts the restoration of Israel from exile and the formation of a new covenant community, he draws from and transforms the Exodus.[91] Although the early chapters of Isaiah (1–39) contain many oracles of judgment, and

---

Just as Joseph's elevation showed God's favor toward his people, though it did not result in a return to their homeland, so Jehoiachin's elevation showed God's sovereign action towards his people, though it did not result in a return from exile. Joseph's elevation presaged the exodus, even though years of bondage still lay ahead for the people of God. Similarly, Jehoiachin's elevation presaged the second exodus, the return from exile, even though years of exile still lay ahead for the people of God.

Paul S. Evans, 'The End of Kings as Presaging an Exodus: The Function of the Jehoiachin Epilogue (2 Kgs 25:27-30) in Light of Parallels with the Joseph Story in Genesis', *McMaster Journal of Theology & Ministry* 16 (January 2014), pp. 65-100 (85).

[89] This study will follow David Pao in rejecting the modern designations of First-, Second-, and Third-Isaiah. He notes that 'recent discussions on the redactional, thematic, and structural unity of the Isaianic corpus have pointed to the possibility that the relationship between various sections within Isaiah is much more complex than has previously been assumed'. David W. Pao, *Acts and the Isaianic New Exodus* (WUNT 130; Tübingen: Mohr Siebeck, 2000), p. 19. In addition, from a canonical perspective, the book of Isaiah should be treated as a unified whole. Scripture is unanimous in affirming Isaiah as the author of all parts of the book (Isa. 1.1; 2.1; cf. quotes from Isa. 1, 6, 10, 40, 42, 53, and 65 in Mt. 3.3; Lk. 3.4; Acts 8.28-33; Jn 12.23-24; Rom. 8.27-29). John Wesley Adams, Quentin McGhee, and Roger Douglas Cotton, *Survey of the Old Testament* (Faith & Action; Springfield, MO: Faith & Action Team, 2010), p. 183.

[90] Clifford, 'The Exodus in the Christian Bible', p. 351. While most scholars agree that Isaiah employs the Exodus motif extensively, others believe Isaiah's motifs are broader. For example, Horacio Simion-Yofre argues that certain themes are too broad to restrict them to Second Exodus interpretation: (*'Una observación más atenta da como resultado que la mención del desierto contiene siempre peculiaridades teles, que la imagen finalmente obtenida no es simplemente la del cruce del desierto, y no ciertamente la de un segundo éxodo'* ['A closer observation results in the conclusion that the mention of the desert always contains peculiar/specific themes, so that the final image is simply that of crossing the desert, and not certainly that of a second Exodus']). Some vocabulary may likewise not apply exclusively to the Exodus; texts that contain commands to 'leave' or 'come out' (e.g. Isa. 51.9-10) are from the point of view of Jerusalem, not from that of exile, and may have more of a liturgical purpose; and other texts (e.g. Isa. 48.20-21) demonstrate more affinity to the wonders of Meriba, the crossing of the Jordan, or the language of Psalms than to the Exodus directly. Horacio Simian-Yofre, 'Exodo En Deuteroisaias', *BIB* 61.4 (1980), pp. 530-53 (551-52); see also Hans M. Barstad, *A Way in the Wilderness: The 'Second Exodus' in the Message of 2 Isaiah* (JSS; Manchester: Manchester University Press, 1989); Øystein Lund, *Way Metaphors and Way Topics in Isaiah* (Forschungen Zum Alten Testament II 28; Tübingen: Mohr Siebeck, 2007).

[91] Pao, *Acts and the Isaianic New Exodus*, p. 51.

the Exodus motif is more prominent from ch. 40 onward, there are several noteworthy appropriations in chs. 1–39.[92]

Isaiah 4.5-6 speaks of a time when, after Israel has undergone a time of judgment and purification, YHWH will cover Jerusalem with a cloud by day and fire by night (cf. Exod. 13.21-22); he will be to them shade (literally, a *booth*, סכה, cf. Lev. 23.42-43) from the heat and a refuge from the storm and rain (cf. Exod. 13.21; Ps. 78.14).[93]

Isaiah 11.11–12.6 announces that after the coming of the Davidic ruler (Isa. 11.1-10; cf. Num. 24.17), 'YHWH will *again* recover *the second time* with His *hand* the remnant of His people' (Isa. 11.11, ital. mine) and bring judgment on the inhabitants of Canaan (the Philistines, Edomites, Moabites, and Ammonites, Isa. 11.14-16; cf. Num. 24.17-18; conquest in Joshua).

> And YHWH will utterly destroy [חרם] the tongue of the Sea of Egypt; and He will wave His hand over the River with His scorching wind; and He will strike [נכה] it into seven streams and make men walk over dry-shod. And there will be a highway from Assyria for the remnant of His people who will be left, just as there was for Israel in the day that they came up out of the land of Egypt (Isa. 11.15-16).[94]

This is followed by a song of celebration, which Buchanan believes is a midrash on the Song of Moses and Israel in Exodus 15.[95]

---

[92] These earlier chapters of Isaiah often receive less (if any) attention in the analysis of the Exodus motif (since many scholars begin with ch. 40). However, they add significantly to the development of the motif and showcase Isaiah's unified personification of return from exile as New Exodus. Therefore, this study will include more details from these chapters

[93] Daniélou, *From Shadows to Reality*, p. 155; Daube, *Exodus Pattern*. Isaiah 10.24-27, also uses Exodus language to describe judgment on Assyria and deliverance for Israel: 'YHWH will arouse a scourge against him like the slaughter of Midian at the rock of Oreb; and His staff will be over the sea and He will lift it up the way He did in Egypt. So it will be in that day, that his burden will be removed from your shoulders and his yoke from your neck, and the yoke will be broken because of fatness' (Isa. 10.26-27).

[94] See John Goldingay, *The Theology of the Book of Isaiah* (Downers Grove, IL: IVP Academic, 2014), p. 147; Daniélou, *From Shadows to Reality*, p. 13. Fishbane suggests a textual correction of בעים to בקע ים, 'cleave the Sea', which produces a reading closely parallel to Exod. 14.21 and Ps. 78.13.

[95] George Wesley Buchanan, 'Isaianic Midrash and the Exodus', in Craig A. Evans and James A. Sanders (eds.), *The Function of Scripture in Early Jewish and Christian Tradition* (Sheffield: Sheffield Academic Press, 1998), p. 100.

Isaiah 19.19-25 offers a striking (perhaps shocking) inversion of the Exodus salvation to include not only Israel, but Assyria and even Egypt![96] In the first Exodus, YHWH sees his people's oppression by the Egyptians, hears their cry, sends them a deliverer in Moses, and gives signs and plagues that the Egyptians might know his power. Fishbane notes that here, 'by means of an exegetical-terminological counterpoint, Isaiah 19:19-25 touches on all the foregoing features of the exodus tradition and radically transforms them' to apply to Egypt in her distress![97] YHWH will hear their cry, send them a Savior, deliver them, make himself known to them, and strike ('smite') them for healing. There will be an altar and a sign to YHWH in their land, and they will worship and sacrifice to him. Israel, Assyria, and Egypt will worship together as a blessing among the nations, and YHWH will say, 'Blessed is Egypt My people, and Assyria the work of My hands, and Israel My inheritance'.[98]

Isaiah's use of Exodus language and imagery to describe YHWH's future action intensifies in chs. 40–66 (e.g. 40; 41; 42–43; 49; 50; 51–52; 55; 58; 60; 61; 63; 64; 66), leading some scholars to assert that New Exodus is not merely one of the prophet's themes here, but *the* dominant theme.[99] The Exodus event is infused with eschatological

---

[96] For a detailed discussion of this passage, see Tsong-Sheng Tsan, 'New Exodus'': A Theological Enquiry of the Exodus Motif in Isaiah 19.16-25', *Taiwan Journal of Theology* 32 (2010), pp. 1-22.

[97] Fishbane, *Biblical Text and Texture*, p. 129. He remarks that 'such a transfer of a designation used pointedly of Israel (e.g. Exodus 3:10) weighed heavily on ancient Jewish translators. Unable to tolerate such a theological paradox, the Septuagint and Targum traditions renationalized the text and substituted Israel for Egypt.'

[98] See also Isa. 15–16, which tells of a time when the Spirit will be poured out, the wilderness will become a fertile field, and justice will tabernacle in the desert. Isaiah 35.1-10 pictures the blossoming of the desert at the coming of the glory of YHWH; waters will break forth in the wilderness, and the ransomed of YHWH will return with joy and singing. See Hahn, 'Worship in the Word', pp. 118–19; Christine Downing, 'How Can We Hope and Not Dream: Exodus as Metaphor: A Study of the Biblical Imagination', *JR* 48.1 (January 1968), pp. 35-53 (49); Watts, 'Exodus', p. 483; Daniélou, *From Shadows to Reality*, p. 13.

[99] Carroll Stuhlmueller, *Creative Redemption in Deutero-Isaiah* (Analecta Biblica 43; Rome: Pontifical Biblical Institute Press, 1970), p. 59; Norman H. Snaith and Harry M. Orlinsky, *Studies on the Second Part of the Book of Isaiah* (VTSup 14; Leiden: Brill, 1967), p. 147; Daniélou, *From Shadows to Reality*, p. 73. Watts comments that the appearance of allusions to the New Exodus in the prologue (40), the end of the first section (48.22), and epilogue (55.12) of the 'Book of Consolation' demonstrate its central significance. Rikki E. Watts, 'Consolation or Confrontation: Isaiah 40-55 and the Delay of the New Exodus', *TynBul* 41.1 (May 1990), pp. 31-59 (33). The proliferation of Exodus language and imagery in these chapters is too widespread to

vision in these chapters,[100] which anticipate that YHWH's action will be not only consistent with his past salvation, but also new and greater.[101]

As YHWH revealed his name to Moses and the people of Israel in the context of deliverance, so in Isaiah he repeatedly states, 'I am YHWH' (frequently attached to גאלכם, 'your Redeemer', or a statement about YHWH as Savior, King, Warrior, Leader, or the one who called/chose Israel, e.g. Isa. 41.13; 43.3, 11, 13; 15; 48.17).[102] The Exodus depicted YHWH's triumph over Pharaoh and the other gods of Egypt, and Isaiah announced earlier that the images of Babylon's gods are fallen (21.9) and that YHWH (vs. impotent false gods, Isa. 36–37) could deliver his people from the hand of the Assyrians. Now Isaiah includes six declarations in chs. 45–46 that 'there is no other' god besides YHWH (45.5, 6, 14, 21, 22; 46.9). Just as through Moses and Aaron, the magicians of Egypt were put to shame, YHWH will make fools of the diviners (Exodus 7–9; Isa. 44.25-26).[103] As in the first Exodus, YHWH's mighty hand will deliver his people and bring them back to Zion (Exod. 15.6; Isa. 40.10; 41.10; 50.2; 51.9; 52.10; 53.1). As he dried up the sea in generations past, he will once again cause his redeemed (פדה, 51.11; earlier, 1.27; 29.22; 35.10; cf. Exod. 6.6; 13.13-15; 14.30; Deut. 7.8; Ps. 77.20) people to pass through the waters with singing (43.1-3, 6-7;

---

provide a passage-by-passage analysis – this study will try to paint the picture in broad strokes.

[100] As is typical with forward-looking prophecy, the distinction is blurred between events that will happen in the near future and those that look ahead to fulfillment during the advent of the Messiah and even in the last days. For a discussion of the eschatological understanding of Isa. 40.3 outside the Hebrew Bible, see Pao, *Acts and the Isaianic New Exodus*, pp. 42-43.

[101] Robin Parry details how Isa. 40–55 takes up themes and texts from Lamentations, announcing YHWH's response to the pain that Lamentations expresses and radically reversing texts from all five chapters of the lament. For example whereas Lamentations 1 pictures Jerusalem as a lady in mourning with no comfort, Isaiah 40 opens by proclaiming comfort to God's people. Robin Parry, 'Prolegomena to Christian Theological Interpretation of Lamentations', in Scott Hahn *et al.* (eds.), *Canon and Biblical Interpretation* (Scripture and Hermeneutics 7; Grand Rapids: Zondervan, Kindle edn, 2006).

[102] Prevallet asserts that here, as in the first Exodus (Daube), YHWH is portrayed as one who 'buys back a kinsman sold into slavery, who vindicates the family cause, who upholds and restores family solidarity'. Prevallet, 'Use of the Exodus', p. 145. Beaudet sees the main concept as protection. Beaudet, 'La typologie de l'Exode', p. 16.

[103] Beaudet, 'La typologie de l'Exode', pp. 13-14.

51.9-11). He will lead the glorious procession along the 'way' (דרך) and be their front and rear guard in the cloud and pillar of fire (Exod. 3.21; 13.21; 14.19; 23.20; Isa. 40.3; 10; 42.16; 44.26-27; 43.16-19; 49.10; 52.12).[104] He will shepherd his people (Exod. 15.13; Pss. 77.20; 78.52; Isa. 40.11) and supply food and water for them (Exod. 17.2-7; Isa. 48.20-21; 49.9). The culmination of this event will be YHWH's enthronement in a restored Jerusalem-Zion.[105] Then all nations will see his glory and know that he alone is God (40.5; 43.13; 45.21; 49.23; 52.10; 60.16).[106]

In contrast to the first Exodus, in this event, there will be a transformation of nature (41.9, 17-19) and the people will not go out in haste or as fugitives (Isa. 52.12). Furthermore, there will be a new spiritual depth to this going out: Israel will be refined and purified, and YHWH will offer them forgiveness (Isa. 48.10; 49; 54; 60). God's people will also grow in their understanding of his redemptive work on their behalf (Isa. 41.14; 44.6; 54.8; 63.16). As the community of Israel was formed into a nation at the first Exodus (Exod. 19.6), Isaiah envisions a reconstitution of the community (49.8).[107] Here, the promise to Abraham that Israel would be a means of blessing to all nations also comes into increased focus (e.g. Isa. 2; 19; 42; 55.3-5; 60). As Prevallet observes, Israel returns from exile not with a political mission, but with a 'mission to lead the nations to Yahweh, to be the means of His glory ... the exodus now constitutes not Israel the nation among other nations but Israel the redeemed – and in some sense redeeming – people'.[108]

In addition to this vision of a New Exodus, Isaiah speaks of a Spirit-anointed Servant of YHWH who bears resemblance to Moses

---

[104] Pao comments that the 'Way' points both to the coming of YHWH and to the return of the people from captivity. The 'desert in the highway' is also connected to the first Exodus. Pao, *Acts and the Isaianic New Exodus*, p. 53.

[105] Watts, 'Consolation or Confrontation', p. 34.

[106] Patterson and Travers, 'Contours of the Exodus Motif', p. 34; Bruce, *New Testament Development*, p. 48; Blenkinsopp, 'Scope and Depth', p. 42; Dennison Jr., 'The Exodus'; Reynolds, 'Comparative Study', p. 55; Watts, 'Exodus', p. 483; Bernhard W. Anderson, 'Exodus Typology in Second Isaiah', in Bernhard W. Anderson and Walter Harrelson (eds.), *Israel's Prophetic Heritage; Essays in Honor of James Muilenburg* (Eugene, OR: Wipf & Stock, 2010), p. 182.

[107] See Pao, *Acts and the Isaianic New Exodus*, pp. 55-58. He ties this into creation language in the Exodus account and new creation language in Isaiah. Here, also, the divine word is fused with the Exodus motif.

[108] Prevallet, 'Use of the Exodus', p. 145.

and is described with language drawn from the Exodus.[109] Like Moses, the Servant makes atonement for the sins of the people (Exod. 32.30) and mediates a covenant with Israel and the nations.[110] Isaiah 53 further speaks of the 'arm of YHWH' (53.1) and the Servant's being 'stricken' and 'smitten' (53.4), 'bearing' (נשא, *nasa'*, 53.4; used of Moses' bearing the burden of the people in Deut. 1.12) the 'stroke' (נגע, *nega'* [used as 'plague' in Exod. 11.1]) due to the people, being 'oppressed' and 'afflicted' (53.7), and suffering like a sacrificial 'lamb' (53.7).[111] Just as YHWH was angry with Moses on the people's behalf, and Moses could not enter·the promised land (Deut. 1.37), the Servant is cut off from the land of the living because of the transgression of the people (v. 8).[112] Passages about the coming Exodus also refer to the leadership of a descendant of Jesse, a 'Branch of David' who is mysteriously called by divine names, who will bring liberation and reign with righteousness (Isa. 9.1-8; 11.1; 16.5; cf. 61.1-7).

---

[109] Buchanan calls the Servant the 'antitype' of Moses. Buchanan, 'Isaianic Midrash and the Exodus', p. 101. I concur with Robin Parry, who explains that the Servant figure refers to Israel in chs. 40–48. Because of Israel's sin, she is unable to fulfill her calling as light to the nations (Isa. 42.16-25; 43.24; 46.8-13). Therefore, an individual assumes Israel's identity and mission to deliver Israel and empower her to become a Servant to the nations. In chs. 49–53, the Servant 'embodies the mission of Servant Israel with the goal of rescuing Israel'. This is accomplished in chapter 53, when the Servant takes up the exilic suffering that he does not deserve. He dies the death of exile, is then glorified (52.12; 53.10b-12) and provides peace and healing for Israel through his wounds (53.5). The salvation of chs. 54–55 flow out of the Servant's work in 52–53. Scott Hahn *et al.* (eds.), *Canon And Biblical Interpretation* (Scripture and Hermeneutics 7; Grand Rapids: Zondervan, 2006), loc. 10558. Dale Allison lists additional Mosaic parallels, such as meekness (cf. Num. 12.3) and bringing Torah (Isa. 40.4). Allison, *The New Moses*, pp. 69-72.

[110] Watts, 'Exodus', p. 482. John Day observes that in providing a remedy to the people's spiritual condition for which they went into exile, the Servant initiates the New Exodus. He also compares the language of this 'new thing' (42.9) to identical language in 43.16-17, 19-21, showing that this work is part of the New Exodus. He argues, like Watts, that the placement of the fourth Servant Song indicates that it is through his death that the Servant will inaugurate this New Exodus. Adam Warner Day, 'Lifted up and Glorified: Isaiah's Servant Language in the Gospel of John' (PhD dissertation, The Southern Baptist Theological Seminary, 2016), pp. 216-17.

[111] Dennison notes that the Servant's 'vicarious suffering will be the ransom-price of the people of God in the new Exodus'. Dennison Jr., 'The Exodus', p. 8.

[112] For a discussion of the Servant's identity, see Watts, 'Consolation or Confrontation'.

Jeremiah and Lamentations

The books of Jeremiah and Lamentations,[113] like Isaiah, contain extensive use of Exodus language and imagery, particularly in passages about judgment and in prophecies about future restoration. In Jeremiah, the Exodus motif is concentrated in the first collection of divine oracles (chs. 1–25) and the Book of Consolation (Jer. 30–33).[114] Jeremiah portrays how the people of Judah have broken the covenant (Jer. 7.25-28) and are under a curse (Jer. 11.3; Deut. 28–30). They have forgotten YHWH, the 'fountain of living waters', and his salvation in the Exodus (Jer. 2.5-7), when he led them in *the way* (דרך, 2.17). Now they are *on the way* (דרך) [back] to Egypt, to drink the waters of the Nile (2.18). Even though YHWH brought them out of bondage in Egypt (7.6), where they were aliens, they have oppressed the aliens (7.6) and taken their Hebrew brothers as slaves – not releasing them (34.13-16). Therefore, YHWH declares that he has divorced them;[115] he will also release them – to the sword, pestilence, and famine (34.17). They will cry out (זעק), but he will not answer (Exod. 2.23-24; Jer. 11.11). They will never again invoke the holy name of YHWH (44.26), and he will cast them from his presence (23.39).[116] Now, YHWH is watching over them for harm (as he was twice accused of in Exod. 5.22; 32.12; Deut. 28.63). He will stretch out his hand against them and destroy them (15.6); they will die by the sword or famine (Deut. 28.22). They will be an object of horror (15.4) instead

---

[113] Lamentations is treated here with Jeremiah because 1) historically, Jews and Christians have read them together, assuming that Jeremiah wrote both books; 2) the LXX and many early extant Hebrew manuscripts place them together; and 3) the message of Lamentations and its use of the Exodus motif (judgment, future hope) aligns better with the situation and message of the prophets than with books such as Ezra and Nehemiah, which demonstrate partial fulfillment of New Exodus activity foretold by the prophets.

[114] Hung, 'Relationship and Rebirth', p. 84.

[115] The same verb (שלח) that was used in the Exodus of Pharaoh's *letting* God's people *go* (e.g. Exod. 5.1; 7.16; 8.1) is used ironically in Jeremiah to depict YHWH as a husband divorcing Israel and later Judah (Jer. 3.1, 8). Just as the people were *sent away* to worship YHWH, he now *sends* them *away* to worship their false gods (Jer. 15.1, 'send them away from My presence'; 24.5, YHWH sent the captives out to Babylonia; cf. 16.13, YHWH will hurl the people out of the land to serve other gods).

[116] Just as the building of the temple was the culmination of the Exodus (Watts, 'Exodus', p. 482), the destruction of the temple was the ultimate symbol that the Exodus had been reversed. For a discussion of the significance of the temple, see Wright, *Jesus and the Victory of God*, II, pp. 205-206.

of glory (13.11) and will return 'few in number' (Jer. 44.28; Deut. 28.62). He will bring darkness on them (13.16) and a sign of punishment (44.29; cf. Deut. 28.46, the curses will 'become a sign and a wonder on you'). YHWH will send deadly serpents against them (8.17) and give them poisoned water to drink (Jer. 9.15; 23.15; cf. Exod. 7.17-18). He will scatter them among the nations (9.16) like chaff in the desert (13.24). They will be put to shame by Egypt as Israel was by Assyria (2.37) and will 'go out' (2.37) but with their hands on their heads. As in the Exodus, they will know YHWH's power and might and great name, but now through his judgment (Jer. 16.21).

If the people would return to YHWH, however, he offers to renew his wonders and show them his salvation (15.20; 30.10). He would break the yoke of slavery off their necks and they would again serve YHWH their God (30.8-9; cf. Jer. 2.20 of the Exodus; Exod. 4.23). They would again be his people and he would be their God (Jer. 30.22; 31.11, 33; Exod. 6.7). He would bring them out of captivity (23.3, 7), show them mercy in the wilderness (31.1-4), multiply them and make them fruitful (23.3), and increase them in the land (3.14-17; 12.15-16; 29.10-14; 30.8-10). He would make a new covenant with them and inscribe his law on their hearts and their minds (31.31-34). His presence would once again dwell among them (3.17). YHWH declares of Judah,

> 'I will make them walk by streams of waters, on a straight path in which they will not stumble; For I am a father to Israel, and Ephraim is My firstborn ... He who scattered Israel will gather him and keep him as a shepherd keeps his flock.' For YHWH has ransomed (פדה) Jacob and redeemed (גאל) him from the hand of him who was stronger than he (Jer. 31.9-11; cf. Exod. 4.22; 6.6; 13.13-15; 14.30; Deut. 7.8; Ps. 77.20).

In that day, he would again punish Moab, Ammon, and other enemies of his people (25.15-26). This salvation would also be mediated through a leader (the 'Branch of David', even called יהוה צדקנו, 'YHWH our Righteousness', Jer. 23.6; 33.15).[117]

---

[117] Jeremiah's call seems to be structured so as to place him in Moses' succession (Exodus 3; 4.11-16). In contrast to Moses, because of YHWH's judgment, Jeremiah is instructed not to pray for the people or cry out on their behalf (11.14; 14.11). Childs, *The Book of Exodus*, p. 54; William L. Holladay, *A Commentary on the Book of the*

As in Isaiah, this activity is described as having continuity with Israel's past, but surpassing it to such a degree that it will no longer be said, 'As YHWH lives, who brought up the sons of Israel out of the land of Egypt', but, 'As YHWH lives, who brought up the sons of Israel from the land of the north and from all the countries where He had banished them' (Jer. 16.14-15; cf. 3.16; 23.7-8; 31.8, 33; 33.14-16).[118] This New Exodus will redefine the touchstone act of salvation associated with YHWH's identity.[119]

Lamentations, like Jeremiah, depicts YHWH's judgments and covenant curses on Israel as reversals of the Exodus.[120] The situation of the captives and YHWH's response to them is sharply contrasted with their Egyptian captivity.[121] Among the laments, Israel is personified as lady Jerusalem (1.1-2) and then a man weighed down with suffering (3.1-19). The exiled lady is in distress, under harsh servitude (עבדה, 1.3, 14; cf. Exod. 1.14), groaning (אנח, 1.4, 8, 21, 22; cf. Exod. 2.23) and afflicted (עני, 1.3, 4, 7, 9; cf. Exod. 1.12; 3.7).[122] Her life is bitter (1.4; cf. Exod. 1.14). She is homeless (1.7) and has no rest (1.3; cf. Exod. 33.14; Deut. 28.65). YHWH has given her into the hands of her enemy (1.14; 2.7; cf. Josh. 10.8), and she has become an unclean thing, a profaned kingdom (1.17; 2.2; cf. Exod. 19.6). YHWH fights like a warrior *against* Israel (ch. 2). He has destroyed his tabernacle and

---

Prophet Jeremiah Chapters 1-25 (Hermeneia; Philadelphia: Fortress Press, 1986), p. 27; Leuchter, 'Samuel: A Prophet like Moses or a Priest like Moses?', p. 148; Martens, 'The Echoes of Moses in Judges', p. 114.

[118] Fishbane notes that it appears that when someone swore by the power of God, he did so by 'God's historical attribute', making 'the force of YHWH as the guarantor of an oath … related to remembrance of His power at the exodus'. In the future, people will swear by this New Exodus. Fishbane, *Biblical Text and Texture*, p. 130.

[119] Hung, 'Relationship and Rebirth', pp. 96, 119.

[120] For further discussion on Deuteronomistic theology in Lamentations and the relationship of judgment to covenant curses, see Bertil Albrektson, *Studies in the Text and Theology of the Book of Lamentations with a Critical Edition of the Peshitta Text* (Studia Theologica Lundensia; Lund, Sweden: C.W.K. Gleerup, 1963); Norman K. Gottwald, *Studies in the Book of Lamentations* (Studies in Biblical Theology; Chicago, IL: A.R. Allenson, 1954).

[121] F.W. Dobbs-Allsopp, *Lamentations* (Interpretation; Louisville, KY: Westminster / John Knox Press, 2002), p. 79. He observes that in Lamentations, Egyptian captivity is the standard for measuring Israel's current situation; he finds at least a dozen specific parallels in language.

[122] Dobbs-Allsopp points out that the word for 'distress' (מצרים) is a pun on the word for Egypt (מצרים). *Lamentations*, p. 59.

abandoned his sanctuary (2.6-7), causing the appointed Feast and the sabbath to be forgotten (2.6).

The man of sorrows is afflicted and in chains (3.1-20). YHWH plagues him with darkness, sickness, bondage, and crooked paths. YHWH does not hear when he cries (זעק, 3.8); he devours him like a lion and shoots at him with arrows (vv. 10-13). YHWH is no longer the cloud guiding his people in the wilderness; he has covered himself with a cloud so that no prayer will be heard (3.44). Israel's inheritance has been given to strangers (5.2), and they are subject to Egypt and Assyria (4.6). Now, even slaves rule over them, and there is none to deliver them (5.8). Mount Zion is desolate (5.18).

Lamentations is not devoid of hope, however. The author brings these sorrows as a prayer to YHWH and asks for him to remember his people (cf. Exod. 6.5), restore them, and renew the days of old (5.1, 21). The man of sorrow consoles himself with YHWH's covenant faithfulness (3.21-23). He knows that YHWH has redeemed (גאל) his life and seen his oppression (3.58-59); he will not reject his people forever. YHWH will once again harden the heart of Israel's enemies (3.65; cf. Exod. 14.8) and pursue them in anger to destroy them (3.66).

Ezekiel

Like Isaiah and Jeremiah, Ezekiel offers a vision of Israel's restoration that frames the events as a New Exodus.[123] The Exodus motif is mostly concentrated in 20.33-38 and 37.21-28. Leading up to the first passage, which is patterned after Exod. 6.6-8,[124] YHWH focuses on the continual, cyclical rebellion of the people that he brought out of Egypt and of their children: he delivered them (vv. 5, 10) and instructed them how to keep the covenant (vv. 7; 11-12; 18); they rebelled and worshiped idols (vv. 8; 13; 16; 21); and he resolved to 'pour out' his 'wrath' and 'accomplish' his 'anger against them' 'in the wilderness' (vv. 8; 13; 21). However, he acted for the sake of his name 'that it should not be profaned in the sight of the nations, before whose sight [he] had brought them out' (vv. 9; 14; 17; 22), although he swore that they would not enter the land (vv. 15; 23).

---

[123] Walther Zimmerli, *Ezechiel* (Biblischer Kommentar Altes Testament 8; Neukirchen-Vluyn: Neukirchener Verlag, 1979), p. 455; Balentine, 'Death of Jesus', p. 28.

[124] Fishbane offers a chart detailing the close intertextual relationship between these texts. He interprets the tone of this passage as sarcastic and bitter. Fishbane, *Biblical Text and Texture*, p. 132.

Again, the people of Ezekiel's day have defiled themselves after the manner of their fathers (vv. 30-33). But YHWH will not allow them to become a nation that worships wood and stone. As before, he will purify them in the wilderness:

> 'As I live', declares the Lord YHWH, 'surely with a mighty hand and with an outstretched arm and with wrath poured out, I shall be king over you.[125] I will bring you out from the peoples and gather you from the lands where you are scattered, with a mighty hand and with an outstretched arm and with wrath poured out; and I will bring you into the wilderness of the peoples, and there I will enter into judgment with you face to face. As I entered into judgment with your fathers in the wilderness of the land of Egypt, so I will enter into judgment with you', declares the Lord YHWH. 'I will make you pass under the rod,[126] and I will bring you into the bond of the covenant; and I will purge from you the rebels and those who transgress against Me; I will bring them out of the land where they sojourn, but they will not enter the land of Israel. Thus you will know that I am YHWH' (Ezek. 20.33-38).

As before, the desert will be a place of testing and entering into covenant; those who rebel and disobey will not enter the land. This Exodus, however, will result not in the worship of idols (Exodus 32), but in faithful worship on God's holy mountain – Mount Zion (Ezek. 20.40-44).[127]

The second passage likewise follows a recounting of YHWH's dealings with Israel (their rebellion and idolatry, his wrath in scattering them among the nations, and his concern for his name, Ezek. 36.17-23) and a prophecy about purification and renewal. It has two repetitions of the promised restoration with a vision in

---

[125] For a discussion of the kingship of YHWH, see Ralph W. Klein, 'Theology for Exiles: The Kingship of Yahweh', *Dialog*, 17.2 (1978), pp. 128-34.

[126] The verb 'to pass' (עבר) is associated with the Exodus tradition in several ways (Exod. 12.12, the angel will 'pass through' the land of Egypt and strike down the firstborn; Exod. 12.23, YHWH will 'pass through' to smite the Egyptians; the Israelites are to 'pass over' [devote] to YHWH the firstborn of their animals; Exod. 15.16, the people of Israel 'pass over' the Sea). Here, 'pass under the rod' seems to refer to the people's passing under the shepherd's staff (see. Lev. 27.32; Mic. 7.14, also a New Exodus text), perhaps with the meaning of judgment and/or consecration, with echoes of the Exodus event.

[127] McKeating, 'Ezekiel the "Prophet Like Moses"', p. 103.

between. Ezekiel pictures this New Exodus as a resurrection and a recovery of Eden (37.1-14; 36.33-36). [128] Beginning in 36.24, YHWH declares that he will gather his people from the nations, save them from their uncleanness, give them a new heart, put his Spirit within them, and cause them to walk in his statutes. YHWH will bring them into the land he gave to their forefathers and bless them with abundance. As in the Exodus, he says, 'they will be My people, and I will be their God' (36.28), and 'Then they will know that I am YHWH' (36.38). This is followed by Ezekiel's vision in which dry bones are infused with the breath of life, representing how YHWH will cause his people to come up out of their graves and be reformed as one nation (37.1-20). Once again, YHWH solemnly declares that he will gather his scattered people and bring them into their own land (37.21). He will deliver them and cleanse them, and he says, 'They will be My people, and I will be their God' (37.23). His servant David will be king over them and shepherd them (37.24-25). YHWH will make an everlasting covenant with them, multiply them, and set his sanctuary in their midst forever (37.26). [129] He closes, 'My dwelling place also will be with them; and I will be their God, and they will be My people. And the nations will know that I am YHWH who sanctifies Israel, when My sanctuary is in their midst forever' (Ezek. 37.27-28).

As in Isaiah and Jeremiah, Ezekiel's future Exodus repeats key elements from Israel's first deliverance, yet also transforms and transcends it. It is becoming clearer that while some parts of the prophecies will be fulfilled as people return from exile, the prophet's words express hopes that can only be realized through the Messiah or in the eschaton (note the growing use of absolute promises like *universal* knowledge of YHWH, an *eternal* covenant, YHWH's dwelling with his people *forever*). In addition, while the prophets themselves are shown to stand in the line of Moses (particularly, Jeremiah, and Ezekiel), [130] there has been a fusion of a separate prophetic expectation

---

[128] Watts, 'Exodus', p. 483. Dumbrell notes the use of Edenic language here with the recreation motif and the prospect of a 'wholly recreated Israel'. Dumbrell, *The End of the Beginning*, pp. 78, 119.

[129] Other passages in Ezekiel (e.g. 43.7, 9) include the concept of God's eschatological dwelling/tabernacling with his people (cf. Joel 3.17; Zech. 2.10; 8.3). Dennison Jr, 'The Exodus', p. 8.

[130] McKeating suggests that the second half of Ezekiel (chs. 40-48), which may seem puzzling otherwise, should be understood in the context of presenting Ezekiel's

with the theme of the Exodus: the major prophets emphasize that the leader of the New Exodus will resemble not only Moses – deliverer, prince, and prophet – but also David, shepherd and anointed king (Isa. 11.1-16; Jer. 23.5-8; Ezek. 37.24-25; cf. Num. 24.17-19).

Hosea

Hosea, like other prophets, turns to the Exodus as a paradigm of both judgment and salvation.[131] He sees the historical Exodus as the warrant for Israel's loyalty to YHWH (Hos. 11.1-4; 13.4-5) and as the vision for Israel's future renewal (Hos. 2.14-15; 12.9). He portrays Israel as the unfaithful wife of YHWH and employs the Exodus motif to speak to her about infidelity and redemption.

Hosea speaks of YHWH's judgment against Israel in terms of covenant curses (Deuteronomy 28–30) and, like Jeremiah, in ironic language of Exodus reversal (typological bondage).[132] Hosea recounts that Israel does not acknowledge God as her husband and provider and has forsaken him for idols (2.8, 13). Therefore, instead of having compassion on her, making her fruitful, leading her in 'the way', and settling her in a land of abundance, YHWH will make her barren (v. 3), have no compassion on her (v. 4), cause her to be lost in a hedge of thorns (v. 6), take back his blessings (v. 9-13), and destroy her 'vines and fig trees'.[133] Israel will be oppressed and crushed (Hos. 5.11; Deut. 28.33). In the past, YHWH carried his people in loving arms (Hos.

---

ministry as parallel to that of Moses: both go up on a high mountain, see the pattern for the tabernacle/renewed temple, and deliver laws about the function of the sanctuary and those who care for it, the division of the land, and the leadership of the nation. Moses and Ezekiel, through prophecy and law-giving, establish the sanctuary worship and form/reform the people. McKeating, 'Ezekiel the "Prophet Like Moses"'.

[131] Pearce argues that the Exodus from Egypt functions in Hosea as 'the predominant paradigm by which the prophet discloses God's message to His people'. He notes that

> Hosea discloses God's message to Israel by recalling his former redemptive activities on their behalf, and subsequently reinterprets them in the light of their future circumstances. In other words, Israel's first Exodus from Egypt supplies Israel's imminent exile with meaning and prefigures the blessings inherent in the second Exodus-event (Pearce, 'Redemptive Function', pp. 118, 126).

[132] Pearce, 'Redemptive Function', p. 128. Ehlen remarks that 'since Yahweh's people had failed to fulfill the demands arising out of the Exodus, that very event would be reversed and Israel would go back into bondage'. Ehlen, 'Deliverance at the Sea', p. 169.

[133] These are symbols for abundance (1 Kgs 4.25; Isa. 36.16; Jer. 8.13; Joel 1.7; Mic. 4.4; Zech. 3.10).

11.3; Exod. 19.4; Deut. 32.11; Isa. 63.9), but now he will carry them off as a lion carries its prey (Hos. 5.14; 13.7-9). The mighty hand that struck Egypt (Exod. 3.20) and brought the Israelites salvation (Exod. 13.14) will now turn against Israel, and no one will be able to deliver (נצל, Exod. 3.8; Hos. 2.10) the people from it.

Hosea further laments that Israel has become like a senseless dove, seeking salvation from her oppressors (Egypt and Assyria, 7.11; 12.1) instead of from the one who would again show her his mighty power. YHWH is willing to ransom/redeem (פדה) his people, but they do not look to him or cry (זעק) to him from their hearts (7.13-14). Therefore, since they have turned back to Egypt in their hearts (like their forefathers, Acts. 7.39), they will return to 'Egypt' in punishment for their sins (8.13, 9.3, 6; 13.3; Deut. 28.68). Hosea 13.14-15 foretells that instead of ransom (פדה, Exod. 13.13; 34.20) and redemption (גאל, Exod. 6.6), YHWH will send an east wind (קדים, cf. Exod. 14.21) from the wilderness (מדבר) and cause Israel's fountain[134] and spring to be dried up (חרב, 13.14-16; cf. Ps. 106.9, Isa. 51.10 of the Exodus). As Israel plundered Egypt (Exod. 3.22) of her articles of gold, YHWH will plunder Israel of her precious articles (כלי, 13.15).

Hosea, especially in contrast to Ezekiel, paints the story of Israel's first time in the wilderness with the tender language of parenting and nurture:

> When Israel was a youth I loved him, and out of Egypt I called My son ... Yet it is I who taught Ephraim to walk, I took them in My arms ... I led them with cords of a man, with bonds of love, and I became to them as one who lifts the yoke from their jaws; and I bent down and fed them (Hos. 11.1, 3-4).[135]

---

[134] Perhaps there is further ironic contrast between Israel's forsaking YHWH, the fountain of living water (Jer. 2.13; 17.13; Ps. 36.9), and his causing their fountain to be dried up.

[135] G.K. Beale observes that Hosea likely draws this imagery of Israel (and Israel's king) coming out of Egypt along with the personification of the lion from Num. 23.24 and 24.9. Based on the structure of Hosea 11 and Hosea's overall Exodus/New Exodus context, Beale believes that Hosea likely understood that Israel's past coming out, together with the lion image, would be 'recapitulated again in the eschatological future' (p. 703). Beale relates this to the prophecy in Hos. 1.10-11, which states that the people of Israel will be called 'sons of the living God' and will 'go up' [out of Egypt] led by one leader, who appears to be further described in 3.5 as a latter-day Davidic king. This sets the stage for Matthew's quotation of Hos. 11.1 in Mt. 2.15. G.K. Beale, 'The Use of Hosea 11:1 in Matthew 2:15: One More Time', *JETS* 55.4 (December 2012), pp. 697-715.

After a time of punishment, YHWH says that there will be another Exodus: Israel will 'go up' (עלה) from the land of her exile (Hos. 1.11; Exod. 12.38). YHWH will cause Israel to recapitulate her wilderness experience.

> Therefore, behold, I will allure her, bring her into the wilderness and speak kindly to her. Then I will give her vineyards from there, and the valley of Achor[136] as a door of hope. And she will sing there as in the days of her youth, as in the day when she came up from the land of Egypt (Hos. 2.14-15).

In the New Exodus, just as Hosea buys back Gomer and shows her love, YHWH will gather Israel from the nations. He will make her dwell in tents again, as in the days of the appointed festival (12.9).[137] Israel, like a faithful bride, will call YHWH 'my husband' and be betrothed to him forever (2.16, 19). She will recognize that salvation comes neither from Assyria nor from idols, but from YHWH (14.3), whose paths/ways (דרך) are right (14.9). YHWH will make a covenant (2.18) with her and restore the blessings of the land (2.21-22; 11.8-11),[138] and David will again reign over Israel (Hos. 3.5). YHWH will have compassion on the people and call them 'My people', and they will say, 'You are my God!' (2.23; Exod. 6.7).[139]

---

[136] Watts notes that this was the site of Israel's first infidelity in Canaan – now, it is a doorway of hope. Watts, 'Exodus', p. 482. Fishbane further interprets the word עכור ('Achor') as 'sorrow' – now even sorrow would be turned to joy. Michael A. Fishbane, *Text and Texture: Close Readings of Selected Biblical Texts* (New York: Schocken Books, 1979), p. 125.

[137] Foulkes sees this as a return to a life of simplicity, trust, and obedience to YHWH. The nation had to again learn to know YHWH, be dispossessed of the land, and live in tents. Foulkes, *The Acts of God*, p. 354. Daniélou likewise associates this with the booths of the desert (although it is not the word סכת [e.g. Lev. 23.42-43]). Daniélou, *From Shadows to Reality*, p. 155. Pearce sees it as further judgment; the people will dwell in tents as homeless wanderers, dispossessed of their land. Pearce, 'Redemptive Function', p. 123.

[138] Blenkinsopp voices that in Hosea's understanding, the historical Exodus was such a constitutive event in the forming of the first covenant that without a renewal of that activity, a future renewal of the covenant would not be possible. This is partly what qualifies its use here as typological. Blenkinsopp, 'Scope and Depth', p. 43.

[139] von Rad notes that in these passages and many others, 'already within the Old Testament the dumb facts of history had become prophetic, and had come to be viewed as prototypes to which a new and more complete redemptive act of God would correspond'. Gerhard von Rad, 'Typological Interpretation of the Old Testament', *Interpretation* 15.2 (1961), pp. 174-92 (34).

Joel

There are several glimpses of the Exodus motif in Joel's prophecies that rebuke Israel for her unfaithfulness to the covenant (implied in 2.12-14). As other prophets, Joel tells of judgment in terms of covenant curses (e.g. locusts in 1.4; barrenness in the land and failure of crops in 1.7-12; desolation, lack of rain, and fire in 1.16-20). Joel envisions the Day of YHWH in the language of the Sinai theophany (blowing of a trumpet on the holy mountain, trembling, darkness, a cloud, gloom, and fire, 2.1-2; Exod. 19.9-25; cf. Deut. 4.11; Heb. 12.18-19). Finally, he looks forward to a day when YHWH will gather his scattered people, judge their enemies, pour out his Spirit (with 'signs' and 'wonders'), and again dwell among them (2.12-32). YHWH declares, 'Then you will know that I am in the midst of Israel, and that I am YHWH your God and there is no other' (Joel 2.27).

Amos

Amos begins his oracles by speaking against Israel's enemies (Damascus, Gaza and the Philistines, Tyre, Edom, Ammon, and Moab). Then in a shocking twist, he turns to condemn Judah and Israel, who have followed in the sins of their fathers and rejected the law of YHWH (especially committing injustice against the poor and helpless, 2.4-8). Amos prophesies YHWH's words against the house of Israel with pervasive, typological use of the Exodus motif. Beginning in chapter 2, YHWH reminds Israel of her special election (2.9-11; 3.1-2), which is the basis for the impending judgment.[140] YHWH has already 'smitten' (נכה) them with covenant curses – hunger, no rain, scorching (שדפון), blight of crops, mildew (ירקון), and locusts (Amos 4.9; Deut. 28.22-24). He then 'sent a plague among [them] after the manner of Egypt' and slew them by the sword (4.10; Exod. 9.3), but still they did not return to him.

---

[140] He chose only her among all the families of the earth, brought her up from Egypt, and 'raised up' some of her sons to be prophets (cf. Deut. 18.18). The language of 3.1, which includes the current generation among those whom YHWH brought up out of Egypt, corresponds to Exod. 13.8 ('It is because of what YHWH did for me …').

Amos tells that this will be followed by further curses, reversals of the Exodus, and ironic judgments.[141] Whereas YHWH had given the people's fathers 'houses full of all good things which [they] did not fill, and hewn cisterns which [they] did not dig, vineyards and olive trees which [they] did not plant' (Deut. 6.10-11; Josh. 24.13), now 'they will not live in the houses they have built or drink the wine of their vineyards' (Amos 5.11). Just as their fathers went out of Egypt, the people will now 'go out' (יצא) in captivity (4.3). YHWH will send darkness (8.8-9) and biting serpents (9.3; cf. Num. 21.6). People will go into mourning, as for an only son – it will be a bitter day (Amos 8.10; cf. Exod. 1.14; 11.15; 12.8; Zech. 12.10). YHWH will 'pass through' (עבר) their midst for judgment (Amos 5.17; Exod. 12.12, 23). As a result, 'will not the land quake and everyone who dwells in it mourn? Indeed, all of it will rise up like the Nile, and it will be tossed about and subside like the Nile of Egypt' (Amos 8.8).

In a final word, Amos takes up the Exodus motif to offer hope to the remnant of Israel. He says that YHWH, who commands the waters of the sea, will 'raise up the fallen booth (סכה) of David', and his posterity will take possession (ירש) of 'Edom and all the nations who are called by My name' (Amos 9.11-12; Deut. 30.1-9).[142]

Micah

Micah is replete with Exodus language and typology. The prophet builds on the historical Exodus as the foundation of YHWH's relationship with Israel (6.3-4) before announcing judgment in similar terms.[143] Before he introduces future hope, Micah says that

---

[141] The people ironically tell Amos not to prophesy in Bethel, where YHWH's sanctuary (מקדש) was (for it is 'a sanctuary (מקדש) of the king and a royal residence', Amos 7.13). Their idolatry is further seen in how their fathers 'carried along Sikkuth [their] king' (an idol) with them (Amos 5.26). Now, this will be reversed: they and their king will be carried into exile (Amos 5.27; cf. Deut. 28.36, 'YHWH will bring you and your king, whom you set over you, to a nation which neither you nor your fathers have known, and there you shall serve other gods, wood and stone').

[142] Amos reinterprets the promise of Deuteronomy 30 to include not simply the land, but other peoples' worshiping YHWH as a possession or inheritance of Israel. For a discussion on potential Exodus parallels in Jonah, see Alastair Hunter, 'Jonah from the Whale: Exodus Motifs in Jonah 2', in Johannes C. De Moor (ed.), *The Elusive Prophet: The Prophet as a Historical Person, Literary Character, and Anonymous Artist* (Oudtestamentische Studiën 45; Atlanta: Society of Biblical Literature, 2005).

[143] Micah predicts sickness, people being smitten and struck down by the sword, and desolation. As in Amos 5.11, Micah tells the people, 'You will sow but you will not reap. You will tread the olive but will not anoint yourself with oil; and the grapes, but you will not drink wine' (Mic. 6.13-15; cf. Deut. 6.10-11; Josh. 24.13). In 1.9,

the people will 'cry out' (זעק) to YHWH, but he will not answer them. First, they will 'go out' (יצא) of the city, dwell in the field, and go to Babylon (4.9-10; cf. Exod. 3.10). There, he says, after a time of judgment, 'you will be rescued (נצל); there YHWH will redeem (גאל) you from the hand of your enemies' (Mic. 4.10; cf. Exod. 6.6). YHWH will once again *pass over* his people in mercy (Mic. 7.18; Exodus 12).[144] As Micah cries out to YHWH for deliverance, 'Shepherd Your people with Your scepter, the flock of Your possession … Let them feed in Bashan and Gilead as in the days of old' (7.14), YHWH answers him with the promise of a New Exodus: 'As in the days when you came out from the land of Egypt, I will show you miracles (פלא)' (Mic. 7.14-15; Exod. 3.20).[145] When he gathers the remnant of Israel like a flock, YHWH says, 'The breaker goes up before them; they break out (פרץ), pass through (עבר) the gate and go out (יצא) by it. So their king goes on before them (לפניהם) and YHWH at their head' (Mic. 2.12-13; Ps. 77.20; Exod. 13.21).[146] Finally, Micah offers hope of the messianic deliverer who will arise to shepherd his brothers in the strength and majesty of YHWH (Mic. 5.3-4; cf. Moses in Exod. 2.11). This ruler will go forth (יצא) for YHWH (Exod. 3.10, 11, 12; 6.6); his 'goings forth' (Greek, ἔξοδοι) are from long ago, from the days of eternity (Mic. 5.2).

Habakkuk

Habakkuk recalls the Exodus and conquest in a poetic cry for mercy (3.2-15). He pictures YHWH's going before his people as a warrior for their salvation, bringing pestilence and plagues on their enemies. The prophet calls out for a renewal of this activity: 'I have heard the report about You and I fear. O YHWH, revive Your work (פעל) in the midst of the years, in the midst of the years make it known; in wrath

---

Micah laments that the people's 'wound' (מכה) is incurable – this is the word for 'plague' in Deut. 28.61.

[144] 'Who is a God like You, who pardons iniquity and passes over (עבר) the rebellious act of the remnant of His possession?'

[145] Fishbane writes that 'the reference to exodus here serves to articulate the felt inner unity of Israel's history with God … Assurance lay in references to times past.' Fishbane, *Text and Texture*, p. 126. Boulton calls the past Exodus the 'prologue' of what YHWH will do here. Boulton, 'Supersession or Subsession?', p. 23.

[146] YHWH is depicted as one who 'broke out' against people in judgment (plagues in Num. 25.4; tumors in 1 Sam. 5.9; Ps. 60.1; Isa. 5.5). The same word describes Israel's 'spreading out' or 'multiplying' in Exod. 1.12 (cf. Hos. 4.10).

remember mercy' (Hab. 3.2; Ps. 44.1, 95.9 of the Exodus). He closes his prayer with an affirmation that YHWH is still the one who brings salvation (3.18).

Zephaniah

Zephaniah describes a time of judgment for Israel in terms similar to Amos 5.11: 'Their wealth will become plunder and their houses desolate; yes, they will build houses but not inhabit them, and plant vineyards but not drink their wine' (Zeph. 1.13; cf. Deut. 6.10-11; Josh. 24.13). He also looks ahead to a time when people will 'call on the name of YHWH, to serve (עבד) Him shoulder to shoulder' (3.9; Exod. 7.16), and he portrays YHWH as Israel's King and a victorious warrior in their midst (3.15, 17).

Haggai

Haggai reiterates the judgment of YHWH against his people's covenant unfaithfulness in terms of plagues and curses.[147] He also proclaims that YHWH has not forgotten the promise he made to his people when they came out of Egypt (Hag. 2.5): YHWH will again fight for Israel, overthrowing kingdoms and chariots and riders (2.22; Exod. 15.1). Like Joel, Haggai picks up the language of the Sinai theophany to describe an eschatological repetition of YHWH's activity: 'For thus says the LORD of hosts, "Once more in a little while, I am going to shake the heavens and the earth, the sea also and the dry land. I will shake all the nations; and they will come with the wealth of all nations' (Hag. 2.6-7; Ps. 68.7-8; Jer. 49.21; 2 Sam. 22.8; Ps. 18.7 of the Exodus; Exod. 3.22; 12.35). Not only will YHWH 'fill [that] house with glory' (2.7; Exod. 40.34), but the glory of that house will surpass that of the first (2.9).[148]

---

[147] "'I smote (נכה) you and every work of your hands with blasting wind, mildew and hail; yet you did not come back to Me," declares YHWH' (Hag. 2.17; cf. Exod. 3.20; 9.18; Deut. 28.22); 'You have sown much, but harvest little; you eat, but there is not enough to be satisfied; you drink, but there is not enough to become drunk; you put on clothing, but no one is warm enough; and he who earns, earns wages to put into a purse with holes' (Hag. 1.6; cf. Deut. 8.2-4).

[148] For a full discussion of how Haggai draws on the Exodus themes, see Dongyoun Ki, 'The Temple, Holy War, and Kingship in Haggai: A Text-Linguistic and Inner-Biblical Study' (PhD dissertation, Trinity Evangelical Divinity School, 2001). Ki's summary of his findings begins on p. 306.

Zechariah

Throughout his proclamations, Zechariah offers a weary, exiled people hope of the renewal of YHWH's wonders in the past. Whereas other prophets' appropriation of the Exodus motif is often weighted with language of judgment, Zechariah's is largely positive.[149] He announces that YHWH will judge Israel's enemies with his hand and make them plunder for their slaves (2.9). Then he tells the people to sing for joy, because YHWH will arise to fight for Israel.[150] He will have compassion on his people, deliver (ישע) them, treat them as his sheep, redeem (פדה) them, and bring them back from 'Egypt' into the land of their fathers (9.16; 10.3-10). They will also receive silver and gold and other valuable articles from their enemies (14.14; cf. Exod. 12.35-36). Zechariah 10.8-12 depicts another passage through the sea on dry land:[151]

> And He will pass through the sea of distress, and strike the waves in the sea, so that all the depths of the Nile will dry up; and the pride of Assyria will be brought down, and the scepter of Egypt will depart. And I shall strengthen them in YHWH, and in His name they will walk.

In addition, YHWH assures that he will once again make his people numerous and cause them to be a blessing to others (8.7; 8.13; 9.16; 10.6, 8; Gen. 12.2-3; Isa. 49.6). Not only Israel, but many nations will be called his people in that day, and he will be their God (Zech. 2.11; 8.8; 13.9) and King (14.3, 9). As he promised in the Exodus, he would dwell among them (2.10; 8.3; Exod. 25.8). The last ch. of Zechariah foretells that all nations will come to Jerusalem to worship YHWH and celebrate the Feast of Tabernacles (Zech. 14.16-18), remembering YHWH's Exodus-like deliverance (cf. Lev. 23.43).[152]

---

[149] Some of the judgments are described in the past (e.g. 7.13-14).

[150] 'Then YHWH will appear over them, and His arrow will go forth like lightning; and the Lord GOD will blow the trumpet, and will march in the storm winds of the south. The LORD of hosts will defend them' (Zech. 9.14-15; Num. 24.8; Ps. 18.14; 77.17 of the Exodus). See also 14.3.

[151] Perhaps this is under the leadership of the messianic 'Branch' (3.8; 6.12-13). The initial 'He' in 10.8 is ambiguous; grammatically, it could refer back to Israel. However, 'He' is acting in ways parallel to Moses (Exod. 14.16), whose staff parted the waters and who led the Israelites through the Sea. This suggests that it is an individual.

[152] Zechariah 14.18 warns that YHWH will 'smite' those who do not come with a pestilence/plague.

Zechariah also tells of the coming of YHWH's servant, the 'Branch' (3.8; 6.12-13). This priestly leader will build YHWH's temple and sit on the throne to rule. Joshua, the high priest in Zechariah's vision,[153] is a sign (מופת, cf. Exod. 4.21) pointing to his coming (Zech. 3.8). Like his antitype, Joshua is appointed to govern YHWH's house and have charge over his courts (3.7).

Malachi

Malachi draws language from the Exodus to speak of YHWH as a Father and a King who deserves honor (1.6; 14) and whose name will be great among the nations (1.11; 14), yet to whom Israel has been unfaithful. The prophet describes the curses that YHWH has brought and will continue to bring on his people for not keeping the covenant (2.1-3) in terms of Exodus-reversal: YHWH will rebuke their offspring, carry them away from the land into exile, and make them despised and abased before all the people (2.3-4, 9). Malachi 3 and 4 (or 3.1-24 LXX) echoes words and themes from Isaiah's New Exodus prophecies[154] to close the OT with a vivid expectation of the coming of YHWH (4.5), the coming of the Lord to his temple (3.1), the coming of the 'messenger of the covenant' in whom the people delight (3.1), and the rising of the 'sun of righteousness' with healing in its wings.[155] This would be preceded by the messenger who would prepare his way (Mal. 3.1; Isa. 40.3), 'Elijah the prophet', who would turn the hearts of fathers to their children and the hearts of the children to their fathers (Mal. 4.6). YHWH promises that on the day he prepares his own possession (Mal. 3.17; cf. Exod. 19.5), those who fear him will be his, and he will spare them 'as a man spares his own son who serves him' (Mal. 3.17; cf. Exod. 4.23; 12.12-13).

---

[153] יהושע ('YHWH saves', cf. Mt. 1.21).

[154] Malachi 3–4 echoes multiple themes from Isaiah 40–42, such as preparing the way of YHWH (40.3), the glory of YHWH revealed (40.5), the coming of YHWH (40.10), the coming of a Righteous one (41.2), God's chosen people (41.9), the rising of the sun (41.25), the messenger of the covenant/Servant of YHWH in whom someone delights (42.1), the burning of chaff (41.2, 15-16), and the destruction of enemies (41.10-12).

[155] The coming of the messenger/Lord seems to be equated with the coming of YHWH himself: the coming of the great (גדול) and terrible/feared (ירא) 'day of YHWH' in 4.5 is preceded by the coming of the prophet Elijah, just as the coming in 3.1 is preceded by the messenger. It is noteworthy that forms of these words appear together in several texts about the Exodus (Gen. 46.3; Exod. 14.13; Deut. 7.19, esp. 7.21; Neh. 1.5).

The Writings

Psalms

Many of the books grouped as 'The Writings'[156] do not allude to or echo the Exodus account as frequently or as explicitly as the Prophets. By contrast, Exodus language and imagery permeate every type of Psalm.[157] Many Psalms look back to YHWH's salvation and mighty deeds in the Exodus as they exhort God's people to praise him or not to repeat the sins of their fathers (e.g. Psalms 78; 81; 95; 103; 104; 105; 114; 135; 136).[158] These are prophetic history lessons; they serve to establish YHWH's character, sovereignty, and great name. They call for loyalty on the basis of his past works as they document (and often lament) YHWH's faithfulness and Israel's persistent rebellion. Moreover, as Pearce observes, 'those who forget his works ... find their culpability intensified and their sufferings wrought by the devastating wrath and judgment of God, which ... is described by the psalmist as a penetrating reversal of God's deliverance' (e.g. Ps. 106.40-43).[159]

On a more motific and paradigmatic level, some psalms praise YHWH for personal salvation, portrayed as a repetition of the Exodus

---

[156] These traditionally include Psalms, Job, Proverbs, Ruth, Song of Songs, Ecclesiastes, Lamentations, Esther, Daniel, Ezra–Nehemiah, and Chronicles. Lamentations has been treated with Jeremiah to preserve canonical order and to demonstrate more natural development of the Exodus as a motif.

[157] Clark Hyde, 'The Remembrance of the Exodus in the Psalms', *Worship* 62.5 (September 1988), pp. 404-14 (411). Hyde adds that the psalms with the Exodus tradition appear to be among the most important ones. For more detailed analysis of Psalms 23, 104, 105, 143, and 149 and Exodus themes, see (respectively) M.L. Barré and J.S. Kselman, 'New Exodus, Covenant, and Restoration in Psalm 23', in Carol L. Meyers and Michael P. O'Connor (eds.), *The Word of the Lord Shall Go Forth: Essays in Honor of David Noel Freedman in Celebration of His 60th Birthday* (Special Volume Series; Winona Lake, IN: Eisenbrauns, 1983); Buchanan, 'Isaianic Midrash and the Exodus', pp. 92-93; William Nelson Wilder, 'Freed from the Law to Be Led by the Spirit: Echoes of the Exodus Narrative in the Context and Background of Galatians 5:18' (PhD dissertation, Union Theological Seminary in Virginia, 1996); Anthony R. Ceresko, 'Psalm 149: Poetry, Themes (Exodus and Conquest), and Social Function', *Biblica* 67.2 (1986), pp. 177-94.

[158] Watts notes that Psalm 78 presents David's shepherd-kingship as the solution for Israel's constant unfaithfulness. Perhaps this looks forward to the eschatological kingship of David's Son. Watts, 'Exodus', p. 484.

[159] Pearce, 'Redemptive Function', p. 108. Susan Gillingham examines the Exodus tradition in the Psalms with an eye to the relationship between liturgy and ideology (how the community established its election and claims to nationhood/statehood). See Susan Gillingham, 'The Exodus Tradition and Israelite Psalmody', *Scottish Journal of Theology* 52.1 (1999), pp. 19-46.

(e.g. Psalm 18), cry out for personal or communal salvation, remembering YHWH's faithfulness in the Exodus (Psalms 74 and 77), or call for a renewal of YHWH's deliverance at the Exodus (Psalms 80 and 106).[160] In Psalm 68, David combines celebrating God's past deliverance in the Exodus (vv. 7-10, 18, 22-25), describing God's character in typical Exodus language ('he leads out the prisoners into prosperity' (v. 6); he 'daily bears our burden' and 'is our salvation' (v. 19); he judges his enemies, (v. 21); he is awesome in his sanctuary (v. 35), and calling for YHWH to continue to act on behalf of his people ('show yourself strong', v. 28). In Psalm 80, Asaph intertwines memories of the Exodus (YHWH's removing a vine from Egypt, driving out the nations, and planting it, vv. 8-10), poetic variations of Israel's wilderness experience (feeding people with the bread of tears [vs. bread of angels], making them drink tears [vs. water from the rock], vv. 5-6), and cries for deliverance ('Oh, give ear, Shepherd of Israel, You who lead Joseph like a flock; You who are enthroned above the cherubim, shine forth! ... Stir up Your power and come to save us!', vv. 1-2). Psalm 106 presents a detailed recounting of the Exodus, the crossing of the Sea, YHWH's judgment on the Egyptians, the people's continual rebellion, and YHWH's salvation for the sake of his name (v. 8); 'many times he would deliver them' (v. 43); 'nevertheless he looked upon their distress ... and relented according to the greatness of his lovingkindness' (v. 45). This is bracketed by a confession at the beginning ('We have sinned like our fathers', v. 6) and a plea for deliverance at the end: 'Save us, YHWH our God, and gather us from among the nations!' (v. 47). The author of Psalm 144 uses Exodus language (esp. the divine warrior motif) to entreat YHWH for salvation from threatening waters and foreign enemies.[161] As the psalmist remembers the past, it becomes present liturgically in his prayer for divine help.[162]

---

[160] Bruce places Psalm 66 in this category, in which a worshiper implies that the individual experience of YHWH's salvation is 'all of a piece with the national salvation' that YHWH's people have encountered from the Exodus onwards. Bruce, *New Testament Development*, pp. 45-46.

[161] For example, 'Touch the mountains, that they may smoke. Flash forth lightning and scatter them; send out thine arrows and confuse (המם) them. Stretch forth Thy hand from on high; rescue me and deliver (נצל) me out of great waters, out of the hand of aliens' (vv. 5-7).

[162] Clifford notes that Psalms of communal lament especially entreat God to renew the Exodus (44.7-14; 74.12-17; 77.12-21; 80.9-12; 83.10-13; 89.2-38). Clifford, 'The Exodus in the Christian Bible', p. 350.

Moses and the Exodus tradition are especially prominent in Book IV of Psalms. The first Psalm in this Book (Psalm 90) is attributed to Moses, and 'the Mosaic motif or context brackets this collection at beginning and end'.[163] Psalms 104–106, which conclude Book IV, resonate with the major themes that thread their way through it. Wilson designates these Psalms as the 'editorial center' of the Psalter, since they effectively provide the 'answer' to the problem of the failure of the Davidic covenant posed in Psalm 89 and focused on in Books I–III.[164] They show that YHWH is King; he has been the refuge of Israel since long before the monarchy; he will continue to be a refuge now that the monarchy is gone; and those who trust in him are blessed.[165] In these Psalms, the use of the Exodus motif illustrates the 'already-not yet' eschatological tension that is present throughout the Psalms. N.T. Wright notes that Psalm 105 depicts the Exodus story in classic style, concluding with no ambiguity but only a continuing task: 'Praise YHWH and keep his commandments'. Psalm 106, in contrast, portrays the time of the Exodus and the monarchy as a time of ambiguity and sin. Wilson observes that it shifts the focus to Israel's rebellious response to each of YHWH's acts.[166] It concludes, 'Save us, O YHWH our God, and gather us from among the nations' (Ps. 106.47). Until that happened, the story would not be complete.[167] YHWH's saving victory of the past, repeatedly reproduced in the present lives of the faithful, would have its climax in the future.[168]

Ezra

The returns from exile represent a significant moment, a *recapitulation*, in the understanding of the Exodus as a repeatable event.[169] The story of God's people in Ezra and Nehemiah embodies much of what the prophets foretold in New Exodus language.[170]

---

[163] Gerald Henry Wilson, *The Editing of the Hebrew Psalter* (SBLSDS 76; Chico, CA: Scholars Press, 1985), p. 215.

[164] Wilson, *Editing,* pp. 126-27.

[165] Wilson, *Editing,* pp. 187-88; 213-19.

[166] Wilson, *Editing,* p. 219.

[167] Wright uses this to argue that 'the great story of the Hebrew Scriptures was therefore inevitably read in the second-temple period as a story in search of a conclusion' (N.T. Wright, *The New Testament and the People of God* (Christian Origins and the Question of God 1; Philadelphia: Fortress Press, 1992), pp. 216-17.

[168] Bruce, *New Testament Development,* p. 46.

[169] Clifford, 'The Exodus in the Christian Bible', p. 345.

[170] Nehemiah interprets the history of Israel in relation to the covenant blessings in Deuteronomy 28–30. He asks YHWH to remember that the people are his people,

Against this backdrop, there are two passages about the returns from Babylon in Ezra that seem deliberately to include details meant to mirror the Exodus and entry into Canaan.[171] The first return (Ezra 1–2) was led by Zerubbabel and Jeshua.[172] Ezra 1 begins with the account of Cyrus' decree to the exiles, in fulfillment of Isaiah's prophecy (Isa. 44.28), to 'go up' (עלה) to Jerusalem to build YHWH's house (Ezra 1.2-3; Exod. 12.38).[173] In accordance with the rest of the decree, 1.6 states, 'All those about them encouraged them with articles of silver, with gold, with goods, with cattle and with valuables, aside from all that was given as a freewill offering'. This loosely parallels Exod. 12.35, which records that the Egyptians gave the Israelites articles of silver and gold and clothing, and 12.38, which says they went up 'with flocks and herds, a very large number of livestock'.

Ezra led the second return himself, as recorded in Ezra 7–8. As well as repeating the decree of Cyrus for the people to give the exiles silver and gold and offerings (7.15-16), this passage includes further details that evoke the Exodus from Egypt and the entry into the promised land. Ezra 7.9 says, 'For on the first of the first month he began to go up from Babylon' (Ezra 7.9); 8.32 adds, 'thus we came to Jerusalem and remained there three days' (Ezra 8.32). Since the Exodus marked the first day of the first month (Exod. 12.2; Num. 33.3), and Joshua and those with him rested for three days after crossing the Jordan (Josh. 3.1-2), this return parallels these events.

---

his servant, whom he redeemed by his great power and by his strong hand (Neh. 1.10). Nehemiah, like Ezra, shows YHWH once again granting his people favor as they renew the covenant and celebrate the Feasts of the Passover and Tabernacles.

[171] See Jacob M. Myers, *Ezra, Nehemiah* (New Haven: Yale University Press, 1995), p. 9; Johanna W.H. van Wijk-Bos, *Ezra, Nehemiah, and Esther* (WBC; Louisville, KY: Westminster John Knox, 1998), pp. 20-21; Mark A. Throntveit, *Ezra–Nehemiah* (Interpretation; Westminster John Knox, 1992), p. 16. For alternate explanations of these details, see Melody D. Knowles, 'Pilgrimage Imagery in the Returns in Ezra', *JBL* 123.1 (Spring 2004), pp. 57-74.

[172] 'Jeshua' in Ezra is spelled 'Joshua' in the book of Zechariah.

[173] Just as in the first Exodus, YHWH effects this 'going up' through a pagan ruler who does not know him (Exod. 5.2; Isa. 45.4). David Isbell further compares Pharaoh and Cyrus. Whereas Pharaoh – whose will caused oppression and death – became the epitome of an oppressive ruler, Cyrus – the agent of freedom and restoration – is actually described as YHWH's anointed (משיח, Isa. 45.1). From a biblical perspective, neither king was acting on his own initiative nor even fully grasped the consequences of his actions. These characterizations emphasize that it is only YHWH who creates history. Isbell, *The Function of Exodus Motifs in Biblical Narratives: Theological Didactic Drama*, pp. 163-65.

In addition, there are repeated statements that the 'hand of YHWH' was upon Ezra (7.6; 7.9; 7.23), and 7.23 adds that Cyrus issued the decree 'so that there [would] not be wrath against the kingdom of the king and his sons' (cf. Exodus 4–12). Toward the end of the book, Ezra more explicitly compares the situation of the exiles to that of the Israelites in Egypt ('For we are slaves; yet in our bondage our God has not forsaken us', 9.9) and to Israel's immanent entry into Canaan, in which YHWH commanded the people to separate themselves from the Canaanites (9.11; 6.21). Moreover, in ch. 6, the community is finally able to dedicate the temple, the symbol of God's presence with his people (Exod. 29.45), and to celebrate the Passover (6.19-22).

Cumulatively, it seems likely that Ezra deliberately made use of the Exodus motif in order to reinforce the connections with YHWH's earlier deliverance and the prophetic promises of restoration that envisioned New Exodus activity.

Summary

The saving acts of God at the Exodus are the kerygmatic nucleus of the OT.[174] The Exodus is woven into the fabric of the OT not only as historical fact but as a pattern for new situations, typifying both judgment and salvation. Voices of OT authors in every genre and every time period echo the language of Israel's founding event as they describe their history, celebrate YHWH's faithfulness, remember his character, lament his judgment, cry out for deliverance, and prophesy about the future. Along the way, the motif becomes intertwined with the cycle of covenant faithfulness and unfaithfulness, blessings and curses of Deuteronomy 28–30. In addition, it carries with it the expectation of a prophet like Moses and later, the kingly Branch of David. In the writings of the prophets, it becomes evident that YHWH's future Exodus activity will surpass the first, even replacing it as the definitive act associated with his name (Isa. 43.18-19; Jer. 16.14-15; Hag. 2.9). The language of the motif also ascends to a universal and eschatological horizon. Even as the returns from exile partially

---

[174] Augustine Stock, *The Way in the Wilderness: Exodus, Wilderness and Moses Themes in Old Testament and New* (Collegeville, MN: The Liturgical Press, 1969), p. v. Hyde also notes this function in Israel's liturgy. Hyde, 'The Remembrance of the Exodus in the Psalms', p. 413.

fulfilled this New Exodus anticipation, they 'fell short of the glorious vision of the prophets'.[175] The true end of Israel's exile, the new covenant written on people's hearts and minds, the radiant temple filled with YHWH's glory, the purified people of God, the pouring out of the Spirit, and the pilgrimage of the nations to worship YHWH in Zion – these must await greater fulfillment in the future.

---

[175] Parry, 'Prolegomena to Interpretation of Lamentations', loc. 10638.

3

THE EXODUS MOTIF IN THE GOSPELS AND ACTS

Introduction

Just as the motif of the Exodus is developed and reimagined throughout the OT, the NT is replete with Exodus allusions and typological fulfillments. As Haugen observes, 'the theme of the Exodus is a continual thread running through the Scriptures'.[1] Yet in the NT, beginning in the Gospels, the Exodus motif acquires new dimensions and a christocentric focus. This chapter will examine the distinct nuances and contributions of each Gospel writer to the overall development of these motific elements.[2]

Matthew

The Gospel of Matthew, with its clear and frequent links to the OT, serves as a canonical bridge between the past experiences and traditions of Israel and the fulfillment of Israel's hope through the life of Jesus the Messiah. As Matthew interacts with Israel's Scriptures, he employs the familiar typological hermeneutic of the OT, focusing on discerning recurring patterns in God's activity that point to God's same hand working in the past and the present.[3] This section will focus

---

[1] Haugen, 'Consummation of the Exodus', p. 11.

[2] Due to the overlap of content in the Gospels, sections on individual books will not cover every parallel. Rather, they will focus on the overall appropriation of the motif and the emphases of each author.

[3] Craig Blomberg, 'Matthew', in G.K. Beale and D.A. Carson (eds.), *Commentary on the New Testament Use of the Old Testament* (Grand Rapids: Baker Academic, Kindle

especially on the first six chapters of Matthew to demonstrate how he carefully constructs his Moses/Exodus typology through the use of explicit statements, reminiscent circumstances, key words and phrases, and structural parallels.[4] It will conclude by analyzing Jesus' words about 'rest' in Mt. 11.28-30.[5]

Before he comes to the Exodus, Matthew evokes the beginning of history with the words 'a record of the genealogy (γένεσις) of Jesus Christ' (1.1).[6] He continues, '... the Son of David, the Son of Abraham'.[7] These words show that Jesus embodies the fulfillment of OT promises related to a Davidic king and to God's blessing all nations of the earth through Abraham's seed (Gen. 49.10; 2 Sam. 7.8-16; Gen. 12.3). In the OT prophets, these promises had become intertwined with prophecies of New Exodus events (e.g. Isa. 9.6-7; Jer. 23.5-6; Hos. 1.10-11; Mic. 5.3-4; Zech. 2; 6.12-13; 8; Mal. 3.17), and it is from this tradition that Matthew continues to draw with four quotations from the OT and one ambiguous quotation from 'the prophets'.

At the end of ch. 1, Matthew emphasizes Jesus' miraculous birth, his vocation as Savior of his people, and his divine identity through a combined quotation of Isa. 7.14 and Isa. 9.6-7. Jesus would lead his people not out of physical bondage or exile, but out of bondage to sin, and in him, God would once more dwell among his people.[8]

---

edn, 2007), loc. 514. This was consistent with the typological understanding and use of Scripture that was already present within the OT.

[4] Allison, *The New Moses*, p. 140. Allison provides additional examples of parallels between Moses and Jesus that will not be covered here (e.g. Matthew's 'transition formula' and the close of the Pentateuch; the miracle stories of chs. 8-9 vis-à-vis the plagues).

[5] The Prologues of all four Gospels lay out the hermeneutical frameworks of the entire narratives. For this reason, I will devote more careful attention to the Prologues as representative samples of the authors' particular interests. For example, Richard Hays notes how Matthew 'frontloads' Matthew's early chapters with statements about Jesus' life fulfilling what was written in Scripture (7 out of 10 of these formulaic quotations occur before ch. 5). Hays contends, 'This cluster of fulfillment quotations near the beginning of the Gospel conditions readers to expect that nearly everything in the story of Jesus will turn out to be the fulfillment of something pre-scripted by God through the prophets'. Richard Hays, *Reading Backwards*, locs. 996-1012.

[6] Cf. Mk 1.1, 'The beginning (Ἀρχὴ) of the Gospel of Jesus Christ, the Son of God'; Jn 1.1-5.

[7] Perhaps this title, in addition to pointing to Jesus as the coming Davidic King or 'Branch', indicates how Jesus, like Solomon – the 'son of David' – will establish the new temple of YHWH (Zech. 6.12; cf. 2 Chron. 35.5).

[8] Scholars like Pao and Wright suggest that the announcement of God's presence among his people, after 400 years of silence, was effectively the announcement of

In ch. 2, Matthew builds on this by establishing Jesus as the King of the Jews (Mt. 2.2) and the eternal Shepherd of Micah 5 (Mt. 2.6).[9] These roles of King and Shepherd, ascribed to YHWH in the first Exodus, are extended to Jesus to build anticipation of a renewal of Exodus miracles (1 Sam. 12.10 of the Exodus; Exod. 15.13; Pss. 77.20; 78.52; Isa. 40.11; cf. Mic. 7.14-15). Matthew then adds a unique citation from Hos. 11.1 (Mt. 2.15) that attributes to Jesus the identity of the Son of God (cf. Exod. 4.4). This indicates that in some sense, Jesus is reliving Israel's history[10] as well as embodying Israel's messianic hopes: he is YHWH's 'chosen' one (Isa. 41.8; 42.1). It also signals the imminent fulfillment of the New Exodus that pervades Hosea's writings.[11]

In a more subtle way, Matthew intimates three additional claims about Jesus: he is the star and scepter of Balaam's prophecy (Num. 24.8, 9, 17), the Branch of David, and the new Moses. In regard to the first, Number 23–24 seems to lie behind Hosea's text (Hos. 11.1, 10-11), and the combination of the quotation from Hosea, the application of the Exodus to Israel's king (as in Numbers), and the statement

---

the end of the exile of the true Israel. Pao, *Acts and the Isaianic New Exodus*, p. 146; Wright, *Jesus and the Victory of God*, II, p. 371. Cf. promises such as Ezek. 37.27, 'I will be with them; I will be their God, and they will be my people'. See Hays for a discussion of how in Matthew, Jesus may be seen as replacing *Torah* and embodying God's presence among the people (like the Shekinah, cf. Mt. 18.20 in light of *m. Ab.* 3.2). Hays, *Reading Backwards*, loc. 1186.

[9] The accounts of Jesus' birth and death, both of which contain special quotations and titles to establish Jesus' identity, bracket his ministry in Matthew. Note the repetition of the titles 'King of the Jews' (27.11), 'Shepherd' (26.31), and 'Son of God' (27.54) at the end of the Gospel.

[10] Enns comments, 'Jesus is to be understood as living out Israel's experience. He is the final, concrete focal point for Israel's experience, the "ultimate Israel"'. Peter Enns, 'Exodus/New Exodus', in Vanhoozer, *Dictionary for Theological Interpretation of the Bible*, p. 217.

[11] I agree with Beale, who sees this as a typological interpretation based to some degree on what Hosea already recognizes: 'Hosea sees that these Numbers allusions about the past coming "out of Egypt" together with the "lion" image [Num. 23.22, 24; 24.8, 9] will be recapitulated again in the eschatological future'. Beale notes that the Numbers passage also provides the precedent for applying the Exodus/Israel's experience to Israel's king. Beale, 'Hosea 11:1 in Matthew 2:15', p. 703. Further, Beale points to a connection between Hos. 10.14-15 (a time of tumult, mothers and infants' being dashed to pieces, and the king of Israel's being completely cut off) and Mt. 2.13-21, where the slaying of male children is followed by Herod's death (p. 711). Beale also observes that Hos. 1.10-11 provides the closest parallel to Jesus' being called 'Son of the living God' (Mt. 16.16). Here also, Jesus is seen as the 'individual kingly son leading the sons of Israel, whom he represents' (p. 709).

about the wise men's vision of the king's star point unmistakably to this passage. In regard to the second, the LXX usually translates the word נצר ('Branch') as ἀνατολή, which means 'east' and can refer to the 'rising' of the sun or a star or to the 'dawn'.[12] Matthew's description of a rising eastern star using this word (Mt. 2.1; 2; 9), in the context of the birth of David's kingly son in Bethlehem, evokes prophecies of New Exodus activity related to the Branch (Isa. 60.19; Jer. 23.5; Zech. 3.8; 6.12, LXX; cf. Lk. 1.78). The possibility of this double entendre is strengthened by the puzzling statement that Jesus' birth fulfilled the prophets' words that 'he should be called a Nazarene' (Mt. 2.23). As Craig Blomberg observes, no OT (or apocryphal/pseudepigraphal) text predicts that anyone will be called a Nazarene![13] However, Matthew could be making a pun on the Hebrew word for 'Branch' (נצר) and the Greek word for 'Nazareth' (Ναζαρέτ).[14] This would account for Matthew's attributing these words to multiple prophets. Could it be that Matthew intended two puns about the Branch in ch. 2? In regard to the third, similarities between the early life of Jesus and the life of Moses reinforce the image of Jesus as Israel's Savior.[15] King Herod, like Pharaoh, issues a decree to kill Jewish children.[16] Joseph is warned in a dream and flees with Mary and Jesus to safety (ironically) in Egypt (cf. Moses' flight from Egypt after he killed an Egyptian).[17] Here they stay until an angel tells Joseph, 'those who sought the child's life are dead' (cf. Exod. 4.19, 'those who were seeking your life are dead').

---

[12] It seems that the idea connecting this to 'Branch' or 'shoot' is that of *upward movement*.

[13] Blomberg, 'Matthew', loc. 823.

[14] Blomberg, 'Matthew', loc. 823. Blomberg does not discuss the use of ἀνατολή.

[15] Simon Kistemaker details more parallels between Moses and Jesus. Simon J. Kistemaker, *Acts* (New Testament Commentary; Grand Rapids: Baker Academic, 1991), p. 251.

[16] Here, Matthew again employs a typological hermeneutic (Jer. 31.15), noting what he believes is more than a coincidence between similar situations – especially in the messianic age spoken of in the rest of Jeremiah 31. Blomberg notes that Jewish readers may have also heard echoes of the hopeful promise in Jer. 31.16 that Rachel's children would one day return from exile (just as the holy family would return one day from Egypt). Blomberg, 'Matthew', loc. 791. Matthew's strategic quotation also suggests that the New Exodus of Jeremiah 31, including the new covenant and gift of the Holy Spirit, is on the horizon. Hays shows how Matthew is 'thinking about the *shape* of Israel's story and linking Jesus' life with key passages that promise God's unbreakable redemptive love for his people'. Hays, *Reading Backwards*, loc. 1123.

[17] Stock points to the use of the same verbal form (ἀνεχώρησεν) in Exod. 2.15 LXX and Mt. 2.22. Stock, *A Way in the Wilderness*, p. 26.

Chapters 3–5 continue to herald the arrival of the New Exodus and portray Jesus' life as recapitulating the history of Israel. Like the other Gospel writers, Matthew identifies John as the one Isaiah spoke of who would prepare the way for the coming of the Lord (3.3; Isa. 40.3).[18] N.T. Wright asserts that by gathering people in the wilderness, John was symbolically saying, 'This is the New Exodus'. John was declaring that the forgiveness people would usually obtain through the temple cult, they could have through water baptism. Here was the new Israel that YHWH would vindicate.[19] John's sharp words introduce the conflict with the religious leaders that will culminate in Jesus' death (3.7-10) and the eventual break with Israel's religious system and foreshadow the ingathering of the nations (Abraham's true children – not only sand [Gen. 22.17], but rocks, 3.9) that was proclaimed in the OT (Gen. 22.18; Isa. 2.2; 42.6; Jer. 3.17; Dan. 7.14). John introduces Jesus as the one who will baptize with the Holy Spirit and fire as well as execute judgment (3.11-12). These words about fire and chaff evoke Scriptures such as Exod. 15.7 ('You overthrow those who rise up against You; You send forth your burning anger, and it consumes them as chaff'), Isa. 41.2 ('Who has aroused one from the east [ἀπὸ ἀνατολῶν, LXX] whom He calls in righteousness to His feet? He delivers up nations before him and subdues kings. He makes them like dust with his sword, as the wind-driven chaff with his bow'), and Mal. 4.1-2 (which tells of a coming day of judgment on the wicked and the advent of the sun of righteousness), all with Exodus/New Exodus contexts.

At Jesus' baptism, he 'comes up' out of the water, is anointed by the Spirit, and is declared to be God's Beloved Son. This parallels Israel's crossing through the Red Sea and confirms Jesus' identity as the Servant of Isaiah's writings ('Behold, My Servant, whom I uphold; My chosen one in whom My soul delights. I have put My Spirit upon Him; He will bring forth justice to the nations' Isa. 42.1). Jesus is immediately led by the Spirit into the wilderness to be tempted (cf. Exod. 13.18; Heb. 3.9). These words echo Deut. 8.2: 'You shall remember all the way which the Lord your God has led

---

[18] The themes of the coming of the kingdom of heaven (Mt. 3.2), repentance/forgiveness of sins, and the revelation of God's glory at Jesus' baptism further tie these passages together.

[19] Wright, *Jesus and the Victory of God*, II, p. 160.

you in the wilderness these forty years, that He might humble you, testing you, to know what was in your heart ...' Beale comments that in the desert, Jesus retraces 'Israel's steps up to the point they failed, and then [continues] to obey and succeed in the mission Israel should have carried out'.[20] His fast of forty days and nights parallel Israel's forty years of wandering in the desert.[21] It is not by chance that Jesus' replies to the tempter are all drawn from the Deuteronomic context that emphasizes testing in the wilderness (Deut. 8.3; 6.13, 16; Mt. 4.1-11). Unlike Israel, Jesus follows the leading of the Spirit, resists temptation with God's word, and steadfastly depends upon his Father.

After this time, Jesus begins to preach the good news of the coming of the kingdom of heaven. Matthew draws from Isaiah 9 to establish that Jesus is the Davidic and divine King who will break the yoke of oppression and bring about justice for his people (Isa. 9.1-7; Mt. 4.11-17). As Matthew ties Jesus' healings here to Isaiah 9, he later connects them explicitly with Jesus' role as the Servant (Mt. 8.17 and Isa. 53.5-6; Mt. 11.5 and Isa. 61.1-2).[22] At the end of ch. 4, Jesus calls 12 disciples to represent the establishment of the true Israel and goes up on a mountain to reissue the Law of the new covenant that he will later enact with his blood (Mt. 5; 26.28; cf. Deut. 18.18).[23]

Matthew also contains the longer version of the Lord's Prayer, which demonstrates how Jesus understood his kingdom work in New Exodus terms.[24] N.T. Wright has termed Jesus' words 'the prayer of the new wilderness wandering people', suggesting that the prayer encapsulates and celebrates the greater liberation that Jesus brought.[25] The phrases in the prayer represent a cohesive petition for the God of

---

[20] Beale, 'Hosea 11:1 in Matthew 2:15', p. 710. Later, Jesus will take up Israel's punishment, even though he does not deserve it, to restore the people to God.

[21] Allison believes that the addition of 'and nights' in Matthew is intended to further emphasize parallels between Jesus and Moses, who fasted 40 days and nights when he received the Law on Mt. Sinai (Deut. 9.9). This seems quite plausible in light of the story's details and its placement before the Sermon on the Mount. Allison does not see the need to dichotomize Matthew's Moses and Israel typology in a rigid, Western sense. Allison, *The New Moses*, pp. 165-72.

[22] Watts, 'Exodus', p. 485.

[23] Stock, *A Way in the Wilderness*, pp. 34-35. Allison has a lengthy discussion about the connection between the Messiah and Torah (cf. Isa. 42.1-4) and the Messiah as the prophet like Moses. Allison, *The New Moses*, p. 185.

[24] Wright, 'The Lord's Prayer'.

[25] Wright, 'The Lord's Prayer'.

the Exodus to bring his holy community out of bondage to sin, through a time of testing, and into its promised inheritance.[26] The disciples are to pray that God would make his name great and expand his kingdom according to the prophecies of the OT that looked forward to both something new and something familiar.

- *Our Father* ... From the first words, the prayer echoes the Exodus tradition. Addressing God directly as 'Father' is not common in the OT, yet it occurs first in the Song of Moses and subsequently in texts about the New Exodus with noteworthy consistency.[27] Israel's filial relationship with God is further the basis for Moses' words to Pharaoh: 'Thus says YHWH, "Israel is My son, My firstborn. So I said to you, 'Let My son go that he may serve Me'; but you have refused to let him go. Behold, I will kill your son, your firstborn"' (Exod. 4.22-23).

- *Hallowed be your name* ... This, too, resonates with the Exodus context of the prayer. God first revealed his name, YHWH, to Moses in tandem with God's deliverance. From the Exodus onward, God's people would identify him by this name (Exod. 6.6-7). In the Exodus and through the lives of his people, God purposes, 'Then they [or you] will know that I am YHWH'; his name will be proclaimed 'through all the earth' (Exod. 9.16). In addition, New Exodus texts such as Ezek. 36.23-28 anticipate the vindication of YHWH's great name in the sight of the nations when YHWH restores Israel, gives her a new heart, puts his Spirit in her, and once again calls her his people.

---

[26] R.F. Cyster notes that Jesus was about to give his life as a ransom, and the New Exodus (Lk. 9.31) would free his people to 'begin their journey of faith'. He points to the structure of Exodus 15–17, which discusses 1) the gift of the daily bread, 2) the people's sin, which led to 3) their tempting God, and 4) deliverance from the Amalekites, arguing that these provide the background for interpreting the Lord's Prayer. R.F. Cyster, 'The Lord's Prayer and the Exodus Tradition', *Theology*, 64.495 (1961), pp. 377-81.

[27] Brant Pitre concludes, in fact, that there is a direct connection between praying to 'our Father' about his kingdom and the image of the Kingdom of God's being established in and through the anointed Son of David (based on his study of 1 Chron. 29.10-13; Isa. 63.10-17; and Jer. 3.16-19). He points out that this link also occurs in Hosea, when God refers to the past Exodus in terms of his paternal relationship to Israel: 'When Israel was a child, I loved him, and out of Egypt I called my son' (Hos. 11.1). Brant Pitre, 'The Lord's Prayer and the New Exodus', *Letter & Spirit* 2 (2005), pp. 69-96 (73-77).

- *Your kingdom come, your will be done on earth* ... These phrases call to mind the contest between Israel's God (Exod. 6.7; 1 Sam. 12.10; Ezek. 20.33) and the supposedly divine Pharaoh (along with other gods of Egypt).[28] Throughout the Exodus story, the will of Pharaoh conflicts with the will of YHWH until YHWH's will prevails. Through this, YHWH establishes a holy people over which he will rule: 'You shall be to Me a kingdom of priests and a holy nation' (Exod. 19.6). The hope for the coming of God's kingdom was repeated in New Exodus prophecies like Isa. 9.6-7, Jer. 13.14-18, Mic. 4.1-8, and Zech. 6.12-13, which speak of the ingathering of both Jews and Gentiles under the righteous reign of YHWH and/or the Messiah.

- *Give us this day our daily bread* is an unmistakable reference to manna – a bread that came daily and directly from God (Exod. 16.12) and was expected to reappear in the age of the Messiah (2 Bar. 29.3-8).[29] Pitre comments that 'Jesus is not merely instructing his disciples to pray for the mundane bread of daily existence. Rather, *he is teaching them to pray for the new manna of the new exodus*'.[30] N.T. Wright adds that manna is 'the food of inaugurated eschatology, the food that is needed because the kingdom has already broken in and because it is not yet consummated'.[31] This daily provision surely includes what is

---

[28] Watts, 'Exodus', p. 479.

[29] Richard Bauckham, *The Testimony of the Beloved Disciple: Narrative, History, and Theology in the Gospel of John* (Grand Rapids: Baker Academic, 2007), p. 214. The noun ἐπιούσιος is extremely rare and of debated meaning. The options include *'daily, necessary for existence, for the following day, for the future'* (BAGD). If the intended meaning is 'the bread of two days', parallel to the people's gathering manna for the Sabbath (Exod. 16.23), Cyster comments that it points both to God's provision and the coming of the holy Sabbath (rest) that remains for God's people. He connects it also with the bread of communion, which represents God's sustaining presence as well as foreshadows the eschatological meal (Origen, *DeOratione*, 27.9). Cyster, 'The Lord's Prayer', p. 379.

[30] Brant Pitre, *Jesus and the Last Supper* (Grand Rapids: Eerdmans, Kindle edn, 2015), p. 177. Footnote 81 offers an extensive list of ancient and modern commentators who connect 'daily bread' and manna. See also W.D. Davies and Dale C. Allison, *A Critical and Exegetical Commentary on the Gospel According to Saint Matthew: Introduction and Commentary on Matthew I-VII* (ICC; Edinburgh: T. & T. Clark, 1988), p. 609; Cyster, 'The Lord's Prayer', p. 379.

[31] Wright, 'The Lord's Prayer'. Pitre examines Jewish literature (e.g. *2 Bar. 29*) and connects the provision of manna with the coming of the Messiah. See Pitre, 'Lord's Prayer'.

necessary to sustain both physical and spiritual life, not least of which are Christ's body given for us (Jn 6.51) and his word (Jn 5.24; 8.51).

- *Forgive us our debts* ... The corporate context of this petition, the OT background of the prayer, and Jewish expectations of the day point to the connection of this forgiveness with the New Exodus and new covenant (Isa. 53.5; Jer. 31.34). In addition, it is possible that Matthew's Jewish audience heard overtones of the eschatological Jubilee behind this 'remission of debts' (cf. Isa. 61.1-3; Mt. 11.5).[32] Just as the Jubilee provisions were grounded in the Exodus, Jesus' expectation is that his followers will offer to others the forgiveness that they have received.[33]

- *Lead us not into temptation* ... This clause echoes back to the wilderness, to Jesus' own temptation (Mt. 4), and to the trials that God's people face (Heb. 3.8, 9, 15, 16). The Greek word for 'temptation' here is πειρασμός (from πειράζω, 'to test'), and it is used to translate two Hebrew words (נסה and מסה). πειρασμός was used three different ways in the Exodus context (LXX). First, it described the *tests* or *trials* that preceded the Exodus (Deut. 4.34; 7.19, 29.3, all נסה) – YHWH brought his people out with *trials*, signs, and wonders. This seems to refer to the plagues, either in their capacity to challenge Pharaoh and give him an opportunity to conform to YHWH's will or in the suffering they inflicted on the Egyptians. Second, YHWH tested his people in the wilderness, to see whether they would walk in his instruction (Exod. 15.25; 16.4; Exod. 20.20).[34]

---

[32] The word for 'forgive' here (ἄφες) and the one in the LXX that describes the release of debts in the Jubilee (ἄφεσιν, Deut. 15.1; 31.10) are from the same verb (ἀφίημι). N.T. Wright argues that in the OT, forgiveness of sin is tied to God's redemption of individuals as well as the forgiveness of corporate sins that caused them to go into exile. Forgiveness of sin, then, can signal the end of exile. Wright, *Jesus and the Victory of God*, II, p. 268. For a discussion of Jewish writings and expectations about the Jubilee, see Pitre, *Jesus and the Last Supper*, pp. 178-82.

[33] Wright, 'The Lord's Prayer'. For parallel contemporary Jewish prayers, see Davies and Allison, *Matthew I-VII*, I, p. 610.

[34] Most commentators, in light of Jas 1.13, reject this meaning for the Lord's Prayer. However, Jas 1.13 must be interpreted in light of other Scriptures that plainly state that God tested people or allowed them to be tested (Gen. 22.1; the book of Job; Zech. 13.9; Mt. 4.1). Perhaps the key lies in the motive (i.e. God never wills for

Third, the people put YHWH to the test (Exod. 17.2; Num.
14.22; Deut. 6.16).[35] Some interpret this clause in the Lord's
Prayer against the Exodus background and with the first
meaning – as a petition for God to keep his people from
eschatological tribulation (the 'messianic woes') or the
judgments associated with the New Exodus (parallel to the
plagues).[36] However, as Wright observes, salvation for the
Church consists not in being spared suffering, but in
persevering under trial (Jas 1.2). He argues for the third
meaning, interpreting this as a prayer for God to enable his
people to be faithful to him and not put him to the test. The
people of the New Exodus must follow Jesus' lead and succeed
where their predecessors failed (Mt. 4.7; 1 Cor. 10.9; Heb. 3.7).[37]

- *but deliver us from the evil one* (or *'evil'*).[38] This final petition, with
  the same verb that was used of the Exodus deliverance

people to do evil or tests them for the purpose of entrapping them in sin) or in the
agency (God does not tempt them himself, but allows them to be tempted). Davies
and Allison suggest that this phrase reflects a Semitic causative with permissive force
– 'do not let us fall victim'. Davies and Allison, *Matthew I-VII*, I, p. 613.

[35] Interestingly, although the place where the people 'tested' YHWH is called מסה,
the verb used to explain the reason for this name is נסה in both texts (Exod. 17.7 and
Deut. 6.16). מסה is used only of God's trials before the Exodus.

[36] Davies and Allison, *Matthew I-VII*, I, pp. 594, 614. This interpretation
would align with Matthew's use of the aorist, indicating a specific tribulation and
evil. Beale argues that the chaos of the Exodus plagues (and later Israel's
tribulation in exile) come to be seen as a pattern for end-time tribulation
(inaugurated in the trials of Jesus' ministry and the church). However, he does
not connect this specifically with the Lord's Prayer. Beale, *New Testament Biblical
Theology*, locs. 4124-26. N.T. Wright's earlier work was along these lines as well.
Wright, *Jesus and the Victory of God*, II, pp. 577-79. See also Pitre, *Jesus and the Last
Supper*, p. 184. Pitre's argumentation is imprecise and has some logical gaps.
Further, he reads this meaning into others' works (e.g. Wright, *The Lord's Prayer*)
and translations (e.g. he asserts that the NEB's 'Do not bring us to the test'
implies they subscribe to the same eschatological interpretation, which seems far
from certain). See n. 99 below.

[37] Wright, 'The Lord's Prayer'. Cyster likewise observes, 'The supreme danger
will always be that the people of God may hesitate, look fearfully backwards,
doubt the power of God to guide, and be led into *the* temptation – tempting God
and saying, "is the Lord among us, or not?"' (Exod. 17.7). Cyster, 'The Lord's
Prayer', p. 380.

[38] I agree with Davies and Allison, who note that 'the evil one' is a favorite
expression of Matthew (he uses the clearly masculine form, ὁ πονηρὸς, in 13.19,
38, and probably 5.37). Davies and Allison, *Matthew I-VII*, 1.614. 'For Yours is
the kingdom ...' is absent in early and significant representatives of the
Alexandrian (א B), Western (D and most of the Old Latin), and other (*f*¹) types

(ῥύομαι, Exod. 6.6 LXX), situates God's people in the position of the Israelites. It elicits a comparison between a powerful but defeated Pharaoh and the one who continues to enslave people to sin, but whom the victorious Second Moses will ultimately overcome (cf. Jn 17.15, 'keep them from the evil one'; 2 Thess. 3.3, 'He will strengthen and protect you from the evil one'; cf. 1 Jn 5.18).

Finally, Matthew alone records Jesus' words, 'Come to Me, all who are weary (οἱ κοπιῶντες, 'the laboring ones') and heavy-laden ([οἱ] πεφορτισμένοι, 'those having been burdened') and I will give you rest (refresh you)' (Mt. 11.28). From the beginning, heavy labor was associated with the curse of sin (Gen. 3.16-17; cf. Gen. 5.29), which also resulted in broken fellowship with God and exile from Eden. In Egypt, God's people were once again far from home and consigned to hard labor (Exod. 1.11) under the burdens of the Egyptians (Exod. 6.6). YHWH freed them from this yoke to bear his ('I broke the bars of your yoke', Lev. 26.13 of the Exodus; cf. Exod. 4.23, 'that he may *serve* me'), offering them covenant fellowship and rest in the land of Canaan ('My presence shall go with you, and I will give you rest', Exod. 33.14; Josh. 1.13; 21.44). The Sabbath day, a haven of Edenic rest from labor, now also symbolized the deliverance and rest that God provided at the Exodus (Deut. 5.15; cf. the 1st day of the 7th month, the seventh year, and the year of Jubilee).

The Israelites enjoyed this rest when they followed the covenant; but when they broke it, they went into exile and found no rest (Deut. 28.64-65). In Mt. 11.28, Jesus quotes from Jer. 6.6, when YHWH had again offered to those who would walk in the ancient paths: 'You will find rest for your souls'. They had refused and were taken into exile (where they found no rest, Jer. 45.3, Lam. 1.3; 5.5). However, YHWH had again promised rest in a future restoration – a New Exodus. Isaiah 14.3 declares that when he restores them, YHWH will give his people 'rest from [their] pain and turmoil and harsh service in which [they] have been enslaved'; Jeremiah says that in that day, YHWH will 'satisfy the weary ones and refresh everyone who languishes' (31.25); and in

---

of texts as well as early commentaries of the Fathers (Tertullian, Origen, Cyprian). Metzger concludes that it was a later ascription for liturgical use. Bruce M. Metzger, *A Textual Commentary on The Greek New Testament* (Stuttgart: Deutsche Bibelgesellschaft, 2nd edn, 1994), p. 14.

Ezek. 34.15, YHWH proclaims, 'I will feed My flock and I will lead them to rest'. Jesus offers the beginnings of this eschatological rest, spiritual return from exile, and restored fellowship to God through a new covenant.

Jesus' words are directly related to the incidents that follow – two confrontations with the Pharisees about the Sabbath, sacrifices, and temple, accompanied by quotations from Hosea (concerning future judgment and restoration) and Isa. 42.1-3 (which tells how YHWH's gentle Servant will bring justice and liberation). Matthew implies here what Luke makes explicit, that Jesus' easy yoke stands in contrast to the heavy burdens that the religious leaders impose on others (Lk. 11.46). He also highlights Jesus' claims that something greater than the temple has arrived and that 'the Son of Man is Lord of the Sabbath' (Mt. 12.6, 8).[39] Just as the Father has given Jesus 'all things', and Jesus is the only one who reveals the Father (11.27), Jesus is sovereign over the Law.[40] Jesus is the fulfillment of prophetic hopes; he has both the authority and the means to proclaim divine judgment and to offer divine rest. The one who shared rest with his creation at the beginning was among them, proclaiming God's favor and freedom.

Mark

In Mark, we find perhaps the most pervasive, although subtle, use of the Exodus motif in the Gospels. Mark, like other Gospel writers, typifies Jesus' life as repeating key experiences of Israel and alludes to the approach of New Exodus salvation and judgment foretold by many OT prophets. However, there is compelling evidence that Mark's structure, themes, and some narrative details derive more specifically from the New Exodus that Isaiah envisions.[41]

---

[39] The order of the sentence makes this statement even more emphatic: κύριος γάρ ἐστιν τοῦ σαββάτου ὁ υἱὸς τοῦ ἀνθρώπου.

[40] Blomberg, 'Matthew', loc. 1887. Allison notes here the continuation of Matthew's 'Moses typology' with Jesus' authority over the Law, exclusive and reciprocal divine knowledge, his meekness/humility, and giving of rest. Allison, *The New Moses*, p. 222.

[41] Hung, 'Relationship and Rebirth', p. 79. Although Mark appropriates Isaiah's concept of a New Exodus in a clear and significant way, his motific use of the Exodus is not limited to Isaiah. He also draws, for example, from Psalms, Jeremiah, Ezekiel, Hosea, Joel, and Malachi.

Mark's carefully-constructed prologue (1.1-15), featuring two clusters of Exodus/New Exodus quotations and allusions (1.2-3, 11) and the Exodus typology in Jesus' life (1.12-13), signals to the reader that this New Exodus will be Mark's 'overall conceptual framework'.[42] It is also possible to understand the progression of Mark's Gospel according to the three-part schema of Isaiah's New Exodus: YHWH's delivering exiled Israel from Babylon and her idols (Jesus' 'evangelistic ministry of powerful words and deeds in Galilee and beyond', Mk 1.1–8.21), a journey to Jerusalem along 'the way' (a journey with Jesus' 'blind disciples' on 'the way', Mk 8.22/27–10.45/11.1), and the arrival in Jerusalem, where YHWH is enthroned (Mk 11.2).[43] As Mark inserts thematic parallels into this broad matrix, he underscores the coming of both YHWH's deliverance to Jews and Gentiles and YHWH's judgment on those who continually refuse to follow him. After examining the prologue, which (in line with ancient literary customs) is of considerable importance to Mark's agenda, this section will briefly survey the development of the New Exodus in these main sections of Mark's Gospel.[44]

Mark brackets the prologue with announcements of good news and affirmations of Jesus' divine Sonship (1.1; 13-15).[45] The enclosed verses focus on three things: the messenger, the coming Lord, and the

---

[42] Rikki E. Watts, *Isaiah's New Exodus in Mark* (Grand Rapids: Baker Academic, 1997), p. 90. Hung describes this as Isaiah's 'primary horizon'. Hung, 'Relationship and Rebirth', p. 78. Thorsten Moritz calls it 'an important hermeneutical key to this Gospel'. Thorsten Moritz, 'Mark, Book of', in Kevin J. Vanhoozer *et al.* (eds.), *Dictionary for Theological Interpretation of the Bible* (Grand Rapids: Baker Book House, 2005), p. 481.

[43] Watts, *Isaiah's New Exodus in Mark*, p. 371. Moritz comments that reading Mark in light of the Exodus motif has the advantage of explaining Jesus' 'wanderings around Galilee and Judea, which may well have the purpose of reliving the desert wanderings of Israel'. Moritz, 'Mark, Book of', p. 482; cf. Piper, 'Unchanging Promises', p. 18.

[44] See Watts for a discussion of the prologue's importance in ancient texts and its relation to the work as a whole. Watts, *Isaiah's New Exodus in Mark*, p. 54.

[45] The Καθὼς γέγραπται ('just as it is written') in Mk 1.2 is epexegetical – it indicates that this good news about Jesus is the good news about which Isaiah wrote. Robert Guelich contends that this 'heading' covers the entire prologue (i.e. vv. 1-15 sketch 'the beginning of the gospel about Jesus Messiah, Son of God, as written by Isaiah the prophet'), and reflects the concerns of the entire work. Robert A. Guelich, *Mark 1-8:26* (WBC 34A; Grand Rapids: Zondervan, 2015), pp. 12-14; Watts, *Isaiah's New Exodus in Mark*, p. 56.

wilderness, all with New Exodus overtones.[46] Mark brings these together through a quotation from 'Isaiah the prophet' that will be programmatic for his Gospel. This is a composite citation, a fusion of Exod. 23.23, Mal. 3.1 (already a reworking of the Exodus passage), and the prologue (40.3) of Isaiah's 'Book of Consolation'.[47] In Exodus 23, YHWH promises to send an angel/messenger who bears YHWH's name before the people to guard them and bring them into the land (Exod. 23.20-21). Malachi 3, speaking of a future 'going out,' adds an ironic twist: YHWH will send a messenger before the sudden coming of the Lord (האדון)/the messenger of the covenant (הברית מלאך) to the temple *to judge* and *refine* (and possibly *curse*) unfaithful Israel (Mal. 2.2-3; 3.2; 4.5-6). This casts the threat of judgment forward onto Isaiah's message, which speaks of YHWH's coming, preceded by a messenger, to reveal his glory, comfort his people, and shepherd them with his mighty arm.

This quotation identifies John the Baptist as the *messenger* (Mal. 3.1; 4.5) and the *voice* (Isa. 40.3).[48] However, he is identified in a penultimate way – his coming ultimately points to the coming of Jesus, the 'stronger one' (Mk 1.7). In Malachi, the forerunner heralds the coming of YHWH himself (note in Mal. 3.1, 'he will clear the way before Me' and Mal. 3.5, 'I will draw near to you for judgment') as well as YHWH's presence in representative form ('the Lord' and 'the messenger of the covenant' are spoken of in third person, 3.1).[49] Isaiah's words leave no doubt that the messenger prepares YHWH's way ('clear the way for YHWH …; make smooth in the desert a highway for our God', 40.3). By substituting αὐτοῦ ('his', of Jesus' path) for the τοῦ θεοῦ ἡμῶν ('of our God') of the LXX (Isa. 40.3) in 1.3, Mark boldly claims that Jesus is 'the one through whom Yahweh's delivering presence and kingly reign is manifest;' in him, Israel's New Exodus hopes have been

---

[46] Ulrich Mauser, *Christ in the Wilderness: The Wilderness Theme in the Second Gospel and Its Basis in the Biblical Tradition* (Studies in Biblical Theology 39; London: SCM Press, 1963), p. 81. The messenger and the wilderness are subordinate to the coming of the Lord, which is the main focus.

[47] Rikk E. Watts, 'Mark', in G.K. Beale and D.A. Carson (eds.), *Commentary on the New Testament Use of the Old Testament* (Grand Rapids: Baker Academic, Kindle edn, 2007), loc. 4564.

[48] Mark provides only enough information about John the Baptist to characterize him as a prophetic man of the desert who is identified with Elijah (leather belt around his waist, cf. 2 Kgs 1.8; Mal. 4.5). Mauser, *Christ in the Wilderness*, p. 82. Mauser comments that Mark includes nothing else about John except his death.

[49] Watts, *Isaiah's New Exodus in Mark*, p. 69.

inaugurated.[50] Jesus is not just a protagonist of Israel's New Exodus, but 'Israel's returning God'.[51] Throughout his Gospel, Mark shows Jesus' fulfilling his mission in this light: liberating, restoring, shepherding, and judging.

The wilderness in Mark's Gospel is of theological significance.[52] Matthew and Luke add further details about the location of John's activity in the desert. Mark, however, sees the wilderness in its correlation to religious tradition and prophecy. The wilderness signifies the place of Israel's relationship with YHWH, and the prophets understood that a 'renewal of the exodus into the desert was necessary for the restoration of Israel's status as the son of God'.[53] This would be a time of both judgment and salvation (Ezek. 20.35-38; Hos. 2.14; 12.9; Isa. 40.3-4; 41.18-19; 43.19-20; 48.20-21). In the wilderness, God would purify his people, renew his love to them, and make a new covenant with them. John thus calls people to come out in repentance, acknowledging Israel's history of disobedience and longing for a fresh start. In Mark, the call to the wilderness and the call to repentance are one and the same; it is time for the New Exodus.[54]

Old Testament motifs continue to coalesce in Mark's prologue as he integrates more components of Isaiah's New Exodus hope and fleshes out implications (1.1, 10, 11, 13, 15). Watts follows Stuhlmacher in asserting that in Mark, εὐαγγέλιον ('gospel/good news') is closely linked to OT texts, with Isaiah foremost in view (e.g. 40.9; 52.7; 61.1).[55] The concept of God's kingdom coming near

---

[50] Watts, 'Mark', loc. 4781.

[51] Moritz, 'Mark, Book of', p. 482.

[52] Unlike Matthew, Mark does not explicitly state that these things 'fulfilled' what was spoken through the prophets. Rather, he employs a typological hermeneutic that discerns similarities in setting and significance. References such as 'by the sea', 'on the mountaintop', 'at home', and 'in the wilderness' evoke the places of Israel's deliverance, the giving of her Law, her idolatry, and her rebellion.

[53] Mauser, *Christ in the Wilderness*, pp. 87-88. The prophets spoke of the wilderness as the place where people would whole-heartedly return to YHWH (Jer. 24.7; Ezek. 11.19; 36.25-26). Mauser offers the Qumran community as an example of the connection between repentance and wilderness.

[54] William L. Lane, *The Gospel According to Mark* (NICNT; Grand Rapids: Eerdmans, 2nd rev. edn, 1974), pp. 50-51. George Balentine argues that Jewish proselyte baptism functioned as initiation into the community of Israel via symbolic passing through the waters of the Red Sea. Balentine, 'Death of Jesus', p. 37.

[55] Peter Stuhlmacher (ed.), *Das Evangelium Und Die Evangelien* (WUNT 28; Tübingen: Mohr Siebeck, 1983), pp. 122-53. Cited in Watts, *Isaiah's New Exodus in Mark*, pp. 98-99.

(ἤγγικεν, 'has come near', Mk 1.5) could be associated with the coming near (ἤγγισα) of God's presence, righteousness, and salvation of Isa. 46.13; 51.5; and 55.6 (LXX).[56] John's proclamation that Jesus is the 'stronger one' (Mk 1.7) echoes language of YHWH as Israel's warrior, who delivered Israel at the Exodus by his strong arm and who would again come 'in strength' (μετὰ ἰσχύος, Isa. 63.1/63.5 LXX).[57] Many commentators see the background for the rending (σχίζω, 'cleaving' or 'tearing') of the heavens at Jesus' baptism in Mk 1.10 as Isa. 63.19 LXX/64.1 MT, 'Oh, that You would rend the heavens and come down'.[58] The descent of the Spirit and the voice declaring Jesus to be God's Son mark Jesus as the royal son of God of Psalm 2,[59] YHWH's true son, Israel,[60] and Isaiah's Servant (Israel's corporate representative), in whom YHWH is 'well pleased' (Isa. 42.1; 63.11).[61] Jesus is both anointed with the Spirit

---

[56] Marshall connects Mark's theme of 'Kingdom of God' with Isaiah and comments that Mark's allusions 'indicate that the broad theme of the Isaianic New Exodus, which is widely attested in the New Testament, has shaped Mark's presentation'. I. Howard Marshall, *New Testament Theology: Many Witnesses, One Gospel* (Downers Grove, IL: InterVarsity Press, Kindle edn, 2004), p. 78. Wright sees Jesus as announcing that Israel was experiencing true return from exile, YHWH was returning to Zion, and judgment would soon befall those who had failed to be loyal. Wright, *Jesus and the Victory of God*, II, p. 371.

[57] Watts, *Isaiah's New Exodus in Mark*, p. 142. Mark's use of 'Son of Man' and his implications that Jesus' coming fulfilled some prophecies of the 'Day of YHWH' further connect Jesus to the divine warrior motif. See B.A. Stevens, 'Why "Must" the Son of Man Suffer?' The Divine Warrior in the Gospel of Mark', *BZ*, 31.1 (1987), pp. 101-10 (108); Tremper Longman, 'Divine Warrior: The New Testament Use of an Old Testament Motif', *WTJ* (October 1982), p. 295.

[58] Guelich, *Mark 1-8:26*, p. 32; Watts, *Isaiah's New Exodus in Mark*, p. 103; Lane, *Mark*, p. 55. Interestingly, a form of this verb is used in Exod. 14.21 (LXX): ἐσχίσθη τὸ ὕδωρ ('the water was divided').

[59] Marshall comments that the effect of these words is 'to initiate Jesus into the office of God's coming king' in light of both Psalm 2 and Isaiah 42.1-4. Marshall, *New Testament Theology*, p. 59. If Psalm 2 is indeed behind this allusion, it reiterates the threat of judgment inherent in Malachi 3 ('Do homage to the Son, that He not become angry, and you perish in the way, for His wrath may soon be kindled' [Ps 2.12]).

[60] Bretscher contends through linguistic analysis that the language of the voice from heaven (here and at the Transfiguration) is drawn primarily from Exodus 4. Paul G. Bretscher, 'Exodus 4:22-23 and the Voice from Heaven', *JBL* 87.3 (September 1968), pp. 301-11. See Watts for a discussion of Mark's presentation of Jesus both as Israel (indicated by surrounding context) and as the agent of YHWH's eschatological victory (indicated by the words of affirmation). Watts, *Isaiah's New Exodus in Mark*, pp. 112-15.

[61] Although the LXX translates רצה ('to be well-pleased, accept favorably') with προσδέχομαι ('to accept, welcome'), εὐδοκέω ('to be well-pleased') is the 'natural and

and identified as the one who, with divine prerogative, will bestow the Spirit upon others (also connected to the wilderness/New Exodus; cf. Isa. 32.15; 44.3; Ezek. 36.27; Joel 2.28).[62]

After Jesus 'comes up' from the water, the Spirit impels him to go into the wilderness, where he is tempted for forty days.[63] Mark omits the details of the temptations, noting only that Jesus was 'with the wild beasts' and that 'the angels were ministering to him' (1.13). Traditionally, this verse has been interpreted in connection with the paradise motif (signifying victory of the New Adam over Satan and temptation so that paradise is restored).[64] Mark could also have Isa. 43.19-20 in mind.[65] However, Lane offers a more comprehensive interpretation. He believes that Mark is emphasizing the character of the wilderness in connection with the realm of Satan, commenting that 'Jesus confronts the horror, the loneliness and the danger with which the wilderness is fraught when he meets the wild beasts'.[66] Moreover, just as angels helped and guided Israel in the wilderness (and sustained Elijah in 1 Kgs 19.5-7), they now strengthen Jesus for his difficult task. Just as here, Jesus triumphs over temptation and enters his ministry full of the Holy Spirit, he will continually face temptation and opposition with dependence on God and faithful obedience.

Within the framework established in this prologue, Mark overlays Israel's familiar metanarrative – including its history and its prophetic

---

most common rendering' in the LXX and is found in Theodotion and Symmachus. Beale and Carson note that the descent of the Spirit and New Exodus context make an allusion to Isa. 42.1 'almost certain'. Watts, 'Mark', loc. 4905.

[62] Macchia, *Justified in the Spirit*, p. 129.

[63] Balentine notes the common Greek phraseology of Jesus' 'coming up' in Mk 1.10 (ἀναβαίνων) with Israel's crossing of/'coming up out of' the Jordan (ἀνέβη, Josh. 4.19 LXX), which was a counterpart to the Red Sea crossing, as well as Jesus' speaking of his Passover death as a 'baptism' (10.38). Balentine, 'Death of Jesus', p. 37.

[64] Guelich, Mark *1-8:26*, p. 39.

[65] This speaks of the 'beasts of the field' glorifying God when he makes a roadway in the wilderness and rivers in the desert at the time of the New Exodus. The combination of the LXX's ἡ ἔρημος ('the wilderness') with τὰ θηρία ('the wild beasts'), against the backdrop of the New Exodus quotations, lends support to this.

[66] He notes that in the OT, blessing is associated with inhabited land; the wilderness is a place of curse, where humankind cannot live. Only frightening and unwanted kinds of animals live there. 'Significantly, when the wilderness is transformed into a paradise no ravenous beast will be in it (Isa. 35:9; Ezek. 34:23-28).' Lane, *Mark*, p. 62.

expectations – with the story of Jesus' life, death, and resurrection. In the first section of Mark (1.1–8.21), some of Jesus' actions and words parallel events from the first Exodus as well as relate to Isaiah's New Exodus expectations. Jesus is identified as Israel's bridegroom (2.18; Isa. 62.5; 54.5) and the one who forgives her sins (2.5-10; Isa. 43.25), heals her (1.34; 3.10-11; 6.5-13; Isa. 30.26; 53.5), and offers her rest (2.28; 6.34-44; Isa. 63.14).[67] Through Jesus' exorcisms, he fulfills the role of Israel's divine warrior.[68] In ch. 3, Jesus performs a sign before the people and the leaders. However, the leaders' hearts are hard, and they attribute his work to Beelzebub and take counsel to destroy him (3.6, 23-30; cf. Exod. 4.29-31).[69] This rejection is analogous to Israel's rebellion against God's Spirit (Exodus 17; Isa. 63.10) and will result in division and judgment (Isa. 29.13-14; Mark 7). After this confrontation, Jesus withdraws to the sea with a great crowd of people, goes up on a mountain, and invests the 12 with authority (cf. Moses' actions in Exodus). [70] Jesus begins teaching in parables, effecting 'judicial blinding' judgment on Israel's leaders, who continue to reject God's truth (Mk 4.2-20; Deut. 28.28-29; Isa. 6.9-10).[71]

Mark 4.35–5.20 contains another sequence of Exodus parallels. Jesus crosses the sea and commands the winds and the waters to be still (cf. Exod. 14.21;[72] also a likely allusion to the Exodus language

---

[67] Watts observes that the restoration of sight and hearing is especially characteristic of Isaiah's New Exodus (e.g. 35; 42.7; 32.1; 61). Watts, *Isaiah's New Exodus in Mark*, p. 171.

[68] Watts, *Isaiah's New Exodus in Mark*, p. 171. Watts ties Jesus' words in 3.27 about binding the 'strong man' and his exorcisms, which deliver people from oppression of enemy demons, to Isa. 49.24-25. He also points to an intertestamental connection (made explicit in the LXX) between idols and demons (e.g. Isa. 65.3 and 11 speak of burning incense and preparing a table τοῖς δαιμονίοις/τῷ δαίμονι ('to/for demons'). See Watts, p. 157.

[69] Watts emphasizes the connection between exorcisms and plundering in light of contemporary Jewish traditions that associate the binding of Beliar and liberation of Beliar's prisoners (presumably by a priestly Messiah) and deliverance of the captives by the 'anointed' of Isa. 52.7 during an eschatological Jubilee (p. 147). See *T. Levi* 18.2; *T. Sim.* 6.6; *T. Dan.* 5.10-13; *Jub.* 10.8; *1 En.* 10.11; 54.4; *Ass. Mos.* 10.1; *Pes. R.* 36 (161a); 11QMelch.

[70] Edward Craig Hobbs, 'The Gospel of Mark and the Exodus' (PhD dissertation, The University of Chicago, 1958), pp. 37-38.

[71] Watts ties this judgment to Mark's initial citation, with its threat of judgment. The authorities reject John and denounce Jesus, leading to increasing conflict and judgment (tied to Isaiah 6, 29). Watts, *Isaiah's New Exodus in Mark*, p. 219.

[72] Lane comments with regard to this passage that God's power over the forces of nature 'was never more evident than in the Exodus and the crossing of the Red Sea'. Lane, *Mark*, p. 168.

of Psalm 65, 89, or 107).[73] He rebukes his disciples, who grumble that they are going to perish, on their perpetual lack of faith (4.40; cf. Exod. 14.11-12; 15.24; 16.2). On the other side, with the Gerasene demoniac, Jesus faces a host ('Legion') of enemies.[74] At his directive, they are drowned in the sea that the 12 had just safely crossed. This causes the people of the region to be seized with fear, and they ask him to leave their region (5.15-17, cf. Exod. 15.14-16; Num. 22.3; Deut. 2.25).[75] Moreover, the combination of tomb-dwelling and swine has led commentators to suggest that Isa. 65.1-7 lays behind Mark's story.[76]

Chapter six is especially full of Exodus parallels and typology.[77] In v. 31, Jesus offers his disciples rest (ἀναπαύσασθε, 'be refreshed') in a wilderness place (ἔρημον τόπον). When the people recognize and follow them, Jesus feels compassion for the people, because they are

---

[73] Psalm 65.7 says that YHWH, who created the mountains, 'stills the roaring of the seas'. The context speaks of God's answering with might in righteousness and salvation; it contains Exodus language of signs and wonders and speaks of God's visiting the earth and causing the wilderness to drip with abundance. Psalm 89.9 seems even more appropriate. The Psalmist writes, 'You rule the swelling of the sea; when its waves rise, you still them'. The Psalm focuses on God's mighty arm of salvation for Israel as well as his covenant with David. Verses 20-29 speak of YHWH's upholding David's royal descendant, strengthening him, and crushing his enemies: 'He will cry to Me, "You are my Father, My God, and the rock of my salvation." I also shall make him My firstborn the highest of the kings of the earth' (Ps. 89.26-27). Psalm 107 speaks of God's faithfulness to Israel in the Exodus. The Psalmist writes, 'He caused the storm to be still, so that the waves of the sea were hushed' (Ps. 107.29). This Psalm also speaks of bringing rivers in the desert and guiding YHWH's people to their desired haven. In Mk 4.39, Jesus rebukes the wind and tells the sea, 'be silent' (σιώπα) and 'muzzled' (πεφίμωσο). These ideas align best with Psalm 89 (καταπραΰνεις, 'he made the waves become meek') or Psalm 107 (the waves had to 'be silent', ἐσίγησαν [also from σιγάω] at the sound of his voice).

[74] Watts and others note the striking presence of military language/imagery in this passage, depicted as a battle against a host of enemies (λεγιών ['legion'] usually referred to troops; ἀποστείλῃ ['to send'] could be a military command; ἀγέλη ['herd'] could depict a band of military recruits; and ὥρμησεν ['to rush'] could describe rushing into battle). Watts, *Isaiah's New Exodus in Mark*, p. 159.

[75] Hobbs, 'The Gospel of Mark and the Exodus', p. 39.

[76] Watts, *Isaiah's New Exodus in Mark*, p. 157. This is an indictment of idol-worshiping Israelites – dwelling in tombs and eating pork seem to be 'some of the more repugnant *tupoi* of idolatry behind which, according to the LXX, stand the demons' (p. 158).

[77] Some commentators also note parallels to Exod. 12.11 in Jesus' instructions to the 12 when he sends them out (6.8-9). Just as God sustained Israel in the wilderness, the disciples are to trust in God's provision. Mauser, *Christ in the Wilderness*, p. 133; Lane, *Mark*, p. 208.

like sheep without a shepherd (6.34). After teaching them many things, he miraculously satisfies them with bread and fish. This is followed by Jesus' walking on the water (6.45-51). These actions parallel certain points of the first Exodus and indicate that the time of the second Exodus foretold by the prophets has arrived.[78] For example, Zechariah 2 mourns how the people wander like sheep without a shepherd. YHWH responds with the promise of a cornerstone from Judah; YHWH will once again have compassion on his people, gather them together, redeem them, and cause them to walk in his name (2.1-12).[79] Isaiah concludes his inaugural announcement of salvation in 40.11 by saying that YHWH will gently tend his flock like a shepherd. The surrounding chapters proclaim that YHWH will supply bread/food for them (51.14; 49.10; 48.20) and show them compassion (49.10).[80] Isaiah 63 speaks of YHWH's leading his people like a shepherd, having compassion on them, and giving them rest in the wilderness. Jeremiah 31 likewise portrays a time when YHWH, who gave his people rest before (31.2), will again gather them like a shepherd and renew his covenant. YHWH declares, 'I will satisfy the weary ones and refresh everyone who languishes' (31.25). Ezekiel 34 envisions YHWH's seeking out his flock, delivering them, feeding them, leading them to rest, and setting a Davidic shepherd over them. Ps. 77.19-20 speaks of YHWH's paths and footprints through the sea and of his leading his people like a flock. In ch. 6, Jesus shows himself to be Israel's true Shepherd, leading his people in the wilderness, giving them rest, and providing for them.[81] The people

---

[78] In the first Exodus, God parted the waters, gave the people provisional or partial rest, led them as a shepherd leads a flock, and provided manna and quail. The grouping of the people by hundreds and fifties recalls the division of the Mosaic camp (Exod. 18.21). Qumran documents use these subdivisions to describe true Israel assembled in the desert in the period of the last days (1QS 2.21; 1QSa 1.14; 1QM 4). Lane, *Mark*, p. 229.

[79] Interestingly, Zech. 10.11 speaks of the people's passing through the sea and of the leader's striking the waters (cf. Mk 6.45-51).

[80] Watts, *Isaiah's New Exodus in Mark*, pp. 177-78. Watts notes that 'green grass' could potentially indicate 'new creational restoration of the wilderness' (Isa. 35.1, 6; 43.20; 41.19), although it is far from certain (179). Lane likewise observes that 'the transformation of the desert into a place of refreshment and life through the power of God is an aspect of the wilderness tradition which is prominent in the prophets'. Lane, *Mark*, p. 229.

[81] Hobbs, 'The Gospel of Mark and the Exodus', p. 42; Clifford, 'The Exodus in the Christian Bible', p. 357.

are thus witnesses of his glory as he demonstrates miraculous provision and power over nature.[82]

In Mark's second section (8.21, 26-10.45–11.1), Jesus leads his 'blind disciples' (who perpetually fail to understand his identity and mission, cf. 4.13, 41; 6.52; 7.18ff; 8.17ff) along 'the way' to Jerusalem (Isa. 42.16).[83] This section is bracketed by Jesus' only two healings of the blind in Mark (8.22-26; 10.46-52) and focuses on the disciples' need to perceive the role of suffering in the realization of Jesus' New Exodus work ('Son of Man' sayings in 8.31; 9.12; 10.33, 45; cf. Isaiah's Suffering Servant). Mark emphasizes Jesus' identity as the divine Son of God (Peter's confession in 8.29; transfiguration in 9.1-13) only in tandem with the necessity of suffering, for Jesus as well as for true disciples.[84]

In the last section of Mark (11.1ff), Jesus arrives in Jerusalem with his disciples. Mark, as in his prologue, identifies Jesus' coming with the prophesied return of YHWH to Zion (Isa. 35.3-10) – the ultimate goal of Isaiah's New Exodus as well as the 'hallmark' of her restoration.[85] Jesus enters Jerusalem as its rightful King, and the people joyfully exult, 'Save us! [*Hosanna!*] Blessed is He who comes in the name of the Lord! Blessed is the coming kingdom of our father David!' (Mk 11.10; Ps. 118.9).[86] Indeed, Jesus' death as a ransom (λύτρον, Mk 10.45) to enact a new covenant (14.24) will make possible salvation, freedom, and redemption for Israel as well as the nations.[87] Its significance is presented both in terms of Israel's first Exodus (with the typology

---

[82] Mauser, *Christ in the Wilderness*, p. 143.

[83] Watts points to polemical use of blind and deaf metaphors in Isaiah 40–55, especially centered on Israel's refusal to accept Cyrus as YHWH's chosen deliverer. Watts, *Isaiah's New Exodus in Mark*, p. 244.

[84] Moritz remarks that the cross is shown as the paradoxical 'way' of launching the long-awaited New Exodus of God's people – 'a way of seeming defeat but actual vindication'. Moritz, 'Mark, Book of', p. 482.

[85] Watts, *Isaiah's New Exodus in Mark*, pp. 296-99. He sets this in the context of the portentous judgment that Immanuel's coming signified in Isa. 7.14-17, particularly with regard to Jerusalem (3.1, 26; 6.11-13). However, Isaiah 55–66 also focus on Jerusalem's renewed status as a place of peace, righteousness, praise, and light to all peoples. This is effected by the Servant.

[86] Matthew and John explicitly tie this to Zech. 9.9.

[87] This 'ransom' language most likely refers to 'payment for release of prisoners or hostages' and aligns with Mark's presentation of Jesus as the one stronger than the 'strong man' and 'able to rescue those whom the evil one has taken captive'. Craig A. Evans, *Mark 8:27-16:20* (WBC 34B; Grand Rapids: Zondervan, 1988), p. 122. It echoes language from Exod. 6.6; 13.13-15; Deut. 7.8; Ps. 77.20; and later prophets, such as Isa. 1.27; 29.22; 35.10; 41.14; 51.11.

especially prominent in the thematic combination of redemption, vicarious sacrifice, liberation, covenant, and new temple) as well as later New Exodus texts, such as Zech. 9.11, Jer. 31.31, and especially Isaiah's Servant Songs (Isaiah 53).[88] Jesus ties these separate traditions together, turning the focus of the Passover meal to his coming death. 'Henceforth, it will be his sacrifice, his blood "poured out", comments Watts, 'that is remembered as effecting the Passover of Israel's eschatological redemption'.[89]

However, soon after Jesus' entry, the threat of judgment incipient in Mark's opening quotation materializes. The conflict between Jesus and the religious leaders escalates as Jesus, knowing that the time for his death is approaching (10.33), speaks more openly about his identity and enacts judgment on the religious leaders and the temple cult (cf. Lam. 2.6-7). The leaders have not heeded the words of the forerunner and have rejected the chosen cornerstone (Mk 12.10; ironically also from Ps. 118.22). Jesus thus comes to the temple for New Exodus judgment and purification (Mal. 3.2-5; Zeph. 1.9). In rapid succession, Mark 11–12 presents the cursing of the fig tree, the cleansing of the temple, and the parable of the vine-growers.[90] All three symbolize impending judgment on Jerusalem, who has continued in her apostasy and has not brought forth the righteous fruit that God expects. (Isa. 5.2-7).[91] The fig tree and the vine were symbols for Israel (e.g. Hos. 9.10, 'I found Israel like grapes in the wilderness; I saw your forefathers

---

[88] The 'blood poured out for many for the forgiveness of sins' draws from Exod. 24.8 (the blood of the Sinai covenant), Zech. 9.11 ('because of the blood of My covenant with you, I have set your prisoners free from the waterless pit'), and Isa. 53.12 ('Because He poured out Himself to death, and was numbered with the transgressors; yet He Himself bore the sin of many'; cf. Exod. 29.12). Lane, *Mark*, p. 507; Evans, *Mark 8:27-16:20*, 34B.122; Watts, *Isaiah's New Exodus in Mark*, p. 362. Craig Evans adds the expectation of Jer. 31.31 to this (esp. in light of Lk. 22.20). Craig A. Evans, 'Exodus in the New Testament: Patterns of Revelation and Redemption', in Thomas B. Dozeman, Craig A. Evans, and Joel N. Lohr (eds.), *The Book of Exodus: Composition, Reception, and Interpretation* (VTSup 164; Boston: Brill, 2014), p. 449.

[89] Watts, 'Mark', loc. 8789. See Watts, p. 350, for a detailed analysis of allusions to Isaiah in Jesus' passion. Hicks expounds on the meaning of the cross and the Lord's Supper in light of the covenant sacrifices and Israel's eating and drinking in the presence of God (Exod. 24.5, 11). Hicks, 'A Sacramental Journey', p. 62.

[90] Mark wraps the cursing of the fig tree (11.12-14) and Peter's observation that it had withered from the roots (11.21) around the temple cleansing in an A-B-A structure, indicating that the two events are linked inextricably.

[91] Lane, *Mark*, p. 402. Lane notes that the fig tree's leaves and the magnificence of the temple both conceal the fact that Israel has not brought forth fruit.

as the earliest fruit on the fig tree in its first season'; cf. Mic. 7.1) and figured prominently in both New Exodus promises and New Exodus judgment (e.g. Hos. 2.12; Joel 2.12-32; Amos 5–6). Jesus indicates that Jerusalem's situation is parallel to the times of Jeremiah, when YHWH denounced the people for their unfaithfulness (Jer. 8.5), rebuked the shameful scribes and leaders (8.8-9), and lamented that the people – unlike even the wild animals – did not understand the seasons (8.7; cf. Mk 11.13). Therefore, YHWH would bring judgment on them: 'There will be no grapes on the vine and no figs on the fig tree, and the leaf will wither' (Jer. 8.13; Mk 11.21); what they had would be taken away and given to others (Mk 12.9; Mt. 21.43; cf. Rom. 11.17-24).

In Jesus' day, the temple was the central symbol of Judaism. It was significant for its sacrificial system; it was a symbol of royalty and legitimized leaders who built, rebuilt, or ran it; and it represented a pivotal hope of the Exodus – YHWH's dwelling among his people.[92] It was also connected to the New Exodus in the prophets. Zechariah prophesied that the coming Davidic ruler (the 'Branch') would govern YHWH's house and have charge of his courts (Zech. 3.7) as well as build the temple (6.12-13). Ezekiel likewise taught that in the New Exodus, 'a Davidic king would oversee a reconstituted people and a new sanctuary' (Ezek. 37.15-28).[93]

The temple was at the center of Jesus' agenda and his conflict with the religious leaders. Mark identifies Jesus' cleansing of the temple as the catalytic event that impels the leaders to begin seeking a way to destroy Jesus (Mk 11.18). It was also Jesus' words about destroying the temple (i.e. his body) and rebuilding it in three days that his enemies used to accuse him at his trial (Mk 14.58).[94] Here, he pronounces judgment on Herod's temple. Now, as in Israel's history, God's house had become a 'den of robbers' (Jer. 7.11; Mk 11.17) and would be deserted (Jer. 26.9; cf. Mt. 23.38; Lk. 13.35) and destroyed

---

[92] Wright, *Jesus and the Victory of God*, II, pp. 406-11.

[93] Watts, 'Mark', locs. 8193-8203.

[94] Only Mark records Jesus' words that he would destroy the temple 'made with hands' and build another 'made without hands' (14.58). These words could imply that the temple had become idolatrous (cf. Isa. 2.8; Acts 19.26). Dumbrell, *The End of the Beginning*, p. 67. They could also serve as the foundation for later biblical teaching that God does not dwell in temples made with human hands (Acts 17.24; 2 Cor. 5.1; Heb. 9.11, 24).

(Jer. 7.14; Mk 13.2).[95] At the same time, Jesus' message constituted a 'counter-temple movement'; he offered what had only been available through the temple. He taught his followers a new way to be Israel. As Israel's true king, David's Lord (Mk 12.35-37; Ps. 110.1), he would rebuild God's temple and open salvation to the Gentiles (Isa. 56.7; cf. tearing of the temple veil in two at his death, Mk 15.38; Heb. 9.8).[96] Just as the vineyard could only be 'the obedient reconstituted Israel gathered around Jesus (cf. 3:31-35)', in Mark's New Exodus, 'it is the rejected Davidic son-stone Jesus who through his resurrection becomes the preeminent stone of a new people-temple (14.58; cf. 1 Pet. 2.4-7)'.[97]

Luke-Acts

Luke-Acts narrates one continuous story of the 'things accomplished among us' (Lk. 1.1-4) – all that Jesus began to do and teach (Acts 1.1) as well as the continuation of Jesus' ministry through the apostles and early believers by the Holy Spirit.[98] Luke situates these events within

---

[95] Watts further suggests that the statement about mountain-moving faith moving 'this mountain' into the sea 'adumbrates the ultimate removal of the present Temple establishment which, in its present form, constitutes such a formidable obstacle to the fulfillment of' Isaiah's new Exodus. Watts, *Isaiah's New Exodus in Mark*, p. 368; cf. Wright, *Jesus and the Victory of God*, II, pp. 329-35.

[96] Wright, *Jesus and the Victory of God*, II, pp. 417, 426. Balentine points out that in Matthew, forms of the verb σχίζω ('to cleave/tear open', used of the Red Sea in Exod. 14.21 LXX) are used to describe both the veil's being torn in two and the tombs' being split open (27.51). He argues that these 'alike are regarded as providing an access to God and to life through Jesus' sacrifice'. Balentine, 'Death of Jesus', p. 41.

[97] Watts, 'Mark', locs. 8193-8203. Watts notes that this would be 'by the Lord's doing' and 'marvelous in our eyes' (12.11), the language of which originated in YHWH's salvation and vindication of his people at the Exodus. Note also 'stone', 'building', and 'wonder' in Mk 13.1-2. Pierre Constant concurs – he argues, «*Le Psaume 118 était en fait une reprise d'Exode 15, un appel à célébrer l'Éternel pour le miracle de l'exode*», ('Psalm 118 was in fact a reprisal of Exodus 15, a call to praise the Lord for the miracle of the Exodus'). Pierre Constant, 'Le Psaume 118 et son Emploi Christologique dans Luc et Actes: Une Étude Exégétique, Littéraire et Herméneutique' (PhD dissertation, Trinity Evangelical Divinity School, 2001), p. ix.

[98] Scholars are increasingly acknowledging the fruitfulness and even necessity of reading Luke-Acts as two volumes of a single work. See Henry J. Cadbury, *The Making of Luke-Acts* (New York: Macmillan, 1927), p. 9; I. Howard Marshall, *Luke: Historian & Theologian* (New Testament Profiles; Downers Grove, IL: InterVarsity Press, 3rd edn, 2001), p. 13; Joel B. Green, *The Gospel of Luke* (NICNT; Grand Rapids: Eerdmans, 1997), p. 6; Kurz, *Reading Luke-Acts*, pp. 19-31; David Wenham and Steve Walton, *A Guide to the Gospels & Acts* (Exploring the New Testament 1; Downers

the framework of Israel's new-Exodus restoration, according to God's preordained plan that was revealed in the Scriptures (Lk. 24.25-27; Acts 13.23, 33; 24.25).[99] First, this section will examine some key indicators of this New Exodus context in Luke's extended prologue and some ways that Luke calls attention to Jesus' identity as the prophet like Moses. Then, it will focus on three interrelated themes essential to Luke's program – the salvation and redemption accomplished by Jesus' life, death, and resurrection; the activity and outpouring of the Holy Spirit; and the formation of an inclusive community of believers – to demonstrate how New Exodus constitutes one lens by which to envision Luke's entire narrative schema.

Luke offers much more detailed accounts of the births of John the Baptist and Jesus than the other Synoptic Gospels. As he recounts these stories, he roots the events in Israel's past experiences and prophecies through explicit references and quotations to Scripture as well as pervasive echoes.[100] The songs of Mary (1.46-55) and Zechariah (1.68-79) are suffused with language from the first Exodus as well as the New Exodus hopes of the prophets and Psalms.[101] Mary speaks of how, as at the time of the Exodus, God has seen the state of his servant (1.48; Exod. 3.9) and has done μεγάλα ('great things',

---

Grove, IL: IVP Academic, 2nd edn, 2011), p. 239; Roger Stronstad, *The Charismatic Theology of St. Luke* (Peabody, MA: Hendrickson, 1984), p. 2.

[99] Beale, *New Testament Biblical Theology*, loc. 5275. Mark Strauss, Max Turner, and David Pao argue for a more particularly Isaianic New Exodus in Luke-Acts. While Luke undoubtedly draws heavily from Isaiah, restricting the study to Isaiah (or even Isaiah 40–66) obscures other Exodus/New Exodus contexts and parallels. See Mark L. Strauss, 'The Davidic Messiah in Luke-Acts: The Promise and Its Fulfillment in Lukan Christology' (PhD thesis, University of Aberdeen, UK, 1992); Pao, *Acts and the Isaianic New Exodus*; Max Turner, *Power From on High: The Spirit in Israel's Restoration and Witness in Luke-Acts* (JPTSup 9; Sheffield: Sheffield Academic Pr., 1996). For example, Luke also draws considerably from the Psalms, e.g. Psalms 106 and 118, both of which are set in Exodus contexts. See Constant, 'Le psaume 118 et son emploi christologique dans Luc et Actes'.

[100] Gabriel, Zechariah, Mary, Elizabeth, and Simeon speak words of praise and prophecy that anchor the coming of Jesus and John in Israel's hopes (e.g. 1.33; Isa. 9.6-7; 2 Sam. 7.13-14; Dan. 7.18) as well as presage the judgment and division that will accompany their powerful ministries.

[101] Mary's song especially draws from the words of Hannah in 1 Sam. 2.4-5 and 10 but could also echo the words of Isa. 61.10. Combined with Luke's statement about Jesus' 'increasing in wisdom and stature, and in favor with God and men' (2.52), which closely parallels 1 Sam. 2.26, perhaps Luke subtly adumbrates the judgment on Israel's religious leaders that the birth of Jesus, like the birth of Samuel, signaled (cf. 1 Sam. 2.35, 'I will raise up for Myself a faithful priest who will do according to what is in My heart and in My soul; and I will build him an enduring house').

cf. Ps. 71.19; Deut. 10.21; 11.7).[102] He has brought salvation through the mighty deeds of his arm (1.51; Exod. 6.6). She affirms that God has brought down rulers and exalted the humble (Lk. 1.52; Exod. 15.6-7).[103] Zechariah declares that God has remembered his covenant (Lk. 1.73; Exod. 2.24) and has redeemed his people (Lk. 1.68; Exod. 6.6). He has raised up a 'horn' of salvation, David's royal son (Lk. 1.69; Ps. 132.17) – a new Moses to deliver Israel from the 'hand' of her enemies (Lk. 1.78; Exod. 3.8).[104] The *telos* of this liberation is the same as that of the first Exodus: Israel's 'serving' God (λατρεύειν, Lk. 1.73; Exod. 3.12; 4.23; 7.16) without fear (cf. Lk. 4.17-19, which portrays Jesus as releasing captives).[105] Zechariah further ties this into the New Exodus hopes of the prophets (Lk. 1.76; Mal. 3.6; Isa. 40.1 and the coming of YHWH; 1.77; Jer. 31.34 and the forgiveness of sin in the new covenant; Lk. 1.79; Isaiah 9 and the light of revelation). Zechariah speaks of Jesus as the 'ἀνατολή' ('Sunrise/Dawn') from on high (Lk. 1.78), which calls to mind prophecies of New Exodus activity related to the Davidic 'Branch' ruler (Jer. 23.5; Zech. 3.8; 6.12 LXX).[106] In the accounts of the shepherds and Simeon, Luke introduces more themes that echo Isaiah – a 'sign' child (Lk. 2.12, 34; cf. Isaiah 7, 9) and God's favor extended not just to Israel, but to 'all people' and the 'Gentiles' (Lk. 2.10, 14, 31-32; Isa.42.6; 49.6, 9; 60.1-3).

---

[102] Nolland remarks that 'great things' is language pointing to God's saving intervention in the OT, especially at the Exodus. John Nolland, *Luke 1:1-9:20* (WBC 35A; Nashville: Thomas Nelson, 1989), p. 75.

[103] Her quotation in 1.53 is from Psalm 107, which is also connected to the Exodus.

[104] Strauss's conclusions are helpful here – he looks to Isaiah to hold together Luke's multi-faceted portrayal of Jesus as Davidic Messiah/king, Suffering Servant, and eschatological prophet like Moses. Strauss, 'Davidic Messiah', p. 242. This aligns with the conclusions of this study, that by the time of the major prophets, the New Exodus motif had become intertwined with expectations related to the prophet like Moses and the 'Branch of David' (see concluding remarks under 'Ezekiel' in Chapter 2).

[105] Green, *The Gospel of Luke*, p. 117; Hahn, 'Worship in the Word', pp. 123-24.

[106] Jeremiah 23 speaks of the ἀνατολή as one who will reign as a righteous king, bring salvation to Israel, and bear the name 'YHWH our righteousness' (Lk. 1.69, 75, 77). At that time, Jeremiah says, God's people will not be afraid (23.4; Lk. 1.73) God's new saving activity will surpass the first Exodus (23.7-8). Zechariah looks forward to a time of forgiveness and peace (3.9) and of the Branch's building God's temple and ruling as a priestly king (6.12-13). Green notes the further connections between light and God's guiding presence (Exod. 13.21; Pss. 27.1; 36.9) and between light/illumination and salvation (Ps. 107.9-10; Isa. 2.5; 9.2; 42.7; 60.1-3; Mic. 7.8; and later, Lk. 2.29-32; Acts 26.17-18). Green, *The Gospel of Luke*, p. 119.

In chs. 3–4, Luke follows Mark and Matthew in presenting the events of Jesus' baptism and temptation as recapitulating Israel's wilderness experience. Through two key quotations from Isaiah in Lk. 3.4-7 (Isa. 40.3-5) and Lk. 4.18-19 (61.1-2), Luke introduces what Pao contends is the hermeneutical key for interpreting the corresponding themes that Luke will develop in Luke and Acts.[107] Many scholars thus consider Jesus' sermon in Nazareth as programmatic for his ministry.[108]

Just as the prologue establishes the significance of these events within the context of Exodus/New Exodus, additional narrative details highlight parallels between Jesus and Moses.[109] First, in Lk. 11.15, some people charge that Jesus is performing exorcisms by 'Beelzebul, the ruler of the demons'. Jesus responds that if he does indeed cast out demons by Beelzebul, Satan's house is divided and will fall. Then he says, 'But if I cast out demons by the finger of God, then the kingdom of God has come upon you' (11.20). Here, Jesus alludes to the Egyptian magicians' confession that it was God's power at work in Moses and Aaron (Exod. 8.19) and they could not replicate the miracles. Jesus thus implies that the same power with which YHWH defeated Israel's enemies and brought her deliverance is at work in him; like Moses, 'he proclaims the kingly authority of God'.[110] Second, Acts 2.22 emphasizes that Jesus was a man

---

[107] Pao, *Acts and the Isaianic New Exodus*, p. 45. Pao observes that the appearance of this quotation from Isaiah, in line with other Jewish interpretive traditions, signals the arrival of Isaiah's New Exodus. He concludes that mentioning this text would have evoked Isaiah's wider program, and the discrete events that follow would have thus been viewed through this hermeneutical lens. He believes that the quotations set the stage both structurally and thematically for Acts in particular. Whether or not one agrees with his conclusion about the structure of Acts in relation to four specific themes of Isa. 40.1-11, his statements about the thematic emphases and Luke's overall program are compelling and resonate with a broad consensus of research.

[108] Nolland, *Luke 1*, p. 195; Joseph A. Fitzmyer, *The Gospel According to Luke I-IX: A New Translation with Introduction and Commentary* (The Anchor Bible; Garden City, NY: Doubleday, 1982), p. 71.

[109] Some add to this that the sending of the seventy(-two) in Lk. 10.1 parallels Moses' anointing seventy elders to assist him (Num. 11.16-17, 24-25). See Watts, 'Exodus', p. 485.

[110] Evans, 'Exodus in the New Testament', pp. 460-61. Evans observes that in contemporary Jewish interpretation (e.g. rabbinic midrash and the Damascus Covenant), the magicians of Egypt 'were themselves in league with Satan' and demons (p. 443).

accredited by God with 'miracles and wonders and signs' (2.22).[111]
This language evokes the time of the Exodus and the 'great deeds' and
'signs and wonders' that God performed through Moses (Deut. 34.11-
12).[112] Third, and more explicitly, characters in Luke-Acts repeatedly
imply that Jesus is the 'prophet like Moses' that God promised to 'raise
up' (Deut. 18.15, 18; Lk. 1.69; Acts 2.24, 32; 3.22; 7.37).[113] Stephen's
speech in Acts 7 particularly emphasizes how the people's rejection of
Jesus parallels their rejection of Moses and unwillingness to keep the
Law (7.20-53).

Finally, in Lk. 9.31, at the Transfiguration, Luke records that
Moses and Elijah appeared and spoke with Jesus about his coming
ἔξοδος ('exodus/departure'), which he would accomplish in
Jerusalem.[114] This is only one of many elements reminiscent of the
first Exodus in this story (e.g. the presence of companions, the
mountain setting, the mention of Moses, the radiance of Jesus' face,
the cloud, the voice, the tents/tabernacles, and the clear allusion to
Deut. 18.15)[115]. In interpreting this, some scholars seek to identify
precise points of parallelism between the first Exodus and Jesus'

---

[111] This language also characterizes the ministry of the apostles in Acts 2.43; 4.30;
5.12; 6.8; 7.36; 14.3; 15.12.

[112] Language of 'signs and wonders' or 'wonders and signs' is clustered around
the Exodus and the early Christian movement in the Bible. See Goldsworthy,
According to Plan, loc. 1432; Balentine, 'Death of Jesus', pp. 31-32; David P. Moessner,
'Luke 9:1-50: Luke's Preview of the Journey of the Prophet like Moses of
Deuteronomy', *JBL* 102.4 (December 1983), pp. 575-605 (582).

[113] Although ἀνίστημι (Acts 2.24, 32; 3.22; 26; 7.37; 13.33, 34) and ἐγείρω (Lk.
1.69; Acts 5.30; 9.22; 10.40) are both used in Luke-Acts to speak of God's 'raising
up' Jesus (i.e. bringing him as a Savior) and to speak of his being raised from the
dead, ἀνίστημι, which matches the LXX for Deut. 18.15 and 18, is used in the more
formal contexts that identify Jesus as the prophet like Moses. Acts 5.30 could be an
exception, especially since envisioning Jesus as a 'Prince and Savior' introduces a clear
Mosaic parallel (5.31).

[114] Green notes that this term was used in the LXX and Hellenistic Judaism to
refer to the Exodus from Egypt as well as to a person's death/departure (cf. Wis. 3.2;
76; 2 Pet. 1.15). However, because of the profuse echoes of the Exodus story in this
text, he deems it almost certain to have Exodus connotations. Green, *The Gospel of
Luke*, p. 382.

[115] The story of Peter's being released from prison (Acts 12) also exhibits some
interesting parallels with the Exodus story. It was during the time of the Passover (vv.
3-4); an angel led him out of his bondage with a light (vv. 7-8); he was instructed to
make haste, 'gird' himself, and put on his sandals and his cloak (vv. 7-8); and he
declared that he was 'delivered' 'from the hand of' Herod (v. 11).

life/death/resurrection.[116] Others point to a structural connection, proposing that this frames the travel narrative (Lk. 9.51–19.44) as the New Exodus journey.[117] Most agree, however, that the term points to the redemptive and liberating power of Jesus' death and exaltation (Lk. 24.26) against the backdrop of his being cast as the prophet like Moses.[118] Like Moses, he brought people out of bondage and mediated the voice of God to an unbelieving and perverted generation (Lk. 9.41; Deut. 32.5). Like Moses, he would be rejected (esp. prominent in the speeches of Acts 3.22; 7.37).[119] Finally, like Moses, he would die for the stubborn sins of the people (Deut. 1.37; 3.26; 4.21; cf. 32.30).[120]

In addition to laying a New Exodus framework in his prologue and using specific language to emphasizes parallels between the works of Moses and Jesus, Luke focuses on several inter-related Exodus/New Exodus components as he sketches the story of the fulfillment of Israel's prophecies:[121] salvation and redemption, the anointing and

---

[116] For example, Jindřich Mánek sees Jesus' suffering and cross as 'entering the threatening waves of the Red Sea' (cf. Jesus' speaking of his death as a 'baptism' in 12.50) and says that Jesus' 'exodus' specifically refers to his leaving the sepulcher. Moreover, he sees a parallel between the forty days in the wilderness and the forty days mentioned at the beginning of Acts and notes that Jesus 'led out' his disciples (Lk. 24.50) just as Moses 'led' the people out of Egypt. Jindřich Mánek, 'New Exodus [of Jesus] in the Books of Luke', *NovT* 2.1 (January 1957), pp. 8-23.

[117] So Moessner, 'Luke 9'.

[118] Balentine, 'Death of Jesus', p. 39; Green, *The Gospel of Luke*, p. 379; Watts, 'Exodus', p. 482; Nicholas T. Batzig, 'The Exodus Motif in Luke–Acts', http://feedingonchrist.com/the-exodus-motiff-in-luke-acts/, accessed 14 May 2012; Patterson and Travers, 'Contours of the Exodus Motif', p. 40. David Miller especially emphasizes the importance of hearing the Son (just as the people had to listen to Moses). David Marvin Miller, 'Seeing the Glory, Hearing the Son: The Function of the Wilderness Theophany Narratives in Luke 9:28-36', *CBQ* 72.3 (July 2010), pp. 498-517 (499).

[119] Dale Allison offers a fuller comparison of Jesus and Moses. Allison, *The New Moses*, pp. 97-98. Kurz also discusses a pattern of dual rejection of both Moses and Jesus in Acts. Kurz, *Reading Luke--Acts*, p. 143.

[120] Moessner, 'Luke 9', p. 585. Luke portrays this vicarious suffering especially in terms of the Isaianic Servant, which he has woven together in his Christology with Mosaic prophet and Davidic king motifs. For example, Acts 2.33 uses language of Isa. 52.13 (LXX) to speak of Jesus' being exalted/lifted up (ὑψωθήσεται/ ὑψωθείς), and Acts 8.32 interprets Isa. 53.7, about the Servant's being led like a silent lamb to the slaughter, as pointing forward to Jesus' death. This Servant, like Moses, was 'cut off from the land of the living for the transgressions of [Israel]' (Isa. 53.8).

[121] Hays insightfully notes how Jesus' corrective words to the disciples on the road to Emmaus send the reader back to *reread* the Gospel and the Scriptures together

outpouring of the Holy Spirit, and the reformation of the people of God as an inclusive community.[122] First, Luke shows a particular interest in redemption and salvation, the roots of which drink deeply from the Exodus story (e.g. Zechariah's words in Lk. 1.68-70; Anna's words in 2.38; the words of the disciples in 24.21; and Luke's use of the title 'Savior' [σωτήρ] in Lk. 1.47; 2.11 and Acts 5.31; 13.23).[123] He seems to refer to salvation and redemption in overlapping ways, as in the Exodus account, as well as in connection with consolation and restoration, as described in the prophets (Lk. 1.68; 2.25, 38; Acts 1.6; 15.16; Isa. 40.1; 49.6-8; 59.20; Jer. 33; Joel 9.11-15; Zeph. 3).[124] Luke also carries forward the idea of Jesus as a sacrificial lamb and Isaianic Servant (Acts 8.32-33; Isa. 53.7-8; Exod. 12.3) whose blood 'purchased' his people (Acts 20.28; Exod. 15.16; Ps. 74.2).

(i.e. read *backwards*), to discern how Israel's Scriptures prefigure Jesus' identity and mission. Jesus is indeed 'the One who would redeem Israel' – much more than 'a prophet powerful in deed and word' (Lk. 24.18, 21). Hays, *Reading Backwards*, locs. 1350-85.

[122] Luke-Acts, like many OT prophetic books, also contains repetitions of Exodus judgment along with the emphasis on salvation. For example, Pao discusses how Luke reverses the judgment-salvation scheme of Isa. 6.9-10 and 40.3-5 (Luke first emphasizes salvation through his quotation of Isaiah 40 in 3.6, then judgment through his quotation of Isaiah 6 in Acts 28.27). Luke announces that all people will 'see' God's salvation but closes with a statement about the people's closed eyes (see also the comparison of Isa. 61.1-2 in Lk. 4.18-19 and Acts 28.26-27). Pao, *Acts and the Isaianic New Exodus*, p. 108. In addition, the narratives about judgment coming upon Herod (Acts 12.20-24) and Elymas (13.6-12) make use of Exodus/New Exodus themes and language. An angel of YHWH struck/smote Herod (ἐπάταξεν, 12.23; cf. Exod. 12.23 (LXX); covenant curses of Deut. 29.22), whereas the word of the Lord went and out multiplied (Isa. 55.11). Paul accuses Elymas of opposing New Exodus work: he is a 'son of the devil' and is 'making crooked' the 'straight ways of the Lord' (τὴν ὁδὸν κυρίου εὐθείας, 13.10; cf. Isa. 40.3 LXX, τὰς ὁδοὺς [τοῦ] κυρίου τὰς εὐθείας). He becomes subject to judicial blinding.

[123] There is only one cryptic reference to redemption in Genesis (48.13), after which the Exodus account introduces the verbs גאל ('to redeem') and פדה ('to ransom') and their corresponding nouns (esp. tied to the Passover; see Exodus 12–13; 2 Sam. 7.23). Language about salvation (ישועה) is likewise found once in Genesis and then concentrated in Exodus (Gen. 49.18; Exod. 14.13; 15.2), as with the verb 'to deliver' (נצל) with a salvation-related meaning (Gen. 32.11; Exod. 3.8; 6.6). A few texts (Exod. 15.16; Ps. 74.2) speak of God's purchasing his people (קנה), which is picked up in Acts 20.28 and is especially prominent in Revelation.

[124] Luke's Isaianic lens is evident again here. Isaiah speaks of YHWH as Israel's Redeemer (from גאל) 13 times in Isaiah 40–66; 'Savior' (מושיע) 7 times (as well as about 40 uses of 'save/salvation'); deliver/deliverance (נצל) about 30 times; and 'comfort' (נחם) 15 times. See Green for additional details about the use of Isaianic 'Servant' language in Luke's Prologue. Green, *The Gospel of Luke*, p. 144.

Second, in the events surrounding Jesus' birth, death, and resurrection and the early days of the Christian community, Luke highlights a 'dramatic and unprecedented outburst of the gift of the Spirit'. [125] Luke's Gospel opens with the Spirit's filling/over-shadowing/coming upon John the Baptist, Elizabeth, Mary, Zechariah, and Simeon (Lk. 1.15, 41, 67). The Spirit descends on Jesus at his baptism (3.22), and Jesus goes into the desert 'full of the Spirit' (4.1) and returns 'in the power of the Spirit' (4.14) to conduct his Spirit-anointed ministry (4.18). Just as Jesus is uniquely endowed with and dependent upon the Holy Spirit (Luke 1–4), he then transfers the charismatic Spirit to his disciples to enable them to carry out their mission (Acts 2.8, 23). [126] In Lk. 24.49, he instructs his disciples to stay in Jerusalem and wait for the promised gift of the Father that he will pour out on them. In Acts 2, Jesus baptizes the 120 in the upper room with the Holy Spirit (2.33), and they become witnesses in Jerusalem, Judea, Samaria, and the 'ends of the earth' (1.8). In Acts, many other people are filled with the Holy Spirit (4.31; 6; 8.15; 9.17; 10.44; 19.2); the Spirit enables them to prophesy and actively guides them in their speech, travels, and ministries (e.g. Stephen, Acts 6–7; Philip, Acts 8; Saul, Acts 9; Peter, Acts 9–11; Barnabas and Paul, Acts 13.1-4). In Luke-Acts, the primary *purpose* of the Spirit's bestowal is a charismatic empowering for service. [127]

The primary *backdrop* for this pouring out of the Spirit is Luke's overall framework of the restoration of Israel/New Exodus,

---

[125] Stronstad, *Charismatic Theology of Luke*, p. 34. See Stronstad for a fuller discussion of the language and scope of the Spirit's activity in Luke-Acts vis-à-vis OT precedent.

[126] Frank D. Macchia, *Baptized in the Spirit: A Global Pentecostal Theology* (Grand Rapids: Zondervan, 2006), p. 129.

[127] This is in line with the Spirit's work in the OT, empowering people for service, especially at key junctures in Israel's history (such as the periods of the Exodus and restoration from exile, e.g. Exod. 28.3; 31.3; Num. 11.17, 25-29; 27.18; various times in Judges; 1 Kgs 18.2; 2 Kgs 2; 2 Chron. 20.14; 24.20; Ezek. 2.2, 3.12; 11.15; 37.1). Stronstad, *Charismatic Theology of Luke*, pp. 12-25; F.F. Bruce, *The Book of the Acts* (NICNT; Grand Rapids: Eerdmans, rev. edn, 1988), p. 53. Stronstad notes the association between the gift of the Spirit and the transfer of leadership (e.g. Moses to the 70 elders and later to Joshua in Num. 11 and 27), the anointing of specific people for service (e.g. Saul in 1 Sam. 10), and the vocational endowment with skills for specific callings (e.g. artisans for the temple in Exod. 28.3). Texts such as Neh. 9.20, Isa. 63.10, and Hag. 2.5 depict the activity of the Spirit at the time of the Exodus and returns from exile (the Spirit was in the people's midst, led the people, instructed them, and gave them rest).

grounded in the prophets.[128] The OT looked forward to both the coming of a Spirit-anointed Messiah and Servant (Isa. 11.1-4; 42; 61.1) and the giving of the Spirit in unprecedented ways, to bring righteousness, fruitfulness, peace, and the end of exile (Isaiah 32); to satisfy people's thirst and mark them as belonging to YHWH (Isa. 44.1-8); to cause people to walk in his statutes and to give them life (Ezekiel 36–37); to signal a great day of salvation and enable 'all flesh' to prophesy and experience dreams and visions (Joel 2); to cause the people of Jerusalem to mourn because of the One whom they have pierced (Zech. 12.10) and to open up a fountain of purification and forgiveness (Zechariah 13). Luke connects the outpouring of the Spirit with some of these expectations, especially in Isaiah, through quotations and allusions. For example, the Spirit's being poured out from 'on high' (Lk. 24.49) echoes Isa. 32.15.[129] The words 'to the ends of the earth' in Acts 1.8 exactly match the LXX of Isa. 49.6 (ἕως ἐσχάτου τῆς γῆς).[130] Peter's speech on the day of Pentecost fuses together words from Joel 2 with phrases from Isaiah, such as ἔσται ἐν ταῖς ἐσχάταις ἡμέραις ('and it will be in the last days', Acts 2.17; Isa. 2.2 LXX) and τοῖς [εἰς] μακρὰν ('to those who are far off', Acts 2.39; Isa. 57.19 LXX). Pao, following William Lane, also contends that the 'times of refreshing' offered in Acts 3.19 refer to the pouring out of the Spirit (according to Symmachus's translation of Isa. 32.15), available to the community after the Day of Pentecost.[131] While not

---

[128] Turner provides a thoughtful discussion of this. Turner, *Power from on High*.

[129] Pao and Marshall believe that Isa. 32.15 may also lie behind the words that the Holy Spirit will 'come upon' the disciples in Acts 1.8. Pao, *Acts and the Isaianic New Exodus*, p. 92; Marshall, 'Acts', loc. 19991.

[130] In the context of the restoration of Israel, this verse speaks of the mission of the Servant as a light to the nations for their salvation. Isaiah 45.22 (YHWH's calling to the ends of the earth to turn to him and be saved) contains very similar language: οἱ ἀπ' ἐσχάτου τῆς γῆς ('those from the ends of the earth'). Pao believes that Jesus' words about the disciples' being his witnesses could echo Isa. 43.10-12, which implies that the people of God will be witnesses of God's salvation when the new age arrives. He also argues that the three regions represent 'geopolitical' expansion of the Isaianic New Exodus program (Jerusalem as the center of salvation; Judea and Samaria as the reunified kingdom, and the 'ends of the earth' as the inclusion of the Gentiles in the people of God). Pao, *Acts and the Isaianic New Exodus*, p. 95.

[131] William L. Lane, 'Times of Refreshment: A Study of Eschatological Periodization in Judaism and Christianity' (ThD dissertation, Harvard Divinity

comprehensive, these demonstrate how in Luke's understanding, the gift of the Spirit, as the other events surrounding Jesus' life and the early days of 'the Way', signified the fulfillment of everything to which the OT looked forward, especially through Isaiah's New Exodus lens.[132]

Third, and closely related to this, is Luke's prominent attention to the identity of the people of God. First, through designations such as ἐκκλησία ('community, assembly, church', e.g. Acts 5.11; 8.1) and ἡ ὁδός ('the Way', e.g. Acts 9.2; 19.9, 23), Luke establishes that the fledgling Christian movement is the continuation of the true community of Israel (Isa. 42.16).[133] Luke asserts that prophecies that anticipated Israel's being gathered and reformed in the last days (e.g. Isa. 49 and the mission of the Servant; Jeremiah 30–31; Ezekiel 20; 36; Hosea 12; Joel 2) are inaugurally fulfilled in the events of Jesus' life and the times of the early church.[134] Second, Luke focuses on the

---

School, 1962); Cited in Pao, *Acts and the Isaianic New Exodus*, pp. 132-33. They further point to a parallel between Acts 2.38 and 3.19-20.

[132] For Luke, it is also the gift of the Spirit that signifies the coming of the eschatological age. Bruce, The *Book of the Acts*, p. 61. Pao sees it as the 'dawn of the Isaianic New Exodus'. Pao, *Acts and the Isaianic New Exodus*, p. 93.

[133] Bruce notes that ἐκκλησία is the usual translation for קָהָל ('assembly') in Deuteronomy and all the successive OT books except Jeremiah and Ezekiel (cf. Acts 7.38). Bruce, *The Book of the Acts*, p. 108. Daniélou asserts that 'there was not a needy person among them' (Acts 4.34) fulfills Deut. 15.4 and draws attention to parallels between the episodes of Ananias and Sapphira (Acts 5) and Achan (Josh. 7.19-20), who violated laws of communal property. Daniélou, *From Shadows to Reality*, pp. 161-62. Pao follows Marianne Palmer Bonz and others who recognize the early ecclesiological function of Luke-Acts (as conferring Israel's heritage 'definitively and exclusively upon the church'). Marianne Palmer Bonz, 'The Best of Times, the Worst of Times: Luke-Acts and Epic Tradition' (ThD dissertation, Harvard Divinity School, 1996), p. 33; cited in Pao, *Acts and the Isaianic New Exodus*, p. 3. Pao specifically examines this in relation to 'the Way' terminology, concluding that it is used in polemical contexts where the identity of the true people of God is at stake (p. 59, see esp. Acts 24.24). He then connects it to Luke's broader Isaianic New Exodus framework, noting that in Isaiah, this language signaled 'the presence of the new salvific act of God' (p. 66).

[134] Pao points to the integral connection between the disciples' question in Acts 1.6 about restoring the kingdom to Israel and Jesus' response in Acts 1.8 about making disciples of the ends of the earth. Pao, *Acts and the Isaianic New Exodus*, pp. 228-29. See also Chapter 20, 'The Church as the Transformed and Restored Eschatological Israel', in Beale, *New Testament Biblical Theology*. Beale compellingly argues that Jesus, as the individual messianic king of Israel, represents the true continuing remnant of Israel. All those who identify with him become a part of the Israelite remnant that he represents. He examines this concept in the NT largely through the lens of Isaiah's New Exodus. Kurz observes that some see the 120 that

universality of the gospel and the inclusive nature of this community (e.g. Lk. 2.29; 3.6; 24.47; Acts 1.8; 2.38-39). As God foretold and foreordained (Gen. 22.18; Isa. 19; 49.6; 56.3-7; Jer. 12.15; Amos 9.11-12), this New Exodus community now includes outcasts (e.g. the eunuch in Acts 8) and Gentiles (e.g. the household of Cornelius in Acts 10; 13.46-48), and their membership is dependent not upon their becoming Israelites (circumcision, keeping the Law), but upon their faith in Jesus (Acts 15.7-11).[135] The gift of the Holy Spirit is the evidence that God has accepted them just as they are.[136] While the first Exodus partially brought about God's promises to Abraham, in Jesus, God 'raised up his *Servant*' (παῖς, from Isaiah's Servant Songs, LXX) and sent him to bring salvation and blessing first to the Jews and then to all nations (Acts 3.24-26; Gen. 22.16-18). They too are now 'My people' (Isa. 19.25) 'called by my name' (Amos 9.12; Zech. 2.11; 8.8; 13.9; cf. Exod. 6.7).[137]

Peter addressed in the upper room as 'symbolic of the restored Israel'. Kurz, *Reading Luke—Acts*, p. 76.

[135] Pao, *Acts and the Isaianic New Exodus*, p. 143. Pao contends that Acts shows the promised reconstitution of Israel, which is now to be defined in terms of relationship to Jesus (cf. election of Matthias in Acts 1.12-26; reunification of the divided kingdom shown through the acceptance of Samaritans into the restored people of Israel, Acts 1.8, 8.14; the expected inclusion of the outcasts, Isa. 56.3-5; Deut. 23.1-7). Pao, *Acts and the Isaianic New Exodus*, p. 123.

[136] Peter's words in Acts 15.10 further echo the Exodus. He asserts that the believing Pharisees of Acts 15.5 are 'putting God to the test' (πειράζετε τὸν θεὸν, cf. Exod. 17.2; Num. 14.22 LXX) and subjecting the disciples to a 'yoke' (ζυγός, Lev. 26.13 LXX) of slavery (the Law) that neither the Jews nor their fathers could bear. This points to the provisional nature of the first Exodus event (Jn 8.31-36), casts the liberation from bondage and oppression that Jesus brought in terms of *true* Exodus, and aligns the Pharisees with the Israelites who tested God and longed for Egypt (Exod. 14.11; 17.3).

[137] It is also possible to trace an inchoate 'new temple' theology in Luke-Acts. Wright, for example, looks at Jesus' teachings and claims as a 'counter-Temple movement'. N.T. Wright, *The Resurrection of the Son of God* (Christian Origins and the Question of God; Philadelphia: Fortress Press, 2003). The events on the Day of Pentecost also parallel the giving of the Law at Sinai. Stronstad notes the presence of Sinai theophany language. Stronstad, *Charismatic Theology of Luke*, pp. 53-62. Bruce discusses possible understanding of Pentecost at the time of Jesus and the early church in relation to the giving of the Law. Bruce, *The Book of the Acts*, pp. 49-50. Wright asserts that language related to the indwelling of the Spirit, in Second Temple Jewish thought, belongs in connection with God's tabernacling presence in the temple. Wright, *The Resurrection of the Son of God*, III, p. 256. Marshall observes that Stephen's speech 'cries out for an understanding of the community of believers as the new temple, not made with hands' (Acts 7.8). Marshall, 'Acts', loc. 19722.

John

As Richard Hays has observed, John is the 'master of the carefully framed, luminous image that shines brilliantly against a dark canvas and lingers in the imagination'.[138] His Gospel, rather than laying out a comprehensive account of Jesus' ministry, provides focused illustrations of how Jesus fulfills Israel's Scriptures and feasts. John does not usually indicate this with formal citations or long sequences of words or phrases, but rather with evocative images and figures.[139] Many of these derive from the Exodus and Israel's subsequent time in the wilderness.

John introduces Jesus as God's presence and glory dwelling with his people and the one greater than Moses, the tabernacle/temple, and the Torah. In the central part of the Gospel, he shows how the bronze serpent, manna, water from the rock, and pillar of fire provided veiled glimpses of the true realities that Jesus embodies.[140] He further portrays Jesus as Israel's true deliverer, I AM, and the true Shepherd. Finally, in the passion narrative, John's early depiction of Jesus as the sin-bearing Lamb of God (1.29) culminates in Jesus' death as a Passover sacrifice to effect the true Exodus.

The Gospel of John, like the Synoptic Gospels, identifies Jesus as the Messiah, the coming Lord of Isa. 40.3, the Son of God, the Son of David (cf. Matthew and Luke), the Spirit-baptizer, the one spoken of by the Law and Prophets, and the King of Israel (cf. Matthew). John adds to these some remarkable attributes of Jesus, the Word – he is eternal, divine, uncreated, the agent of all creation, the giver of life, and the true light of men (1.1-11).[141] People are granted special

---

[138] Hays, *Reading Backwards*, loc. 1837.

[139] Hays, *Reading Backwards*, locs. 1843-44. See Andreas J. Köstenberger, 'John', in G.K. Beale and D.A. Carson (eds.), *Commentary on the New Testament Use of the Old Testament* (Grand Rapids: Baker Academic, Kindle edn, 2007), locs. 15941-42.

[140] Craig S. Keener, *The Gospel of John: A Commentary* (Grand Rapids: Baker Academic, 2003), I, p. 278.

[141] For a thorough discussion of the Logos in relation to Jewish and Greco-Roman background, see Keener, *Gospel of John*, I, pp. 333-63. Keener concludes that John is primarily drawing on Jewish traditions about Wisdom and more specifically, Torah. He says that 'Jesus himself embodies the Torah and is its fullest revelation, and the apostolic witness thus delivers a revelation of greater authority than that of Moses (1.14-18; cf. 2 Cor. 3). It is rejecting Jesus, rather than obeying him, that constitutes a rejection of Torah (cf. 1:11-13)' (I, p. 360).

relationship with God as his children by believing in Jesus' name (*not* by following Torah, 1.12-13).[142]

After John recounts the inconceivable rejection of this divine Word (vv. 10-11), he continues in vv. 14-18 to chronicle the extraordinary entry of the Word into human history. He appropriates language and images from the Sinai tradition to emphasize parallels, fulfillment, and contrast. First, John's language of the Word's 'tabernacling' or 'encamping' (ἐσκήνωσεν, 1.14) among his people calls to mind YHWH's presence (in Jewish writings, the 'Shekinah') among the people of Israel in the tabernacle/tent of the meeting (σκηνή, Exod. 25.8-9; 29.45 LXX)[143] and on Mount Sinai. It could also echo New Exodus texts such as Isa. 40.1-11, Ezek. 37.21-28, and Zech. 2.10-12 that look forward to YHWH's dwelling among his people (cf. 'Immanuel', Mt. 1.21) under a new and everlasting covenant (Jer. 31.1; Ezek. 37.26). Second, as the people of Israel and especially Moses saw the glory of YHWH (e.g. Exod. 40.35), John and others beheld Jesus' glory (δόξα). Here, Jesus is not a 'new Moses', who saw YHWH's glory and dimly reflected it (Exod. 34.29-35); Jesus' glory is his own, which he shares with the Father (1.14; 2.11; 12.41; 17.5, 24).[144] Especially in light of this context, some scholars believe that John's reference to 'grace and truth' (χάριτος καὶ ἀληθείας) also derives from the Exodus tradition (Exod.

---

[142] These statements call to mind Scriptures such as Pss. 19.8 (18.8 LXX) and 118.130, which link God's words/commands with light, and Isa. 51.4 and 60.1-2, which anticipate the coming of (a) Torah as light to the peoples and the glory of YHWH's presence rising upon his people.

[143] Many scholars note that the Hebrew verb 'to dwell' (שׁכן), from which was later derived the noun 'Shekinah', sounds similar to the Greek word for 'tabernacle' (σκηνή). This seems to have influenced the translators of the LXX at times, and possibly John as well. J. Ramsey Michaels, *The Gospel of John* (NICNT; Grand Rapids: Eerdmans, 2010), p. 79. Morris notes that the parallels here include both God's *presence* and God's *tabernacle*. Leon Morris, *The Gospel According to John* (NICNT; Grand Rapids: Eerdmans, rev. edn, 1995), p. 92.

[144] Especially because John presents Jesus as the *Word* here, there is at least an implied contrast between the glory of the Mosaic covenant and the glory of Jesus' new covenant. Keener contends that the main contrast of vv. 14-18 is between the Torah, which the Jews called the 'Word of God', and Jesus, the Logos made flesh. See Keener, *Gospel of John*, I, p. 361 n. 343. See also Hays, *Reading Backwards*, locs. 1915-24; T.F. Glasson, *Moses in the Fourth Gospel* (Eugene, OR: Wipf & Stock, 2009), pp. 24-26.

34.6).[145] Third, John emphasizes the special relationship that Jesus has with the Father. Even Moses, who spoke with God in a unique way ('face-to-face', Exod. 33.11), did not truly see God (1.18). But Jesus, in the Father's bosom, eternally beholds the Father's face (1.1, 18).[146] He is the preexistent, 'only begotten' of the Father (1.14-15) and has explained the Father (1.18) in a definitive and full way. Finally, whereas the Law was given through Moses,[147] Jesus brought grace and truth (1.14, 16; possibly the Spirit).[148] As Keener verbalizes, 'The grace and truth present in the law were more fully revealed in Jesus; the restrained glory revealed in the law was now fully unveiled in Jesus of Nazareth'.[149] Through all of these thoughts run the common threads of Jesus' surpassing excellence and the way in which he fully expressed and embodied what was only partially revealed through the Torah, the tabernacle, and Moses.[150]

In the central section of John's Gospel, John continues his Exodus typology against the background of the Jewish Feasts of the Passover, Tabernacles, and Dedication (Hanukkah). Especially through Jesus' *I*

---

[145] See Michaels, *The Gospel of John*, p. 83. In Exodus 34, YHWH says he is 'compassionate and gracious, slow to anger, and abounding in lovingkindness and truth'. The LXX has, 'οἰκτίρμων καὶ ἐλεήμων μακρόθυμος καὶ πολυέλεος καὶ ἀληθινὸς' ('sympathetic, patiently compassionate, very merciful, and true'). While this does not match exactly, the next few verses of John point to precisely this context. In addition, as McGhee *et al.* point out, John is showing how Jesus perfectly *exegetes* the Father and fully reveals him – as the Father is full of grace and truth, so the Son. Quentin McGhee, Steve Eutsler, and John Wesley Adams, *Gospel of John: The Word Became Flesh* (Faith & Action; Springfield, MO: Faith & Action Team, 2016), pp. 34-35.

[146] Evans, 'Exodus in the New Testament', pp. 458-60.

[147] The passive here, along with the choice of different verbs, emphasizes a closer connection among grace and truth and Jesus than between the Law and Moses. Morris, *John*, p. 99. This could be subtly correcting a tendency to ascribe the Law to Moses in the same way that the Jews ascribed to him the miracle of the manna (6.31-32).

[148] The χάριν ἀντὶ χάριτος of 1.16 is better translated 'grace instead of grace' (the normal meaning of ἀντὶ with the genitive). This leads commentators to suggest that 'as one piece of divine grace [the Law] recedes it is replaced by another'. Morris, *John*, p. 98. Thus they believe that in John, there is not so much contrast as continuity between the covenants. So Michaels, *The Gospel of John*, p. 90; Keener, *Gospel of John*, I, p. 361; Hays, *Reading Backwards*, loc. 1915; Evans, 'Exodus in the New Testament', p. 460. Evans asserts that YHWH's giving Israel the Law a second time at Sinai adumbrated a future exchange of the old grace of the Law for a new grace. McGhee *et al.* see the contrast in degree, not in quality. McGhee, Eutsler, and Adams, *Gospel of John: The Word Became Flesh*, p. 34.

[149] Keener, *Gospel of John*, I, p. 361.

[150] I will discuss Jesus as the 'Lamb of God' in the section about his death.

AM statements (cf. Exod. 3.14) and 'sign' (σημεῖον) miracles, which reveal the glory of God and call those who witness to a decision regarding belief (Jn 1.11; cf. Exod. 3.12; 4.8; 16.7 LXX),[151] John points to Jesus as the true reality to which OT symbols pointed.[152] In ch. 2, John accentuates two incidents related to ritual purity at the beginning of Jesus' ministry. Through these, he emphasizes that 'Jesus is the path from religious forms to living faith' and the center of worship.[153] Jesus' first sign miracle occurs at the wedding in Cana (2.1-11). Here, subtle thematic and linguistic elements recall the first plague in Egypt, when the water of the Nile and of 'wooden and stone vessels' was turned into blood (Exod. 7.19-20; cf. 'stone water jars' in Jn 2.6).[154] This story also carries forward contrasts from ch. 1 between Jesus and Moses and between ritual waters and the gift that Jesus gives (the waters of baptism vs. the Holy Spirit, 1.33).[155] Directly following this, the first temple cleansing, recounted only by John,[156] foreshadows the cleansing and deliverance that Jesus will bring at a later Passover. Jesus' statement in 1.19 (explained in 1.21) indicates that Jesus' body is the true temple – 'the place where God dwells, the place where atonement

---

[151] For a detailed examination of the testing function of signs in John against the background of Israel in the wilderness, see Daniel H. Fletcher, *Signs in the Wilderness: Intertextuality and the Testing of Nicodemus* (Eugene, OR: Wipf & Stock, 2014).

[152] Keener meticulously examines Jewish literature, noting a persistent hope for a repetition of 'signs and wonders' in connection with New Exodus activity, salvation and deliverance, and a prophet like Moses. He comments that later Jewish tradition explicitly anticipated that these coming miracles would surpass those done through Moses (*t. Ber.* 1.10; *Exod. R.* 2.6; *Lev. R.* 27.4; *Deut. R.* 9.9; *Pes. R.* 31.10; *Gen. R.* 100.10; *Deut. R.* 9.9; *Pes. K.* 5.8; *Qoh. R.* 1.11; 4Q389 frg. 2; Sir. 33.1-6/36.1-6). Keener, *Gospel of John*, I, p. 403 n. 298. He asserts that John explicitly connects the signs of 2.1-11; 6.32; and 9.28 with a New Exodus.

[153] McGhee, Eutsler, and Adams, *Gospel of John: The Word Became Flesh*, p. 52.

[154] Glasson, *Moses in the Fourth Gospel*, p. 25. Allison mentions this vis-à-vis Moses' sweetening of the waters of Marah (Exod. 15.25). Allison, *The New Moses*, p. 105. Köstenberger sees here a contrast between 'the barrenness of first-century Judaism' and 'the end-time messianic joy inaugurated by Jesus the Messiah'. Köstenberger, 'John', locs. 16146-47.

[155] Michaels, following Moloney, suggests that the words 'on the third day' (2.1) could parallel the giving of the Law on Mt. Sinai (Exod. 19.11, 15-16, based on the Jewish Midrash *Mekilta on Exodus*). Michaels, *The Gospel of John*, p. 140. Keener later comments that at the end of Jesus' journey to the cross that was begun here, he receives sour wine (19.29-30) before giving forth living water (19.34). Keener, *Gospel of John*, I, p. 1147.

[156] Morris, *John*, pp. 166-68. In support of this view, Morris points to markedly different details/language (besides the chronology) between this account and Jesus' temple cleansing in the Synoptics.

for sin occurs, [and] the place where the division between God and humanity is overcome' (cf. 1.14).[157] The Jews' traditional washings and the temple cult could point to the reality of humanity's need for purification, but only the death and resurrection of the 'Lamb of God' could provide a remedy for sin.

Chapters 3–10 contain some of the clearest and most concentrated Exodus typology in the NT. John, with post-resurrection eyes (Jn 2.22; 12.16), reveals how Jesus is the fuller reality that Israel's symbols and liturgical festivals prefigured. Just as YHWH provided deliverance, life and healing, manna, water from the rock, and guiding light for Israel, Jesus – the incarnation of 'I AM' – now provides greater spiritual provision for all who believe. In ch. 3, Jesus talks with Nicodemus about how people receive spiritual *life* and become God's children (Exod. 4.22; cf. Jn 8.12-59). Nicodemus, ironically called 'the teacher of Israel' (v. 10), is shown to hold an inadequate view of Jesus' identity (a 'teacher from God', v. 2) and to speak for those of immature faith based on Jesus' signs (3.2; cf. 2.24-25).[158] Jesus refers to Moses' lifting up the bronze serpent in the wilderness (Num. 21.4-9) in order to help Nicodemus understand that to receive true life, people must look[159] with faith upon the uplifted (i.e. *crucified* and later *exalted*) Son of Man (3.14; cf. 12.32, 34).[160] *Those who believe in him* are the ones who have salvation (v. 17), eternal life (v. 16), and a relationship with the Father (v. 5). Being 'lifted up' in John also seems to echo Isa. 52.11-15, which anticipates that at the time of the New Exodus, God's Servant will be 'lifted up and greatly exalted' (ὑψωθήσεται καὶ δοξασθήσεται,

---

[157] Hays, *Reading Backwards*, locs. 1915-24. Stephen Coxon observes how Jesus' withdrawal from the temple in John 5–10 parallels the withdrawal of God's glory from the temple in Ezekiel and signifies destruction. He ties this new temple motif into ch. 10, in which Jesus is portrayed as the royal priest in charge of building God's house (cf. Rev. 21.22, in which the Lord God Almighty and the Lamb are the temple). John shows that believers are joined to this temple in Christ and through the indwelling of the Spirit (e.g. Jn 14.17, 20, 23). Coxon, *New Exodus in John*, p. 85.

[158] Fletcher, *Signs in the Wilderness*, p. 76. For a chart detailing characters in John with varying levels of faith, see McGhee, Eutsler, and Adams, *Gospel of John: The Word Became Flesh*, p. 64, Figure 2.10.

[159] For a discussion of 'looking' in Numbers 21 and 'seeing' in John's Gospel, see Glasson, *Moses in the Fourth Gospel*, pp. 34-35; Keener, *Gospel of John*, I, pp. 683-84; Köstenberger, 'John', loc. 16576.

[160] Morris examines the full meaning of ὑψόω ('to lift up') in John and the inextricable relationship between Christ's death and exaltation. Morris, *John*, pp. 199-201.

'lifted up and glorified' LXX) to 'sprinkle many nations'.[161] Being born of 'water and the Spirit' (v. 5) is most likely a reference to another New Exodus text, Ezek. 36.25-26. Here, YHWH declares that for the sake of his name, he will gather his people, sprinkle clean water on them, give them a new heart and spirit, and put his Spirit within them.[162]

In the next few chapters, John continues to emphasize Jesus' abundant provision (cf. 2.6; 3.34) against the backdrop of Israel's history and prophetic expectation. In John 6, with the Passover near (6.4), Jesus feeds the 5,000 and teaches that he is the 'true bread from heaven' (6.32) and the 'bread of life' (6.48).[163] As Keener observes, this miracle 'fitted into a new exodus expectation as old as the biblical prophets and amplified in Jewish themes of a future deliverance modeled after the first Passover (as in the Hallel) and exodus, as well as a new Moses'[164] (cf. Isa. 49.8-10). However, Jesus uses this opportunity to correct people's ascription of the manna to Moses (6.32) and to shift their paradigm: the manna, he teaches, 'pointed figurally to a different kind of bread altogether'.[165] Rather than work for food that perishes (Exod. 16.19-21), Jesus tells people to believe and receive *true* bread from heaven – his body – that can give[166] them eternal life (6.33-40; cf. 3.14-15, also connected to the Passover).[167] Here, his words anticipate his paschal sacrifice and the symbolic bread

---

[161] Jesus often speaks of his death (perhaps in tandem with his resurrection) as his being 'glorified' in John (7.39; 12.16; 12.23; 13.31).

[162] Köstenberger, 'John', loc. 16546.

[163] Jesus also asserts that his teaching fulfills prophecies of all people being 'taught of God' (Jn 6.45; cf. Isa. 54.13; Jer. 31.34).

[164] Verse 14 confirms this – when the people see this 'sign', they declare that Jesus is 'the Prophet'. Keener, *Gospel of John*, I, pp. 270-71.

[165] Hays, *Reading Backwards*, locs. 2097-2101.

[166] This is taking ὁ ἄρτος τῆς ζωῆς ('the bread of life') in 6.35 and 6.48 as a genitive of product – as 6.33 specifies, the bread *gives* life (cf. 8.12, τὸ φῶς τῆς ζωῆς, 'the light of life').

[167] Peter Borgen has demonstrated the midrashic form of this discourse following the quotation in 6.31. Furthermore, Borgen shows that among the rabbis, 'bread' represented the Law (Philo, *Moses* 1.201-202; 2.267; *Mekilta* on Exod. 16.4). In this passage, then, as in John's Prologue, Jesus could be claiming to fulfill the Torah/wisdom. Peder Borgen, *Bread From Heaven* (NovTSup X; Leiden: Brill, 1965); cf. Keener, *Gospel of John*, I, pp. 679-80. Wayne Meeks also shows that Jewish midrash connected manna with Passover bread and interpreted both eschatologically. Wayne A. Meeks, *The Prophet King: Moses Traditions and the Johannine Christology* (Leiden: Brill, 1967), p. 92.

that will commemorate its life-giving function.[168]

In John 7-8, John illuminates how Jesus fulfills and surpasses the water and light symbolism of the Feast of Tabernacles, which recalled water from the rock and the pillar of fire in the wilderness. In addition to building booths and carrying branches, the Jewish people had developed ceremonies that involved pouring water from the pool of Siloam onto the altar for seven days and kindling brilliant candelabras in the temple. The focal reading for the water ceremony was Isa. 12.3, 'You will joyfully draw water from the well/springs [πηγῶν] of salvation',[169] likely in connection with Zech. 14.7-8.[170] These texts indicate the eschatological character of the Feast: while it celebrated YHWH's provision at the Exodus, it had become invested with expectations of New Exodus judgment and salvation, ushered in by the reign of the Davidic Branch (Isa. 49.9-10; 35.6; 30.19-21; Ezekiel 47).[171] Rabbinic tradition connected this water to a Moses-like teacher who would duplicate the gift of the 'well' of the Torah (i.e. water from the rock) to Israel.[172] In Jn 7.37-38, Jesus stands in the temple at the climax of the Feast and cries out, 'If anyone is thirsty, let him come to Me and drink. He who believes in Me, as the Scripture said, "From his innermost being will flow rivers of living

---

[168] Just as the Israelites lacked faith and grumbled about God's provision for them (Exod. 15.24; 16.2; Numbers 14, 16), here the Jews *grumble* about Jesus' words (Jn 6.43, 61).

[169] Morris, *John*, p. 372. The Jerusalem Talmud (*Sukk.* 5.1) interprets this as the gift of the Holy Spirit.

[170] Keener, *Gospel of John*, I, p. 725 n. 215. This spoke of a time when all nations would recognize YHWH's kingship and gather in Jerusalem to celebrate the Feast of Tabernacles, and living water (ὕδωρ ζῶν) would flow from Jerusalem.

[171] Coxon, *New Exodus in John*, p. 244. Coxon documents expectation for the end of exile, covenant renewal, deliverance of Jerusalem, judgment on Israel's enemies, the coming of the messianic Branch/teacher, and supernatural light and water coming from the temple. Carson likewise notes that the ceremonies related both to the provision in the desert and to the Lord's pouring out of the Spirit in the last days. He observes, 'Pouring at the Feast of Tabernacles refers symbolically to the messianic age in which a stream from the sacred rock would flow over the whole earth'. He also notes the connection of the Feast to prayers for rain, both material and spiritual. D.A. Carson, *The Gospel According to John* (The Pillar New Testament Commentary; Grand Rapids: Eerdmans, 1991), p. 322.

[172] Jewish tradition taught that the rock had followed the Israelites in the desert and continued to provide water for them. This was associated with the Torah (Num. 21.18; *Targ. Onq.* Num. 21.18; *Suk.* 3.10-12; *Bib. Ant.* 10.7; 11.14; 28.7-8; *Qoh. R.* 1.8, 9); cf. the ref. to Exod. 17.6 in 1 Cor. 10.4. Coxon, *New Exodus in John*, p. 246; Köstenberger, 'John', loc. 16682.

water.'"[173] (Jn 7.37-38; cf. Jn 4.1-14; Rev. 7.15-17).[174] Jesus' words combine the invitation of Isa. 55.1 ('Everyone who thirsts, come to the waters'), the theme of Tabernacles (Isa. 12.3), and the promises of Isa. 58.11 ('you will be like ... a spring of water whose waters do not fail') and 44.3-4 ('I will pour out My Spirit on your offspring and they will spring up among the grass like poplars by streams of water'). Through Moses, God turned bitter waters sweet (Exod. 15.23-25), gave the people of Israel water from a rock (Num. 20.1-12), and instructed them with his Law. But Jesus gives water that quenches thirst and wells up to eternal life (Jn 1.33; 4.14; 6.63; 20.22; Isa. 49.10; Ezek. 47.1-12). From Jesus, the new temple, flows water that reverses the curse of barrenness in the fallen world and purifies from sin (Zech. 14.8).[175] Those who believe in him are satisfied with the abundant goodness (Jer. 31.12-14) 'presaged by the Feast of Tabernacles'.[176]

Again,[177] Jesus proclaims, 'I am the light of the world. He who follows Me will not walk in darkness, but will have the Light of life' (8.12).[178] Here, Jesus continues to draw from Israel's wilderness

---

[173] Alternate punctuation results in this translation: 'If anyone is thirsty, let him come to me, and let the one who believes in me drink. Just as the Scripture says, "From within him will flow rivers of living water."' In the more common English translation, it is unclear whether the pronoun 'his' refers to Christ or the believer as the source of the water. Manuscript evidence is divided, as are the Fathers. For a discussion of supporting evidence and commentators, see Carson, *The Gospel According to John*, pp. 323-28; Michaels, *The Gospel of John*, pp. 463-64. Seeing Jesus as the source, as Keener does, enhances the depiction of Jesus' gift of living water in light of Ezekiel's prophecy (Ezekiel 48) and points to the water flowing from his side on the cross as an announcement of the same promise. Keener, *Gospel of John*, I, p. 730.

[174] Hannah An, based on OT texts (esp. Joel 2.23; Hos. 10.12) as well as the Dead Sea Scrolls, argues for an essential connection in this passage between Jesus' roles of the prophet like Moses and the provider of living water. She especially examines how the ambiguity of the word מורה (which can be rendered 'to rain' or 'to teach' in the hiphil) contributes to this interplay. An, 'The Prophet Like Moses (Deut. 18)'.

[175] Köstenberger, 'John', loc. 16682; Dumbrell, *The End of the Beginning*, pp. 68-69. Keener observes that it is not coincidental that Jesus' announcement stands between two sections of temple confrontation (7.10-36; 7.40-52), considering the role of the temple in eschatological water expectation. Keener, *Gospel of John*, I, p. 724. Cf. Jesus' discourse on 'true worship' in John 4.

[176] Köstenberger, 'John', locs. 17242-43.

[177] Most commentators agree that 7.53–8.11 was a later addition. See Metzger, *Textual Commentary*, pp. 187-88.

[178] Here, Coxon suggests the additional parallel between the light in the dwellings of the Israelites in Egypt and the darkness that covered the land of their enemies (Exod. 10.22-23). Coxon, *New Exodus in John*, p. 261.

experience (Exodus 13–14) and its attendant celebration at the Feast of Tabernacles.[179] The Mishnah describes how during the nights of the Feast, the Jewish people lit four colossal lamps in the temple, visible throughout the city, and sang and danced joyfully.[180] As with water imagery, 'light' evokes a tapestry of biblical traditions. Scripture depicts the light of YHWH's presence and revelation as continuing to guide his people and bring them salvation, just as he led the people of Israel in the desert with a pillar of fire by night (Exod. 13.21; Pss. 27.1; 119.105). The prophets looked forward to a time when the Servant of YHWH would bring the light of salvation to the Gentiles (Isa. 49.6), and texts like Isa. 60.19-22 and Zech. 14.5-7 speak of YHWH's being a light to his people in the last days. Here, Jesus declares that he will lead his people out of darkness, and they will have the light of life (cf. Jn 1.4-9; healing of the blind man in 9.1-41).[181] Those who believe in Jesus walk in his light and clearly see the revelation of God's glory in him.[182]

In contrast, the spiritually blind leaders are unable to see Jesus' light and will die in their sins like their forefathers (8.13-21; 9.1-41; cf. Num. 14.35; Isa. 6.9-10). [183] Still in the context of Tabernacles, which celebrated the realization of Israel's freedom at the Exodus, Jesus explicitly discloses to these leaders both his divine identity ('I AM [He]' 8.24; 28, 53; Isa. 43.13)[184] and his liberating mission (cf. Exodus 3;

---

[179] For a list of scholars who note this wilderness theme, see Köstenberger, 'John', loc. 17330.

[180] *Sukkah* 5.1. Carson says some sources indicate that this took place on every night of the festival. Carson, *The Gospel According to John*, p. 337.

[181] George Beasley-Murray also points out the Exodus background of the 'following' motif with the pillar of fire. George R. Beasley-Murray, *John* (WBC 36; Nashville: Thomas Nelson, 2nd edn, 1999), pp. 128-29.

[182] Jesus' words about supplying living water and light (and implicit claims about being the temple) find their fullest expression in Rev. 21.22; in the new Jerusalem, there is no temple, for 'the Lord God Almighty and the Lamb are its temple'; no sun or moon, for 'the glory of God has illumined it, and its lamp is the Lamb'; and from the throne flows a river of 'living water'.

[183] The Isaianic lawsuits likewise indicate that 'Israel's perception of Babylon's power and of God's apparent inability to deliver them led to disbelief in his sovereignty'. This is the context behind the revelation in Isa. 43.10 LXX, with which 8.58 matches exactly. Coxon, *New Exodus in John*, p. 264.

[184] Carson states that there can be no doubt about 'whether or not *egō eimi* should be taken absolutely' in v. 53. He also refers to strong linguistic connections with YHWH's self-disclosure in Isa. 43.13; 41.1 ('I, YHWH … I am He'). Carson, *The Gospel According to John*, p. 358. Morris concurs: '"I am" must here have the fullest significance it can bear'. Jesus uses the aorist to indicate that Abraham's

Isa. 43.10). As the *Son* of God, Jesus has the authority to release slaves,[185] and he will bring the ultimate freedom from the bondage to sin when he is lifted up (8.28; Isa. 52.13). Abraham's true children will follow this Son greater than Moses (cf. Heb. 3.5-6) out of sin's bondage to the place he has prepared for them in the house of his Father (14.2-3).

Jesus' claims and teaching in ch. 10 are not far removed from this discussion of liberation and leading. John mentions that Jesus was standing in the temple during the Feast of Dedication (i.e. Hanukkah, 10.22). This commemorated the victory of the Maccabean revolt over Antiochus Epiphanes IV, which led to the renewal of temple worship and a brief period of national independence.[186] Surely, as the Jewish people – now under Roman oppression – celebrated this Feast, it was with mixed joy and longing. Amid suspense and controversy about Jesus' identity (10.19-24; 41-42) and the dark backdrop of the 'glaring irresponsibility of the Jewish religious leaders' (9.1-41),[187] he proclaims that he is the 'good shepherd' (10.11; 14) who lays down his life for his sheep.[188]

Shepherd imagery was associated primarily with YHWH's leading his people out of Egypt to serve him as their King (Ps. 78.52; cf. Exod. 15.13; Pss. 77.20; 80.1), with Israel's kings' and leaders' ruling over [or being rebuked for mistreating] God's people (Num. 27.17; 2 Sam. 7.7; Isa. 56.11; cf. Cyrus in Isa. 44.28; Jer. 3.15; 10.21; 23.1), and with the New Exodus coming of YHWH and the messianic 'Branch' of David, who would gather God's scattered flock, reign over them, and judge unfaithful leaders.[189] In particular, Jesus' words evoke Isa. 40.10-11 (YHWH will tend his flock like a Shepherd, gather and carry his lambs) and 49.9-10 (YHWH will release those in darkness, give them pasture; they will not hunger or thirst; he will lead them to springs of water); Jer. 23.3-8 (YHWH will gather the

---

being had a definite beginning, whereas Jesus' did not. Morris, *John*, p. 419; cf. Watts, 'Exodus', p. 485.

[185] Coxon, *New Exodus in John*, p. 264.

[186] Hays, *Reading Backwards*, loc. 2030.

[187] Köstenberger, 'John', loc. 17515.

[188] Coxon sees 10.1-21 as still related to Tabernacles, and 10.22-42 as related to the Feast of Dedication. He explores YHWH as Shepherd-King of Israel, his universal enthronement, and his relationship to his 'sacral king and under-shepherd' against this Tabernacles background. Coxon, *New Exodus in John*, p. 281.

[189] Coxon notes that *gathering* and *scattering* language is further related to the covenant promises and judgments of Deuteronomy 28-30 (e.g. 30.1-6), which establish the Exodus as a paradigm. Coxon, *New Exodus in John*, p. 286.

remnant of his flock, raise up a righteous Branch to reign as king) and 31.10-11 (YHWH will gather scattered Israel, keep him as a shepherd keeps a flock; ransom and redeem Jacob); Mic. 5.2-5 and 7.14-15 (an eternal, messianic Shepherd-ruler will gather the sons of Israel as in the days of the Exodus and perform miracles); and Ezekiel 34 and 37 (YHWH will search for his scattered sheep; lead them to rest; set over them 'one shepherd', his 'servant David'; break the bonds of their yoke; and feed the fat and strong with judgment).[190] John 10 portrays Jesus as the good shepherd who seeks the lost for salvation and lays down his own life to provide abundant life for his sheep (10.10; cf. Rev. 7.15-17). More than this selfless care, the allusions in the text tie it to themes of return from exile, the people of God, and 'religious-political usurpers' vs. YHWH and his under-shepherd.[191] Jesus' claims have undertones of his messianic kingship, his role as deliverer (cf. Ezek. 34.27) and the leader of the New Exodus, and his judgment against the 'false shepherds'.[192] As the fulfillment of the Feast of Dedication, Jesus is also the one who offers true freedom to Israel, who makes possible true worship through his body, and who reigns on the throne of David.[193]

Finally, at the end of John's Gospel, John reappropriates the Lamb imagery that he introduced in 1.29-36 to depict Jesus' death as a

---

[190] Jesus' words about 'lead[ing] them out' and the sheep's 'go[ing] in and out' in 10.9 seem to refer to Num. 27.17. Köstenberger, 'John', locs. 17524-34. Jesus' words about uniting his flock under 'one shepherd' (10.16) seem to be drawn from Ezek. 34.23-24. His saying he will die to 'gather together into one the children of God who are scattered abroad' recalls Isa. 56.8 ('The Lord GOD, who gathers the dispersed of Israel, declares, "Yet others I will gather to them, to those already gathered"'). Zechariah 13.7-9 also speaks of a time when the Shepherd will be struck and YHWH will purify Israel.

[191] Coxon, *New Exodus in John*, p. 303.

[192] Morris notes the connection between shepherd imagery and sovereignty in the Bible. Morris, *John*, p. 445. Hays asserts that Jesus is 'staking symbolic claim to be the new David, the restorer and ruler of Israel'. Hays, *Reading Backwards*, locs. 2052-59.

[193] In Jn 15.1-11, Jesus also calls himself the 'true vine'. In doing so, he appropriates language used of Israel (Ps. 80.8; Isa. 5.1; 27.2-6; Ezek. 19.10), indicating that true Israel is now constituted *in him* (cf. 14.20, 'I am in my Father, and you in me, and I in you'). Jesus brings forth the fruit that Israel as God's people failed to produce; he is now the focal point of God's salvific plan, and faith in Jesus becomes the defining characteristic of membership in the people of God. Köstenberger, 'John', locs. 18563-73; cf. Michaels, *The Gospel of John*, p. 801. As in many of Jesus' other statements in John, this depicts Jesus as the only source of eternal *life*.

Passover sacrifice. In 1.29, John the Baptist testifies that Jesus is the 'Lamb of God who takes away the sin of the world'. Keener rightly contends that John primarily has in mind the Passover lamb (to which, as Keener shows, early Judaism had attached the nuances of sacrifice), possibly in combination with the Isaianic Servant (Isa. 53.7).[194] Both of these died on behalf of others, procuring freedom and averting judgment (Exod. 12.1-17; Isa. 53.4-8; cf. Jn 10.11, 15; 11.50; 18.14; 1 Jn 2.2; 3.16; 4.10; Rev. 5.6, 9).[195]

The Passover symbolism that pervades John's Gospel (John 2; 6; 11; 12; 13) climaxes in the passion narrative. The Synoptics tell that the night before Jesus' death, he had already eaten the Passover meal with his disciples (Mt. 26.17-30; Mk 14.12-16; Lk. 22.7-13), decisively reinterpreting its significance.[196] John, rather than focusing on these symbolic elements, emphasizes the reality that they commemorate. He records how details of Jesus' death fulfilled Scripture and points, as he

---

[194] Keener observes, 'That the Fourth Gospel later portrays Jesus' death in terms of the Passover lamb (18:28; 19:36) and writes in the context of a new exodus and new redemption (1:23) expected by Judaism indicates that this is the sense of "lamb" in view in the Fourth Gospel'. Keener, *Gospel of John*, I, p. 454. Morris and Michaels prefer to see it as a composite representation of OT sacrifices, all of which were fulfilled in Christ. Morris, *John*, p. 130; Michaels, *The Gospel of John*, p. 108. Köstenberger likewise suggests 'multiple levels of meaning', but leans toward Isa. 53.7. Köstenberger, 'John', loc. 16295.

[195] Coxon follows Holland and Howard in asserting that by the time of Second Temple Judaism, Passover had become associated with the Day of Atonement (cf. Ezek. 45.21); thus both the initial and eschatological Passovers were related to the removal of sin. Coxon, *New Exodus in John*, pp. 151-53; J.K. Howard, 'Christ Our Passover: A Study of the Passover-Exodus Theme in 1 Corinthians', *EvQ* 41 (April 1969), pp. 97-108; Tom Holland, *Contours of Pauline Theology: A Radical New Survey of the Influences on Paul's Biblical Writings* (Geanies House, Scotland: Mentor, 2010), p. 161.

[196] While some scholars find irreconcilable contradictions between the Synoptics' and John's chronology of Jesus' death in relation to Passover, I agree with Carson and Köstenberger that the Synoptic chronology is correct, and John's Gospel, when interpreted correctly, does not contradict it. Carson, *The Gospel According to John*, pp. 456, 604; Köstenberger, 'John', loc. 18897. This makes the 'day of preparation for the Passover' in 19.14 refer to the day of preparation for the Sabbath of Passover week (confirmed by the Jews' request in 19.31 to remove the bodies before the Sabbath, which as Keener concludes, would have been 'unconscionable' on a festal Sabbath). Keener, *Gospel of John*, I, p. 1151. As Morris notes, the primary difficulty with this view is that in Jn 18.28, it seems that the Jews did not want to be defiled and thus unable to eat the Passover meal. Morris, *John*, p. 688. Other scholars believe that John intends to depict Jesus' dying at the time when Passover lambs were sacrificed. See Hays, *Reading Backwards*, loc. 18977; Allison, *The New Moses*, p. 256; Stock, *A Way in the Wilderness*, p. 113.

did with other feasts, to how Jesus fulfilled the Feast itself. John uniquely mentions several details about Jesus' death that together portray him as the Passover Lamb: the hyssop branch (19.29; Exod. 12.22), Jesus' unbroken bones (19.33; Exod. 12.45; Num. 9.12; Ps. 34.20), and the blood mingled with water that flowed from his side (19.34; Num. 20.11; *m. Pesaḥ.* 5.5-8; *m. 'Ohal.* 3.5).[197] John's quotation from Zech. 12.10 (19.37; cf. Isa. 53.5), which speaks of mourning the death of a firstborn, further ties Jesus' death to Exodus symbolism.[198] The water flowing from Jesus' side could indicate the availability of the living water of the Spirit (Zech. 12.10; 13.1) that John adumbrated in 7.37-39, with secondary allusions to the rock in the wilderness.[199] Just as at the Passover, YHWH redeemed his people from slavery and spared them from judgment, through Jesus' sacrifice, his people receive true freedom (8.36; cf. Rev. 1.5) and are saved from judgment (3.17; 5.24; 11.50; 12.47).

The following chart summarizes the correspondences between the Exodus motif and the life of Jesus Christ.

Birth, Flight to Egypt	The destruction of male babies in Egypt parallels the killing of male infants in Bethlehem (Mt. 2.16). The lives of both Deliverers are spared. Just as Israel – God's firstborn – went down to Egypt and was brought up again, Jesus – God's only begotten Son – descended to Egypt and was called out (Mt. 2.15; Hos. 11.1).[200] Moses and Jesus returned home after those who sought their lives died.
Name 'Jesus'	Jesus is named for his role as Savior/Deliverer (Mt. 1.21). In Jesus, 'YHWH saves' his people (Exod. 14.30). Jesus will lead his people out of a greater and more terrible slavery than

---

[197] Köstenberger, 'John', loc. 18982; Morris, *John*, p. 727; Hahn, 'Worship in the Word', p. 123; Fisher, 'New and Greater Exodus', p. 77.

[198] The Synoptic Gospels note additional parallels between Jesus' death and Israel's Exodus/wilderness experience. The giving of the Sinai covenant was accompanied by darkness, quaking of earth, and a loud voice; at the crucifixion, when the new covenant was established, there were also darkness, quaking of the earth, and the loud voice of Jesus (Mt. 27). The darkness could also parallel the three days of darkness in Egypt before the last plague (Exod. 10.21-22). This immediately preceded the killing of the firstborn, and the darkness at the cross immediately preceded Jesus' death as the 'firstborn over all creation' (Col. 1.15).

[199] Keener mentions that Jewish tradition taught that when Moses struck the rock in the desert, first blood flowed, and then water. *Exod. R.* 122a (citing Ps. 78.20); *Pal. Targ.* Num. 20.11. Keener, *Gospel of John*, I, p. 1154; cf. Glasson, *Moses in the Fourth Gospel*, p. 54.

[200] Bruce, *New Testament Development*, p. 46.

	the bondage of Egypt. In contrast to the first 'Joshua', Jesus will be able to offer his people rest (Mt. 11.28; Psalm 95; Heb. 4.1-11).
The Tabernacle	Jesus is called *Immanuel*, 'God with us' (Mt. 1.21; Isa. 7.14). John says he 'tabernacles' among his people (1.14; 2.19, 21).[201] He is the new locus of God's presence, the king with royal authority to establish the temple, and the final and perfect sacrifice. All that was available through the temple is now available through him.[202]
Declaration of John the Baptist	John the Baptist prepares 'the way' of the Lord (announcing Isaiah's New Exodus – Exod. 13.21; Isa. 40.3). Christ's coming is the prophesied return of YHWH to Zion.[203] In him, Israel experiences true return from exile.[204]
Baptism	At Jesus' baptism, YHWH's affirmation of Israel's sonship (Exod. 4.22) is applied to Jesus (Mk 9.7).[205] As the Israelites crossed the Red Sea and 'came up' out of the Jordan (Josh. 4.10, LXX), Jesus 'comes up' out of the baptismal water.
Temptation	Jesus' forty days of testing in the wilderness form a parallel to Israel's forty years of testing in the wilderness. Jesus, the true Israel, is faithful and continues to depend on his Father.
Sermon on the Mount	This Sermon is parallel to the giving of the Law at Sinai, yet punctuated with contrast. 'You have heard that it was said …, but I say to you …' (Mt. 5.21, 27, 31, 33, 38, 43).[206]
Signs and Wonders	Linked together, these miraculous events are clustered around two events in Scripture: the Exodus from Egypt (Exod. 7.3) and the ministry of Jesus and his apostles (Acts 2.22; 5.12).[207]
Calling of the 12	Jesus' calling 12 disciples signifies the constitution of the eschatological Israel.[208]
Feeding of 5,000	The provision of bread (and fish) in the wilderness alludes to the giving of manna (and quail) to Israel (Exod. 16.14).
'I AM' statements in John	Israel drank from the rock and Jesus gives living water (Jn 4.10; 7.38); Israelites ate manna and Jesus is the bread of life

---

[201] Hung, 'Relationship and Rebirth', p. 80.

[202] Wright, *Jesus and the* Victory *of God*, II, p. 436; Beale, *New Testament Biblical Theology*, p. 489.

[203] Wright, *Jesus and the Victory of God*, II, p. 371.

[204] Beale, *New Testament Biblical Theology*, loc. 14449.

[205] Bruce, *New Testament Development*, p. 47.

[206] Stock, *A Way in the Wilderness*, p. 35.

[207] Goldsworthy, *According to Plan*, loc. 1432.

[208] Wright, *Jesus and the Victory of God*, II, p. 436; Stock, *A Way in the Wilderness*, p. 35. Cf. Mt. 19.28.

	(Jn 6.51); Israel was led by a pillar of fire and Jesus is the light of the world (Jn 8.12).[209] Jesus is the Good Shepherd (Jn 10.11-14; cf. Exod. 15.13; Ps. 77.20; Isa. 40.11) and the true vine (a symbol for Israel, Jn 15.1-7; Isa. 5; Ezek. 19.10).
Transfiguration	The Transfiguration is invested with Exodus symbolism. Jesus goes up on a mountain, and his glory is revealed (cf. Moses, Exod. 34.29); God's presence appears in the form of a cloud (cf. Exod. 13.21); and Peter offers to build 3 tents/booths (cf. Feast of Tabernacles), perhaps thinking that God would again dwell among his people.[210]
Triumphal Entry	Just as the Israelites saw God's miracles yet murmured and lacked faith, the crowd that 'hailed Jesus as Messiah called out later that same week for his crucifixion'.[211]
Covenant/ Lord's Supper	Jesus institutes a new covenant sealed with a fellowship meal at the time of the Passover (Exod. 24.11; Mt. 27.26-28). His words 'blood of the covenant' (Mt. 26.28) echo Exod. 24.8.[212]
The Bronze Serpent	'As Moses lifted up the serpent in the wilderness, even so must the Son of Man be lifted up; so that whoever believes will in Him have eternal life' (Jn 3.14-15).
Crucifixion	There was darkness for three hours of the crucifixion (Mk 15.33), parallel to three days of darkness in Egypt's penultimate plague (Exod. 10.21-22). The plague on Egypt immediately preceded the killing of the firstborn, and the darkness at the cross immediately preceded Jesus' death.[213] Jesus died as our Passover lamb (1 Cor. 5.7), and not one of his bones was broken (Jn 19.36; cf. Exod. 12.46). The God of Israel had once more 'visited and redeemed his people' (Lk. 1.68). The giving of the Sinai covenant was also accompanied by darkness, quaking, and a loud voice; at the crucifixion, when the new covenant was established, there were darkness, quaking of the earth, and the loud voice of Jesus who bore curse of the law (Matthew 27).[214]

---

[209] Patterson and Travers, 'Contours of the Exodus Motif', p. 26.

[210] Stock, *A Way in the Wilderness*, pp. 37-41. According to Jewish tradition (2 Macc. 2.7-8), the cloud was expected to reappear in messianic times.

[211] Patterson and Travers, 'Contours of the Exodus Motif', p. 42.

[212] Boulton, 'Supersession or Subsession?', pp. 23-24; John Mark Hicks, 'A Sacramental Journey: A Christian-Theological Reading of Exodus', *Leaven* 21.2 (January 2013), p. 4.

[213] Patterson and Travers, 'Contours of the Exodus Motif', p. 43.

[214] Hung, 'Relationship and Rebirth', p. 80.

Resurrection	At the Transfiguration, Jesus spoke about his coming 'exodus' (Lk. 9.31), referring to his death and resurrection (Eph. 4.8; Exod. 12.38).
Jesus pours out the Spirit at Pentecost	During the celebration of harvest and the renewal of the covenants with Noah and Moses,[215] the Spirit is poured out to provide justifying righteousness (Acts 2)[216] and signal the ingathering of exiles and reformation of the people of God (cf. Isa. 44.3-6).[217]

Table 2: Exodus Parallels in the Life of Christ

Summary

The Gospels and Acts mark another advance in the use of the Exodus motif. The Gospel writers appropriate the Exodus on several levels. First, they apply Exodus language and imagery to the life of Jesus with a typological hermeneutic, portraying him as recapitulating Israel's experiences and summing up in himself Israel's true vocation.[218] Second, they show how Jesus is the typological climax toward which the Exodus and other OT events and institutions pointed (e.g. the death of the firstborn, the Passover lamb, the redemption of Israel, the tabernacle/temple, and the feasts).[219] Finally, they depict Jesus as fulfilling prophecies of New Exodus activity that had become intertwined with expectations of a coming prophet like Moses, Branch of David, and Isaianic Servant of YHWH. Jesus' coming represents the coming of YHWH to Zion for comfort and judgment. His reign is inaugurated with signs and wonders and brings restoration, the end of exile, freedom to worship, a new covenant, forgiveness of sins, the gift of the Spirit, and blessing to all nations.

---

[215] I. Howard Marshall, 'Acts', in G.K. Beale and D.A. Carson (eds.), *Commentary on the New Testament Use of the Old Testament* (Grand Rapids: Baker Academic, Kindle edn, 2007), loc. 20116. See *Jub.* 6.17-18.

[216] Frank D. Macchia, *Justified in the Spirit: Creation, Redemption, and the Triune God*, Pentecostal Manifestos (Grand Rapids: Eerdmans, 2010), p. 103.

[217] Pao, *Acts and the Isaianic New Exodus*, p. 131.

[218] For a detailed analysis of this in Matthew, see R. Joel Kennedy, 'The Recapitulation of Israel: Use of Israel's History in Matthew 1:1-4:11' (PhD thesis, University of Aberdeen, 2008).

[219] Hung, 'Relationship and Rebirth', p. 78.

4

THE EXODUS MOTIF IN THE PAULINE EPISTLES

Introduction

Paul's Epistles, while possibly written before the Gospels, build upon them theologically and canonically. The Gospels and Acts introduce Jesus as the true Israel; demonstrate how various aspects of the Exodus were recapitulated and consummated in his experiences; and portray the fulfillment of New Exodus prophecies and expectations in his life, death, and resurrection. Paul's Epistles expound on the theological and practical significance of these events – for Israel, for the Gentiles, for the church, and even for creation. To this end, Paul appropriates the Exodus motif in several ways. Before this chapter turns to consider Paul's specific uses of the motif in his Epistles, it will survey three primary categories of his usage and four contours of the storyline that will serve as an analytical framework for the study.

Hermeneutic

First, Paul uses the Exodus motif for *texture* and *depth* via a network of subtle, metaleptic echoes and allusions. [1] Paul is constantly in conversation with Israel's Scripture, weaving it into the background of his thought. Exodus/New Exodus language and imagery comprise an

---

[1] These bring out implicit resonance between his own appropriations of words or figures of speech and those in earlier texts. Hays, *Echoes of Scripture*, p. 20.

integral part of this symbolic world, this matrix of ideas.[2] Their presence adds resonance, intensified significance, and continuity to Paul's arguments.[3] Second, he invests some texts with explicit New Exodus *quotations* and points to *type/antitype relationships* in others. The events surrounding Jesus' life and those in the early believers' experience, he contends, represent the fulfillment of prophecy and the culmination of hope.[4] Paul especially draws from Isaiah and Psalms to indicate that the New Exodus has been inaugurated. Moreover, he observes that certain elements in Israel's history pointed forward typologically to greater and truer realities. The OT foundations (e.g. the Passover lamb, tabernacle) were but scaffolding and shadows; believers are stewards of spiritual mysteries that were hidden in the past, but disclosed in the fullness of time (Rom. 16.25-26; 1 Cor. 4.1; Eph. 3.9). In these ways, Paul confirms that the things that have happened conform to and reveal God's purpose according to the Scriptures.[5] While the story may have assumed a surprising or even shocking shape, it is not without witness. Third, Paul employs an overarching *Exodus/New Exodus storyline* that this chapter will examine in four movements:

1) Slavery/exile: just as Israel was in bondage to Pharaoh, the entire human race was enslaved to sin before the coming of Christ, groaning for redemption (Romans 6–8; Gal. 4.3-7).

2) Redemption/judgment: in the fullness of time (cf. Exod. 12.40-41), Jesus came as both Deliverer and Passover sacrifice (Rom. 3.24-25; Gal. 4.4-5; 1 Cor. 5.7). He redeemed God's chosen people from slavery and rescued them from God's wrath (Rom. 5.8-10; 1 Thess. 1.10). At the same time, those who reject God's salvation experience

---

[2] Sylvia C. Keesmaat, *Paul and His Story: (Re)Interpreting the Exodus Tradition* (JSNTSup 181; Sheffield: Sheffield Academic Press, 1999), pp. 31-32; 55; Wright, *Jesus and the Victory of God*, II, pp. 268-69; Hays, *Echoes of Scripture*, pp. 35, 57; Holland, *Contours of Pauline Theology*, p. 12.

[3] Wright correctly asserts that this demonstrates the centrality to Paul's thought of the OT context. It is not merely peripheral or illustrative for him. N.T. Wright, *The Climax of the Covenant: Christ and the Law in Pauline Theology* (Philadelphia: Fortress Press, 1993), pp. 7-9.

[4] Paul speaks of 'fulfillment' in broad strokes, asserting, for example, that at the climax of the ages, Jesus' death and resurrection fulfilled the entire Law and its requirements (Rom. 8.4; Gal. 4.4). He does not speak of certain events 'fulfilling' certain Scriptures (e.g. as Matthew does).

[5] Douglas Moo, *The Epistle to the Romans* (NICNT; Grand Rapids: Eerdmans, 1996), p. 610.

various forms of judgment, including hardened hearts and being turned over to follow their evil desires (Rom. 1.18–2.10; 9–10; 1 Cor. 1.18-20; 2.6-9; 10.1-12).

3) Election/sonship: Jews and Gentiles who participate by faith in the death and resurrection of the messianic Son of God are baptized into Christ (Rom. 6.3-4; 1 Cor. 10.2; 12.13). In him, they compose the true Israel and are heirs of Abraham's promise (Romans 9–11; Galatians 3–4; cf. 2 Samuel 7).[6] God calls them into his kingdom (Col. 1.13-14) as his adopted sons and daughters (Romans 8–9; Gal. 4.5; Eph. 1.5), setting them apart as a people for his own possession (Eph. 1.14; Tit. 2.11-14) to worship him in holiness (Rom. 12.1). The Spirit writes the new covenant on their hearts (Rom. 2.29; 2 Cor. 3.6); and seals them for their future inheritance (2 Cor. 1.22).

4) Journey: God's people now walk by/are led by the Spirit (Rom. 8.14; Gal. 5.16-25) and are nourished on Christ (1 Corinthians 10). By the Holy Spirit, God dwells among them (Rom. 8.9), forming them into a holy temple in Christ (1 Cor. 3.16-17; 2 Cor. 6.14-18; Eph. 2.21).

Here, Paul follows in the footsteps of the OT authors, who understood the Exodus as a paradigm for later acts of salvation and judgment. He sees that the overall plotline of the Exodus (and later New Exodus texts) applies to the analogous situation of his audience; it is recapitulated and intensified. He constantly looks backward, to understand and to illustrate (1 Cor. 10.6). Using this narrative framework, this chapter will survey Paul's multi-layered contours of Exodus/New Exodus in his Epistles.

Slavery/Exile

Slavery and exile make an early debut in the pages of Scripture. The first sin of humanity resulted in exile, curse, heavy labor, suffering, and death (Genesis 2–3).[7] After Joseph died, the people of Israel spent 400 years in Egypt, 'enslaved and oppressed' (Gen. 15.13). They clung to God's promise that he would surely deliver them (Gen. 50.24), which he did definitively at the Exodus. However, the cycle of sin, oppression

---

[6] Hans Hübner, *Law in Paul's Thought: A Contribution to the Development of Pauline Theology* (ed. John Riches; trans. James C.G. Greig; London: T. & T. Clark, 3rd edn, 2004), pp. 15-17.

[7] For more background, see prior section on Mt. 11.28.

and exile, and deliverance (thereafter often envisioned as New Exodus activity, cf. Deuteronomy 28–30) continued throughout Israel's history. While God raised up leaders, and Israel experienced partial restoration and return from exile, the people still longed for complete freedom.[8] There was a sense that they were still in exile, awaiting New Exodus deliverance and vindication.[9]

Paul exhibits a keen awareness of this interpretation of exile and restoration. He focuses, however, not on Israel's political situation, but on the spiritual condition of fallen humanity. Herein lies the problem, Paul asserts: the entire human race became enslaved to sin (Rom. 6.6, 16; 7.14; Gal. 4.3),[10] 'shut up under sin' and its power (Gal. 3.22; cf. Rom. 3.9).[11] Through sin, death reigned as master (Rom. 5.27; 6.23). Ironically, though in line with God's purpose, this slavery came about through the Law (Rom. 5.12-13; 7.9).[12] While good and holy, the Law was unable to offer life and righteousness (Gal. 3.21). All those who did not keep the whole Law (i.e. everyone until Jesus) came under its curse (Gal. 3.10;

---

[8] They longed for the prophet like Moses, the messianic Branch of David, and freedom to worship YHWH under a new covenant written on their hearts. They yearned for YHWH to return to Zion, fill the temple with his glory, and exalt his name among the nations, according to the full scope of his promises.

[9] N.T. Wright is a major proponent of this underlying narrative in the NT. See, for example, Wright, *Jesus and the Victory of God*, II, pp. xvii–xviii, pp. 126, 208; Wright, *Climax of the Covenant*, p. 6; N.T. Wright, *What Saint Paul Really Said: Was Paul of Tarsus the Real Founder of Christianity?* (Grand Rapids: Eerdmans, 1997), p. 60. Cf. Tob. 13.5; Bar. 3.6-8; 2 Macc. 1.27-29; 4QSD 1.3-11; 1QS 8.12-16); 1QM 1.2-3. For a list of other scholars who support this view, see James M. Scott, *Adoption as Sons of God: An Exegetical Investigation into the Background in the Pauline Corpus* (WUNT; Tübingen: Mohr Siebeck, 1992), p. 115 n. 248.

[10] In Gal. 4.3, 9, Paul says believers used to be enslaved to τὰ στοιχεῖα [τοῦ κόσμου] ('the elemental things of the world'). Some scholars connect this with cosmological powers (cf. Eph. 2.2) or perhaps angels through whom the Law was given. See Ronald Y.K. Fung, *The Epistle to the Galatians* (NICNT; Grand Rapids: Eerdmans, 1988), pp. 189-190.

[11] Paul draws here from Isaiah, in whose day Israel was sold into exile and slavery because of sin (Isa. 50.1 LXX says ἰδοὺ ταῖς ἁμαρτίαις ὑμῶν ἐπράθητε, 'Behold, you were sold because of your sins').

[12] While Paul's use of 'Law' is not limited to the formal giving of the Law at Sinai (for even Adam received a commandment), Sinai nonetheless epitomizes it. Paul ironically depicts Israel, just released from slavery, as coming under the new slavery of sin with the giving of the Law. Wilder provides an in-depth discussion of Paul's understanding of being 'under the law' as specifically related to the Exodus. Wilder, 'Freed from the Law to Be Led by the Spirit: Echoes of the Exodus Narrative in the Context and Background of Galatians 5:18'.

Deut. 27.26).[13] In the past, God had announced that the Israelites would be slaves in Egypt for 400 years (Gen. 15.13; Acts 7.6). When the time was completed, they went up out of Egypt (Exod. 12.31). In the same way, God spoke through the prophets to proclaim that he would act again to deliver his people in a wondrous way. Paul says in Gal. 4.4 that God's plan was fulfilled when Jesus arrived ὅτε δὲ ἦλθεν τὸ πλήρωμα τοῦ χρόνου ('when the fullness of [the] time had come'; cf. 1 Tim. 2.6).[14]

Paul sharpens his metaphor with language drawn from the Exodus.[15] For example, the word *slavery/bondage* (δουλεία, Rom. 8.15) recalls LXX passages such as Exod. 6.6; 13.14; 20.2; Deut. 5.6; and Lev. 26.45.[16] Paul adds the description 'yoke of slavery' to this (Gal. 5.1; cf. Lev. 26.13). Humanity also *groans* (στενάζομεν) with creation, Paul says, for the completion of redemption (Rom. 8.22-23; 2 Cor. 5.2, 4; cf. στεναγμὸν, 'groaning' in Exod. 2.24 LXX).[17] Finally, believers are not *led* into *fear* (φόβον) such that they wish to return to

---

[13] This categorization shockingly includes Israel, the covenant people, whom he perceives are 'as much in need of an exodus as had been Israel in Moses' day'. Reynolds, 'Comparative Study', p. 199. Holland provides a helpful discussion about the corporate nature of Paul's struggle with sin (either 'acting out the role of mankind in its bondage to Sin, or representing the Jewish nation as it grapples with the consequences of the giving of the law'). Holland, *Contours of Pauline Theology*, p. 97.

[14] This phrase indicates the proper or appropriate completion of a period of time. Johannes E. Louw and Eugene A. Nida (eds.), *Greek-English Lexicon of the New Testament Based on Semantic Domains* (2 vols; New York: United Bible Societies, 2nd edn, 1989), 67.69.

[15] See Chapter 2 for examples of how this language was appropriated in New Exodus texts.

[16] Keesmaat, *Paul and His Story*, p. 66; N.T. Wright, 'New Exodus and New Inheritance: The Narrative Structure of Romans 3–8', *Romans and the People of God: Essays in Honor of Gordon D. Fee on the Occasion of His 65th Birthday* (Grand Rapids: Eerdmans, 1999), pp. 28-29; Craig S. Keener, *Romans: A New Covenant Commentary* (New Covenant Commentary Series 6; Eugene, OR: Wipf & Stock, Kindle edn, 2009), locs. 2934-36; Daube, *Exodus Pattern*, pp. 59-60; contra E.P. Sanders, *Paul and Palestinian Judaism* (Philadelphia: Fortress Press, 1977), p. 512. Keesmaat further contends (pp. 77-78) that κράζω ('to cry out') represents a special kind of cry in times of crisis or oppression (used in texts like Exod. 5.8; Judg. 3.9; Ps. 3.4; Hab. 1.1 (LXX), although Exod. 2.23 uses a different verb) and further echoes the Exodus, especially in combination with 'Father' language (cf. Isa. 63.15-16).

[17] Keener notes that while 'groaning' is 'not limited to exodus or childbirth contexts (e.g. Sib. Or. 3.417, 438, 558, 602, 752), the present context suggests these allusions'. Keener, *Romans*, locs. 3826-29. Although Paul evokes the Exodus with 'groaning' language, he also emphasizes that the Spirit, through these groans, testifies to believers' liberty and sonship (Rom. 8.23; Gal. 4.6).

slavery (Rom. 8.15; cf. ἐφοβήθησαν, 'they were afraid'), as the Israelites in Exod. 14.10-12 and Num. 14.9 (cf. 'Do not fear' of Deut. 1.21, 29).[18]

Paul's use of this cluster of terms from the Exodus shows how he has 'radicalized' slavery and exile to conceptualize the human condition of sin and separation from God.[19] The next section will examine how Paul likewise discerns Exodus typology in the redemption and judgment brought about by Jesus' death and people's response to it.

Redemption/Judgment

Describing what happened at Christ's death according to Paul's writings is admittedly complex. This is due in part to Paul's use of overlapping metaphors (e.g. salvation, freedom, redemption, atonement, and reconciliation) and in part to his use of terms with disputed backgrounds and significance (e.g. ἱλαστήριον ['propitiatory sacrifice' or 'mercy seat'], 'justification', and 'righteousness of God').[20] However, the events of the cross are at the heart of Paul's theology. This section will examine several key terms and concepts in Paul's writings to demonstrate that the Exodus motif pervades Paul's thought in this area and may offer a framework that can account for and provide insight into his mixed imagery.

Liberation from Slavery

Just as Paul depicts fallen humanity as slaves of sin and death, he speaks of their rescue in terms of freedom and liberation from slavery.[21] Several families of words convey this idea. The most general words are ἐλευθερόω and ἐλευθερία, which simply connote

---

[18] Keesmaat, *Paul and His Story*, p. 68. Keener concurs that the language of being 'led' by God's Spirit (Romans 8) particularly evokes the Exodus. Keener, *Romans*, loc. 3509.

[19] Mark A. Seifrid, 'Romans', in Andreas J. Köstenberger, G.K. Beale, and D.A. Carson (eds.), *Commentary on the New Testament Use of the Old Testament* (Grand Rapids: Baker Academic, Kindle edn, 2007), loc. 23251.

[20] Note that this cluster of vocabulary is all drawn from the Exodus motif. Refer to the previous discussion on salvation and redemption in Luke-Acts; the footnotes in that section examine salvation/redemption/deliverance language in the OT.

[21] Bruce, *New Testament Development*, p. 34.

'to set free' and 'to be set free/freedom'.[22] At times, Paul broadly states that believers were 'set free' or that Christ 'set us free' (e.g. Gal. 5.1, 13); at other times, he specifies that we are set free 'from sin' (Rom. 6.18, 22) or from 'the law of sin and death' (Rom. 8.2).[23] More specifically, he uses λυτρόομαι, λύτρωσις, and ἀπολύτρωσις, which imply that a slave has been set free and that something was paid for the release (cf. Exod. 6.6; Deut. 7.8).[24] These words lie behind statements in Tit. 2.14 that Jesus gave himself to *redeem* us from every lawless deed and make us 'a people for his own possession' (cf. Exod. 19.5) and in 1 Tim. 2.6 that Jesus gave himself as a *ransom* for all. Ephesians 1.7 and Col. 1.14 declare that in Jesus and through his blood, believers have *redemption*, which is set in apposition to the ἄφεσις ['forgiveness'] of sins.[25] Finally, Paul employs ἀγοράζω and ἐξαγοράζω, 'to cause release/freedom by a means that proves costly; to redeem', in several verses.[26] Galatians 3.13 and 4.4-5 assert that 'Christ *redeemed* us from the curse of the Law' and came 'to redeem those under the Law'. Paul exhorts believers in 1 Cor. 6.20 and 7.23 to consider the costly price of this *redemption* so that they will not become slaves of men and will glorify God in their bodies.[27]

This language of liberation, purchase, and redemption clearly evokes the events of the Exodus that were recapitulated in Israel's history (e.g. Deut. 13.5; 2 Sam. 7.23; Isa. 44; Mic. 4.10; Zech. 10.8).[28] Moreover, these words are embedded in *clusters* in texts (e.g. Rom. 3.21-26; 6–8; Galatians 4–5; Eph. 1.3-14; and 1 Corinthians 5–6; 10) along with unmistakable references to Exodus history and typology (e.g. adoption as sons, baptism into Moses/Christ, inheritance) that together offer a panoramic view of God's unfolding plan that is

---

[22] Louw and Nida, *Greek-English Lexicon*, 37.133-135.

[23] The context of Gal. 1.5 makes clear that this is freedom from the Law (Paul exhorts believers, 'Do not be subject again to a yoke of slavery').

[24] Louw and Nida, Greek-English Lexicon, 37.128.

[25] He notes that although this has been inaugurated, it has yet to be completed (Eph. 4.30; Col. 1.14; Rom. 8.23).

[26] Louw and Nida, *Greek-English Lexicon*, 37.131. These are figurative extensions of words that mean 'to buy' or 'pay a price' (see 57.188).

[27] On occasion, the verb δικαιόω, usually translated 'justified/declared righteous' or 'vindicated', connotes 'freed from' a dominating force (as in Rom. 6.7).

[28] Cf. footnotes under 'Slavery' section. N.T. Wright goes so far as to say that in Judaism, any general story about slaves and freedom is an allusion to Exodus. See Wright, 'New Exodus and New Inheritance: The Narrative Structure of Romans 3–8', p. 29.

increscent, cohesive, resonant, and profound. More specifically, though, *how* does Paul envision this redemption and what OT concepts lie behind it?

Passover and New Exodus Redemption/Propitiation

The previous verses (e.g. 1 Tim. 2.6; Rom. 3.24-25) indicate in general that Jesus' life was the price of believers' redemption. Paul unequivocally points to the cross and to Jesus' blood when he speaks of believers' freedom. He provides more explicit indications, however, that he sees Jesus' death in terms of the Passover sacrifice and New Exodus redemption.[29] This portion of the study will look at several aspects of the Passover that find parallels in Paul's theology of the cross and survey the contours of New Exodus allusions in Paul's letters.

First, there are multiple reasons to assert that the Passover sacrifice and Exodus/New Exodus deliverance lie behind Paul's theology of the cross. Passover was the sacrifice that accomplished Israel's redemption. By the blood of the Passover lamb, Israel was purchased as YHWH's people (Exod. 15.16; Ps. 74.2), was spared from death and judgment (plagues and the death of the firstborn), and passed out of slavery (along with a 'mixed multitude', Exod. 12.38).[30] At the Exodus, YHWH triumphed over Israel's enemies with great judgments, signs, and wonders (Exod. 6.6; 7.3). He took Israel as his holy people (Exod. 19.6), and they experienced a change of ownership (Exod. 4.23).[31] In remembrance of this deliverance, they were to celebrate an annual Passover meal as an eternal ordinance (Exod. 12.14); people from each new generation were to remember the events as if they had been present (Exod. 13.8; cf. Deut. 6.20-25). In addition, the Passover was a public sacrifice, with the lamb's blood presented on the lintels and doorposts of every home (Exod. 12.22-23). Throughout the OT (esp. Ezek. 45.21) and Jewish writings like the Mishnah, the Passover had become associated

---

[29] This is not to say that Paul *always* or *exclusively* has in mind the Passover sacrifice. Some passages, such as Eph. 5.2-3, seem to have in mind the broader concept of sacrifice.

[30] Just as the firstborn of Israel were spared judgment by the *death* of the Passover lamb, they were continually redeemed by the *living service* of the Levites (Num. 3.12-13).

[31] Howard, 'Christ Our Passover', pp. 102-103.

with atonement as well as redemption.[32] Finally, YHWH's mighty deliverance at the Exodus grounded the community's laws and ethics and identity.[33] Eating unleavened bread during the celebration of the Passover and the Feast of Unleavened Bread not only recalled the haste which was necessary at Israel's departure, but also symbolized the people's holy calling and reminded them of the ethical obligations that their redemption imposed upon them.[34]

Likewise, by the one sacrifice of Jesus, believers – Jew and Gentiles together – have been redeemed, and set free.[35] They have experienced a New Exodus.[36] God's own Firstborn bore judgment and curse on his family's behalf (Rom. 8.29; Col. 1.15, 18; Gal. 3.13)[37] and delivered them from wrath (1 Thess. 1.10; Eph. 2.3-4).[38] At the cross, he 'triumphed over' his enemies and made a public display of them (Col. 1.13-15; cf. Exod. 15.1-19).[39] In addition, God 'passed over' (πάρεσιν, Rom. 3.25) sins through Jesus' death as a Passover Lamb (1 Cor. 5.17).[40] Jesus' blood was a propitiatory sacrifice,[41] 'displayed publicly' (Rom. 3.25).[42] Through this sacrifice or 'ransom',

---

[32] Coxon, *New Exodus in John*, pp. 151-53; Howard, 'Christ Our Passover'; Holland, *Contours of Pauline Theology*, p. 161.

[33] See 'The Exodus and Israel's Laws and Traditions' in Chapter 1.

[34] Howard observes that 'The beginning of a new era must be free from any possibility of contamination'. Howard, 'Christ Our Passover', p. 100. It was essential at the beginning of each new year thereafter to break continuity with the past. Fee interestingly connects the sacrificial lamb with cleansing, commenting that 'The slaying of the lamb is what led to the Jews' being "unleavened"'. Gordon D. Fee, *The First Epistle to the Corinthians* (Grand Rapids: Eerdmans, rev. edn, 2014), p. 239.

[35] Keener connects this with Passover/New Exodus (Rom. 3.20). Keener, *Romans*, loc. 2096.

[36] Howard, 'Christ Our Passover', p. 101.

[37] Holland, *Contours of Pauline Theology*, p. 175.

[38] For a discussion on possible Moses typology, see Scott, *Adoption as Sons*, pp. 166-68.

[39] Lundberg demonstrates how the concept of baptism is tied into victory over death and Satan. Per Lundberg, *Typologie Baptismale Dans L'Ancienne Église* (Leipzig, Germany: Alfred Lorentz, 1942), pp. 225-28.

[40] Holland notes that this verb is also used in Isa. 64.10-12; 63.15; and 42.14 to speak of God's keeping back his wrath.

[41] Moo provides a thoughtful discussion of the support for/against translating ἱλαστήριον as 'mercy seat'. Moo, *Romans*, p. 231 nn. 67-68. He remarks that if Paul had 'mercy seat' in mind, Paul would be 'inviting us to view Christ as the New Covenant equivalent, or antitype', to the OT place of atonement (p. 232). Since the covenant was associated with the Exodus, and the Passover and Day of Atonement became interwoven, this interpretation still offers New Exodus implications.

[42] Holland observes that the Passover lamb was the only sacrifice in the OT given public display. Holland, *Contours of Pauline Theology*, pp. 165-66.

God purchased a people to serve him in holiness (1 Tim. 2.6; Tit. 2.14; 1 Cor. 6.20; 7.23). In remembrance of this deliverance, this blood poured out for many, Jesus instituted the new Passover meal (1 Cor. 11.23-26).[43] Paul shows in 1 Corinthians 5 that just as the Passover and the Exodus informed Israel's identity and imposed obligations on them, Jesus' death as Passover Lamb compels the new Christian community to live in holiness.[44] Here, Paul exhorts God's people to 'an obedient response to God's grace in light of the (new) exodus and (new) Passover'.[45] Finally, Paul teaches that just as the Jewish people relived their history as they celebrated the Passover, each generation of believers is to remember Christ's sacrifice and receive blessing as they experience his presence (1 Cor. 10.16).

Second, Paul's letters are infused with allusions to New Exodus texts.[46] Language from Isaiah and other prophets about Israel, the Gentiles, and the Servant of YHWH underlies Paul's arguments. Isaiah looks ahead and sees a coming Savior and 'son' who would bring light to people in darkness (Isa. 9.2; 49.9), breaking the yoke of the people's burden and ruling on David's throne (Isa. 9.2-7; 61.1). The Servant would be a covenant to the nations, bring them light, and sprinkle many of them clean (Isa. 42.6-7; 49.6; 52.15).[47] Paul echoes these texts when he declares Jesus to be the 'Son of God' and a 'descendant of David' in Rom. 1.3, when he repeatedly mentions release from darkness (Col. 1.13; Eph. 5.8; 1 Thess. 5.5; Rom. 13.12), and when he describes Jesus as a Deliverer who makes a covenant of forgiveness (Rom. 11.27). He quotes from Isa. 52.15 in Rom. 15.21

---

[43] Boulton, 'Supersession or Subsession?', pp. 23-24; Hicks, 'A Sacramental Journey', p. 4. See also discussion on the Passover at the end of the section on John's Gospel.

[44] In 1 Cor. 5.7, Paul exhorts the community, 'clean out the old yeast', for 'Christ our Passover [lamb] has been sacrificed'. Fee, *First Corinthians*, p. 236. Cf. 2 Cor. 6.17 (also Exodus context), 'come out' and 'be separate'. For a detailed analysis of this passage, see William J. Webb, *Returning Home: New Covenant and Second Exodus as the Context for 2 Corinthians 6:14-7:1* (Sheffield: Sheffield Academic Press, 1993).

[45] Roy E. Ciampa and Brian S. Rosner, *The First Letter to the Corinthians* (The Pillar New Testament Commentary; Grand Rapids: Eerdmans, 2010), p. 30.

[46] See esp. Hays, *Echoes of Scripture*.

[47] Zechariah 9.9-11 also contains many of these themes (salvation through a humble king, prisoners set free because of the blood of the covenant, peace to the nations).

in the context of describing Christ's bringing the Gentiles to the obedience of faith through Paul's ministry, implying that they have been sprinkled by Jesus' blood. Paul also proclaims in 2 Cor. 6.2 the advent of the 'favorable time' and 'day of salvation' of which Isaiah spoke (Isa. 49.8). Paul adds that Isaiah spoke of a 'root of Jesse' in whom the Gentiles would hope (Isa. 11.10) and points to the fulfillment of YHWH's declaration in Hosea that those who were 'not my people' would be called 'My people', 'beloved', and 'sons of the living God' (Hos. 2.23; 1.10; Rom. 9.24-26).

Furthermore, in Phil. 2.5-11, Paul may be drawing on passages in Isaiah about the Servant of YHWH. He speaks of Jesus as a 'servant', made in the 'likeness' of humanity (Phil. 2.7; cf. 'appearance' in Isa. 52.14; 53.2), who 'humbled himself' unto death (ἐταπείνωσεν ... μέχρι θανάτου, 2.7; cf. ἐν τῇ ταπεινώσει ... εἰς θάνατον, Isa. 53.8 LXX), 'emptied himself' and become obedient to death on a cross (Phil. 2.7-8; cf. 'poured out his soul unto death', Isa. 53.12 [compare Gal. 1.4]; 'pierced', Isa. 53.5; was silent like a lamb led to the slaughter, Isa. 53.7);[48] and was 'highly exalted' (Phil. 2.9; Isa. 52.13-15).[49] In his words 'every knee will bow' (Phil. 2.10), Paul uses words from a New Exodus passage about salvation for the 'ends of the earth' to ascribe to Jesus the universal sovereignty of YHWH:[50]

---

[48] N.T. Wright connects Jesus' obedience to death in Phil. 2, the 'obedience of faith' in Rom. 1.5 and 16.26, and the 'righteousness of God' of Romans (which he interprets as God's faithfulness to his covenant/promises) to the narrative of Israel (esp. the Exodus). See Wright, 'New Exodus and New Inheritance: The Narrative Structure of Romans 3–8'. Holland delves deeper into how Paul draws this from the OT, especially Isaiah. Holland, *Contours of Pauline Theology*, p. 157. Moo offers a well-balanced discussion of the 'righteousness of God', including its OT background. Moo, *Romans*, p. 79; French L. Arrington, 'Justification by Faith in Romans', in Terry L. Cross and Emerson B. Powery (eds.), *The Spirit and the Mind: Essays in Informed Pentecostalism* (Lanham, MD: University Press of America, 2000), p. 107.

[49] Douglas Oss also calls attention to the Isaianic background of Philippians 2, noting specific parallels between Christ's and the Servant's humiliation (Phil. 2.5-8; Isa. 53.2-12) and exaltation (Phil. 2.9-11; Isa. 52.13; 53.12a; 45.23b). Douglas A. Oss, 'Paul's Use of Isaiah and Its Place in His Theology with Special Reference to Romans 9–11' (PhD dissertation, Westminster Theological Seminary, 1992), pp. 159-60.

[50] This aligns with the Gospel writers' application of Isaiah 40 to the coming of Jesus (see earlier discussion). There are further parallels in these passages in the language about salvation and glory/glorification. The surrounding verses in Isaiah

Isa. 45.23 LXX	Phil. 2.10a, 11a
ἐμοὶ ('to me')	ἐν τῷ ὀνόματι Ἰησοῦ ('at the name of Jesus')
κάμψει πᾶν γόνυ ('every knee will bow')	ἵνα ... πᾶν γόνυ κάμψη ('so that every knee should bow')[51]
καὶ ἐξομολογήσεται πᾶσα γλῶσσα ('and every tongue will confess')	καὶ πᾶσα γλῶσσα ἐξομολογήσηται ('and every tongue should confess')
τῷ θεῷ ('God')	ὅτι κύριος Ἰησοῦς Χριστὸς ('that Jesus Christ is Lord')

Table 3: Comparison of Isa. 45.23 (LXX) and Phil. 2.10a, 11a

Lastly, prophets like Isaiah and Micah proclaimed the coming of one who would bring peace to those who were 'far away' and be 'our peace' (Isa. 57.19; Mic. 5.4-5). Paul interprets Jesus' bringing together Jews and Gentiles (Eph. 2.1-22; cf. Col. 1.20), being himself 'our peace' (Eph. 2.14), as the fulfillment of this reconciliation.[52]

Exodus/New Exodus Judgment

Finally, in the tradition of Israel's prophets, Paul's writings resound with warnings of judgment for those who fail to learn from Israel's past and who reject God's New Exodus salvation. This judgment is especially prominent in 1 Corinthians and Romans.

In 1 Corinthians, Paul looks back both to the wilderness generation and to the time of Israel's exile to remind his audience of the judgment that fell on the disobedient. In ch. 10, he notes how the experience of the fathers discloses the outcomes of unbelief. The people of Israel tasted YHWH's goodness, yet 'craved evil' (v. 6). As a result, they did not please God and fell in the wilderness (v. 5). Paul states twice that these things happened as 'an example' for believers (vv. 6, 11). He exhorts them in this way to

---

speak of God's righteousness, salvation, the power of his word, and the vindication of those who trust in him. Verse 25 closes, 'In YHWH all the offspring of Israel will be justified and will glory'.

[51] Here, Paul's use of ἵνα with the subjunctive (κάμψη, 'should bow') is more emphatic than the future indicative of Isa. 45.23. Wallace says it indicates 'purpose-result' – 'both the intention and its sure accomplishment'. Daniel B. Wallace, *Greek Grammar Beyond the Basics: An Exegetical Syntax of the New Testament* (Grand Rapids: Zondervan, 1996), pp. 473-74.

[52] Cf. Peter's speech at the home of Cornelius in Acts 10.36 – 'preaching *peace* through Jesus Christ', in the context of God's not showing partiality, but accepting 'in every nation the man who fears Him and does what is right' (v. 35).

avoid idolatry, immorality, testing God, grumbling, and provoking God to jealousy (vv. 7-22; cf. Exod. 32.4-19; Num. 16.41; 25.1-9; Deut. 32.21).

Earlier in the letter, Paul draws on Isaiah 29 to renounce the wisdom of the 'wise' and proclaim the 'foolishness' of God's salvation in the cross (1 Cor. 1.18-25). In Isaiah's day, YHWH was announcing judgment on the people of Israel, who had drawn near to him in word, but removed their hearts from him. Therefore, he declared that he would once again 'deal marvelously' or 'wondrously' with them (פלא, Isa. 29.14, ironically evoking the Exodus). Before a time of renewed salvation would come judgment. Paul likewise asserts that with the cross, God has destroyed 'the wisdom of the wise' and set aside the 'cleverness of the clever' (1 Cor. 1.19; Isa. 29.14). Christ crucified is a 'stumbling block' (lit., 'scandal') to Jews and foolishness to Gentiles (1 Cor. 1.23), but salvation to those who believe (cf. Isa. 8.14). Paul continues this contrast in 1 Corinthians 2, quoting from three more passages of mixed salvation and judgment (1 Cor. 2.9 and Isa. 64.4; 65.17; 1 Cor. 2.16 and Isa. 40.13).

In Romans, as in 1 Corinthians, Paul notes the dual function of the gospel as 'the power of God for salvation to everyone who believes' (Rom. 1.16) and as the means of judgment on those 'who suppress the truth in unrighteousness' (1.18-32). First, Paul quotes from Hab. 2.4 (Rom. 1.17), who contrasts the life and vindication of the faithful with the impending judgment on the proud and wicked. In the following verses, Paul subtly alludes to the Exodus story of Psalm 106. It details how the people made an image of a calf and worshiped Baal-peor (Ps. 106.19, 28); they 'exchanged their glory for the image of an ox' (καὶ ἠλλάξαντο τὴν δόξαν αὐτῶν ἐν ὁμοιώματι μόσχου ἔσθοντος χόρτον, Ps. 106.20 LXX), 'forgot God their Savior, who had done great things in Egypt' (Ps. 106.21), and despised his word (v. 24). As a result, he gave them what they asked for (v. 15), swore to scatter and destroy them (v. 23), and handed them over (παρέδωκεν) to their enemies (v. 41 LXX).[53] Paul takes up this language to pronounce God's wrath and

---

[53] Stephen's speech in Acts also chronicles this story: the people rejected Moses (Acts 7.35, 39) and turned back in their hearts to Egypt (7.39), and God delivered them up (παρέδωκεν) to serve the host of heaven (7.42; cf. Amos 5.25-27).

judgment against those who were suppressing the truth in his day. They also 'exchanged the glory of the incorruptible God for an image in the form of corruptible man and of birds and four-footed animals and crawling creatures' (καὶ ἤλλαξαν τὴν δόξαν τοῦ ἀφθάρτου θεοῦ ἐν ὁμοιώματι εἰκόνος φθαρτοῦ ἀνθρώπου καὶ πετεινῶν καὶ τετραπόδων καὶ ἑρπετῶν, Rom. 1.23), worshiped idols (v. 25), dishonored God (v. 21), and did not see fit to acknowledge him (v. 28). Therefore, God 'gave them over' (παρέδωκεν, vv. 24, 26, 28) to their depraved passions,[54] for which they would face judgment and spiritual death (1.32; 2.2).[55]

In Romans 9-10, Paul emphasizes once again that Israel's Exodus story and exilic experiences cast their shadows forward onto the events of his own day. In the past, YHWH hardened stubborn Pharaoh's heart and showed mercy to younger-son-Jacob's descendants, making his power and sovereignty known through his wrath as well as his salvation (Rom. 9.6-18). Now, he has once again shown mercy on whom he wills, still honoring the intention of people's hearts. Those who were 'not his people' (Gentiles with Jews) are called 'his people' (Rom. 9.23-26; Hos. 2.31; 1.10; Isa. 10.12). Moreover, those Jewish people who have heard the word and not believed (Rom. 10.8, 16; cf. Deut. 30.14) – called a 'disobedient and obstinate people' (10.21; Isa. 65.2) – have 'stumbled over the stumbling stone' (Rom. 9.33; cf. Isa. 28.16). Paul quotes texts from Deuteronomy, Isaiah, and Psalms to indicate that these people are experiencing the covenant curses of hardened hearts and darkened eyes (Rom. 11.8-10, 25) until the time of the salvation of a remnant (11.1-5; 25-32).[56]

---

[54] The idea in these passages of being made into the image of whatever/whomever one worships (whether God or idols) is prominent in Ps. 115.8 ('those who make them will become like them') as well as passages like Isa. 44.18-20. For a discussion on being made into the image of fallen creation, see Beale, *New Testament Biblical Theology*, ch. 12.

[55] Paul echoes this in 2 Corinthians 4, where he says that believers renounce things hidden because of shame, do not adulterate the word of God, and walk in truth. However, he says that the gospel is veiled to those who are perishing; their eyes are blinded so that they might not see the light of Christ, who is God's image (2 Cor. 4.1-4; cf. Eph. 4.17-24).

[56] Oss observes that Paul pronounces this 'hardening' curse of Isaiah on the Jews in Rome in Acts 28.26-27. Douglas A. Oss, 'A Note on Paul's Use of Isaiah', *Bulletin for Biblical Research* 2 (1992), pp. 105-12 (107 n. 5).

Paul appropriates Exodus/New Exodus in these varied contexts in continuity with the OT prophets. He once again highlights the contrast between YHWH's covenant faithfulness and Israel's disloyalty and apostasy. While he still holds out the hope of mercy and longs for the salvation of the remnant of Israel, Paul declares that God's wrath abides on those who suppress truth. He exhorts those who hear 'the word' to learn from Israel's past, turn their hearts from Egypt, and not 'be conceited, but fear', lest they be 'cut off' (Rom. 11.20, 22) or 'fall' (1 Cor. 10.12).

Election/Sonship

As Paul fleshes out his Exodus storyline, he describes the status of those who have been liberated and redeemed in terms saturated with meaning from Israel's history. He also expounds on and clarifies how believers receive the blessings promised to Abraham and David as they participate in Christ's faithful obedience, death, and resurrection (cf. John 3, 15; Acts 17.28, 39). This section on the third 'moment' in Paul's Exodus storyline will first examine Paul's theology of participation in Christ before turning to highlight how Paul frames believers as true Israel, adopted sons of God, and heirs of the covenant and New Exodus blessings.

Jesus, the Firstborn

The OT offered manifold glimpses of coming figures who would be the means of blessing to others, both to Israel and to the nations. These included the seed of the woman (Gen. 3.15), the seed of Abraham (Gen. 12.3), the seed/son/Branch of David (Isa. 9.1-7; 11.1-10; Jer. 23.5-6; Ezek. 37.24-25; Hos. 3.5; Zech. 3.8; 6.12), the Servant of YHWH (Isa. 53), the messenger of the covenant (Mal. 3.1), and although not usually specified as such (except in Dan. 9), the Messiah.[57] These presupposed the concept of corporate solidarity, prominent from Genesis onward, whereby the actions of heads of families, kings, and prophets represented the nation of Israel or humanity in general.[58] In particular, texts like 2 Sam. 7.12-16 and Pss. 2.7; 89.26-27 portray how YHWH adopted the king of Israel

---

[57] See Chapter 2 for how these concepts were embedded in New Exodus texts and became intertwined in New Exodus expectations.

[58] Beale, *New* Testament *Biblical Theology*, loc. 12912.

as his son. Jewish tradition applied this special election to both the Messiah and eschatological Israel, who expected to share in the Messiah's divine adoptive sonship.[59]

New Testament writers discerned that these mixed prophecies and types, while sometimes maintaining previous historical referents, reached their ultimate fulfillment in Jesus. As a result, Paul, like the Gospel writers, depicts Jesus as the corporate representative of humanity (the last Adam); the Son of God and true Israel; and the promised Savior, Servant, and King.[60] In Romans 5, Paul details how just as through 'one man', all sinned and came under the power of death (5.12), through the 'one man Jesus', God's grace abounded to many, resulting in justification (5.15-18; cf. 1 Cor. 15.45; Isa. 52.15; 53.11). Jesus reenacted in a faithful way the failed experiences of Adam and Israel (Rom. 8.1-4; cf. 5.12-19; 6.10; 16.20; 1 Cor. 15.45).[61] He summed up in himself Israel's vocation as a light and a means of blessing to the nations (Rom. 15.9-12).[62] He is God's obedient Son (Rom. 1.3-4) who makes available the obedience of faith to others (Rom. 1.5; 3.21; 16.26) and the 'seed' of Abraham to whom the promise was made (Rom. 3.19).[63] In him, God will soon crush Satan under foot (Rom. 16.20). Jesus fulfilled the righteous requirements of the Law and bore the curse of the Law on behalf of others (Rom. 7.4; 8.3-4; Gal. 3.13-14; cf. Isa. 53.1-12), Paul proclaims, receiving subsequent vindication through the resurrection and taking his seat at the right hand of the Father (Rom. 8.34; Ps. 110.1).[64] He is also the Firstborn Son and thus heir of all things (Rom. 8.17, 29; Eph. 3.6; Col. 1.15-20). The next section will examine how Paul envisions believers' sharing in Christ's obedience, death, resurrection, and inheritance.

---

[59] Scott references 4QFlor 1.11; 4QTJud 24.3; Jub. 1.24. Scott, *Adoption as Sons*, p. 104. See also Keesmaat, *Paul and His Story*, p. 60.

[60] VanDrunen, 'Israel's Recapitulation of Adam's Probation under the Law of Moses', p. 316.

[61] Wright, *Jesus and the Victory of God*, II, p. 517; Wright, *The Resurrection of the Son of God*, III, p. 223.

[62] See previous discussion on the Servant in Isaiah, esp. n. 111.

[63] Paul uses 'seed' of Abraham in this specific way only in Galatians (its meaning in Rom. 4.3; 9.7-8; 2 Corinthians 11 is clearly plural or means 'descendant'). This is parallel to Acts 3.25-26, which describes Jesus as the 'seed' of Abraham who brings the blessing of forgiveness.

[64] Hübner, *Law in Paul's Thought: A Contribution to the Development of Pauline Theology*, pp. 19-20.

Participation 'In Christ'

Paul lays out a nuanced theology of participation in his writings, whereby believers are joined to Christ and share in his actions:[65] they die with him (Rom. 6.8; Col. 2.20); are crucified with him (Rom. 6.6; Gal. 2.20); are buried with him (Rom. 6.4; Col. 2.12); are raised with him (Col. 2.12; Eph. 2.6); coming to life with him (Col. 2.13; Eph. 2.5); are seated with him in the heavens (Eph. 2.6); and are 'with' him in various ways in this life and in the future.[66] This concept is grounded in Paul's 'understanding of Christ as a representative, even inclusive, figure',[67] and believers experience this identification through faith and baptism.

First, Paul teaches that salvation comes by faith in Jesus Christ (Rom. 1.16-17; 3.21-22, 26; 4; Gal. 2.16, 20; 3.8-9, 26; Eph. 2.8; Col. 2.12).[68] He discerns that faith has always been the means by which believers receive God's promises of life and justification.[69] Abraham is the prototype of this believing – he 'believed God, and it was credited to him as righteousness' (Gen. 15.6). His true descendants and those who receive the blessing promised to come through his Seed are those who believe like he did (Rom. 4.1-25; Gal. 3.7-9). Paul finds in David and the prophets additional witnesses that faith is the means of receiving righteousness (Rom. 4.6-8; cf. Ps. 32.1-2). He quotes, for example, from Hab. 2.4 ('My righteous one by faith shall live')[70] in Rom. 1.17 and Gal. 3.11 and from Isa. 28.16 ('whoever believes in him [the precious cornerstone] will not be put to shame') in Rom. 9.33; 10.11 to show that God's righteousness is a matter of faith from start

---

[65] Paul often expresses this idea by prefixing σύν ('with') to various verbs or by using ἐν Χριστῳ ('in Christ'). Bruce gives a more thorough analysis of this 'corporate or communal mysticism', which includes sharing in Christ's sufferings. F.F. Bruce, *Paul, Apostle of the Heart Set Free* (Grand Rapids: Eerdmans, 2000), p. 136.

[66] Moo, *Romans*, p. 392. Moo's list includes 9 items and more extensive references.

[67] Moo, *Romans*, p. 393.

[68] Keener rightly notes that 'faith' for Paul involves more than mental assent – it involves dependence on God's righteousness and faithfulness or loyalty to him. Keener, *Romans*, locs. 1101-19.

[69] See Arrington, 'Justification by Faith in Romans', pp. 110-11.

[70] I concur with scholars like Frank Macchia that this translation, which emphasizes that faith is the means of receiving life/justification and is integrally connected to it, is preferable. Furthermore, the Old and New Testament contexts contrast this faith that leads to life with shrinking back that leads to destruction (e.g. woes upon the wicked in Habakkuk 2; Heb. 10.39). Macchia, *Justified in the Spirit*, p. 201.

to finish (Rom. 1.17).[71] By faith, the believer 'puts on Christ' (Gal. 2.26-27), is united to him, and shares in his sonship.[72]

Second, Paul proclaims that believers become one with Christ at the moment of baptism: more specifically, in baptism, they are united with him in his death (Rom. 6.3-6). This rite of passing through the waters evokes the crossing of the Red Sea. This was Israel's national baptism ('into Moses', 1 Cor. 10.2) and was the decisive moment at which God's people were cut off from the old world and stepped into new redeemed existence.[73] Jewish proselyte baptism around the time of Christ exhibited a keen awareness of this connection. At baptism, the convert essentially 'became a part of the Israel which was baptized at the Red Sea' and could thereafter eat the Passover meal.[74] Paul likewise envisions believers' being baptized into Christ, thus becoming part of the redeemed community and dying to their previous way of life. This is the critical moment in the story of New Exodus liberation (Romans 6–8).[75] At baptism, the New Exodus is sealed, as the 'whole renewed people', no longer in slavery to sin, is 'baptized into the Messiah' (Gal. 3.27; Rom. 6.3-6) and walks in 'newness of life'.[76]

---

[71] For a discussion of the New Exodus undertones in Paul's 'stone', see Hyukjun Kwon, 'The Reception of Psalm 118 in the New Testament. Application of a New Exodus Motif?' (PhD thesis, University of Pretoria, 2007).

[72] G.R. Beasley-Murray, *Baptism in the New Testament* (Grand Rapids: Eerdmans, 1973), pp. 147-49.

[73] Howard, 'Christ Our Passover', p. 104.

[74] Holland, *Contours of Pauline Theology*, p. 289; cf. Reynolds, 'Comparative Study', p. 198. Beasley-Murray, while cautioning that this concept was still in development, offers some evidence from the Mishnah that it could have pre-dated the destruction of the temple. He asserts that both the form and theology of Christian baptism depend on those of Jewish proselyte baptism (in being baptized into a name, in the significance of death/new life and Exodus crossing, and in requiring immersion). Beasley-Murray, *Baptism in the New Testament*, pp. 24-28.

[75] Wright contends that when Paul speaks of baptism in Romans 6, he has in mind the crossing of the Red Sea. This has the advantage of demonstrating the continuity of Romans 6 as a whole as well as Paul's story of liberation from slavery in chs. 6–8. Wright, 'New Exodus and New Inheritance: The Narrative Structure of Romans 3–8'. This also follows the pattern of Jesus' own baptism, which the Gospel writers portrayed as a New Exodus (accompanied by declaration of Sonship, followed by wilderness temptation and being led by the Spirit).

[76] N.T. Wright, 'The New Inheritance According to Paul: The Letter to the Romans Re-Enacts for All Peoples the Israelite Exodus from Egypt to the Promised Land – from Slavery to Freedom', *Bible Review* 14.3 (1998), pp. 16-47 (18); cf. Hahn, 'Worship in the Word', p. 125.

New Exodus Blessings

In this way, those who believe become partakers of New Exodus covenant blessings in Christ (cf. Acts 13.39; 17.28). They constitute the eschatological community of God (Isa. 42.14-16; Jer. 31.8-9), the true Israel.[77] Paul, through a catena of Exodus/New Exodus texts about this special covenant relationship, applies the sonship of Israel and the Messiah to all those who believe in Jesus (2 Cor. 6.16-18).[78] As they are 'clothed with Christ', they become 'Abraham's descendants and heirs according to the promise' (Gal. 3.29; cf. Romans 4). 'Since *we* have these promises', Paul says to mixed Jewish and Gentile believers in 2 Cor. 7.1, 'let us cleanse ourselves …' (Acts 18.1-8; cf. 'our fathers' in 1 Cor. 10.1). He also asserts that believers have the 'Spirit of sonship' (Rom. 8.14-15; 9.25-26; Gal. 3.13; 4.6-7; cf. Hos. 1.10).[79] This gift of the Holy Spirit signifies covenant renewal (Jer. 31.31-34; Ezek. 11.17-20; 36.24-28) – the Spirit writes the new covenant on the hearts of believers (2 Cor. 3.1-18; 5.17).[80] Paul also speaks of this as inward circumcision (Rom. 2.29), which enables faithfulness to the covenant. This fulfills the promise of Deut. 30.6 ('YHWH your God will circumcise your heart and the heart of your descendants, to love YHWH your God with all your heart and with all your soul, so that you may live') as well as passages such as Jer. 31.31-34 and Ezek. 36.26-27, which anticipate the internalization of the new covenant. Paul further indicates that whereas Moses' face was veiled to conceal that

---

[77] Holland, *Contours of Pauline Theology*, p. 289; Beale, *New Testament Biblical Theology*, p. 653; Dumbrell, *The End of the Beginning*, pp. 157-58. Dumbrell discusses Paul's use of the 'Israel of God' in Gal. 6.16. Also, see previous discussion of ἐκκλησία ('church/community') in section on Luke-Acts.

[78] Keesmaat comments on how Paul uses Israel's narrative as in identity claim for Christians:

> The Spirit which leads them is the Spirit that was promised to Israel; the sonship which they now have is the sonship first given to Israel; the father they cry to and witness concerning is Yahweh, the father of Israel; the glory which they anticipate is a glory identified with Israel; the inheritance for which they wait is that which was promised to Israel; and the image to which they are to be conformed is that of Jesus, the messiah of Israel … Israel's story is their story (Keesmaat, *Paul and His Story*, p. 151).

[79] For a detailed and convincing argument about New Exodus participatory sonship of believers, see Scott, *Adoption as Sons*; cf. Keesmaat, *Paul and His Story*, p. 60. Keesmaat examines echoes of Deuteronomy 32 in Romans 8-10; 1 Corinthians 10.

[80] Wright, 'New Exodus and New Inheritance: The Narrative Structure of Romans 3–8', p. 35. Webb offers an extended discussion of New-Exodus background in 2 Corinthians, especially in relation to Moses typology and the new covenant. Webb, *Returning Home*.

the glory of the previous covenant was fading away even as it was given (2 Cor. 3.12), believers behold with unveiled faces the unfading, greater glory of the new covenant in Christ (3.8). They are continually transformed into his image (2 Cor. 3.18) and receive life (2 Cor. 3.6) and righteousness (2 Cor. 3.9) through the Spirit.[81]

Journey

Finally, Paul – much like the author of Hebrews – visualizes believers as New Exodus sojourners. God has already acted on their behalf and inaugurated their deliverance. For a time, however, they are in between their past life and their future inheritance. Three aspects of this include being led by the Spirit, being nourished by Christ, and being built into a holy temple.

Led by the Spirit

First, Paul writes that 'all who are being led by the Spirit of God' are 'sons of God' (Rom. 8.14; cf. Gal. 5.18).[82] Ignace de la Potterie has demonstrated that 'leading' verbs (ἄγω, ἐξάγω, εἰσάγω, and ὁδηγέω) represent technical Exodus vocabulary in the NT.[83] Paul's words evoke a collage of texts, such as Exod. 13.21 ('YHWH was going before them in a pillar of cloud by day to lead them on the way, and in a pillar of fire by night to give them light'), Exod. 15.13 ('In Your lovingkindness You have led the people whom You have redeemed'), and Ps. 104.37, 42 (LXX)/105 MT ('He led out his people …') about the Exodus and Jer. 38.8 (LXX)/31.8 MT ('Behold, I am bringing them from the north country, and I will gather them from the remote parts of the earth') and Ps. 143.10 (LXX)/142 MT ('Your good Spirit will lead me on level [εὐθείᾳ, 'straight'; cf. εὐθείας in Isa. 40.3]

---

[81] Paul says Moses' face was veiled πρὸς τὸ μὴ ἀτενίσαι τοὺς υἱοὺς Ἰσραὴλ εἰς τὸ τέλος τοῦ καταργουμένου ('so that the sons of Israel would not gaze at the *end* or *outcome* of what was being abolished', 2 Cor. 3.13).

[82] Paul uses the parallel language, 'walk by the Spirit', in Gal. 5.16, 2 and 'walk according to the Spirit' in Rom. 8.4 (contrasts throughout chs. 6–8).

[83] Ignace de La Potterie, 'Le chrétien conduit par l'Esprit dans son cheminement eschatologique (Rom 8:14)', in Lorenzo De Lorenzi (ed.), *Law of the Spirit in Rom 7 and 8* (Rome: St. Paul's Abbey, 1976).

ground') that are embedded with future expectation.[84] As God's sons make their way through the present wilderness (1 Cor. 10.1-13), with its temptation/testing and suffering (1 Cor. 10.9; Rom. 8.12-13, 17-25; Gal. 6.1), the Holy Spirit takes the place of the Shekinah in bringing them to their promised inheritance.[85] Sealed for this inheritance (2 Cor. 1.22; Eph. 1.13-14) and enabled to live in righteousness (Rom. 8.4-6; Gal. 5.18, 16-23), they must not turn back to Egypt (Rom. 8.12-17) or receive God's grace in vain (2 Cor. 6.1-18).

Nourished on Christ

Second, Paul offers a parallel between the spiritual food and drink of the fathers in the desert (Exod. 16.4-30; 17.1-7; Num. 20.2-13) and that of believers, in combination with their 'baptism'. Because the Corinthians, like the Israelites, were facing the perils of idolatry (1 Cor. 6.9-11; 10.1-33; cf. 2 Cor. 6.14-18), Paul draws from Israel's past both to remind them of God's supernatural provision for them and to warn them not to repeat Israel's mistakes. Building on the rabbinic tradition that the rock followed the Israelites in the wilderness,[86] Paul boldly asserts that the people of Israel partook of Christ for their spiritual food and drink (1 Cor. 10.4).[87] Even though they shared table fellowship with YHWH (Exod. 24.11), and he continually supplied for them in miraculous ways, the people craved evil and were not faithful to him (1 Cor. 10.7). The Corinthians, who have shared in the body and blood of Christ (10.16; cf. Jn 6.27-58; 7.37-38; Heb. 13.10), must surely cherish this spiritual fellowship and live in holiness, unity, and devotion to God.

---

[84] Keesmaat, *Paul and His Story*, pp. 57-59. Cf. Ps. 77.20; Isa. 35.8-10; 49.8-13. She provides a more detailed discussion about the 'leading' language in connection with the concepts of sonship, suffering, glory, new creation, and new inheritance.

[85] As N.T. Wright notes, the tabernacling presence of God traveled with the people in the original Exodus story as their guide and companion. As Paul retells the story, the Spirit takes the place of the Shekinah and leads the people to the promised land – the new/renewed creation (Wright, *Paul*, p. 98). Frank Macchia likewise notes that 'the indwelling of the Spirit through Pentecost fulfills the OT Shekinah, the presence of God tabernacling with the faithful from the Exodus to the promised land' (Macchia, *Justified in the Spirit*, pp. 214-15. See also Jesús Luzarraga, *Las Tradiciones de la Nube en la Biblia y en el Judaismo Primitivo* (Analecta Biblica 54; Rome: Pontifical Biblical Institute Press, 1973).

[86] See Chapter 3, n. 191, for discussion about the rock/well following the Israelites in the desert.

[87] Fee provides a more extended analysis of this meaning. Fee, *First Corinthians*, pp. 448-49.

A Holy Temple

Finally, Paul discerns that just as at the Exodus YHWH called his people out of bondage to dwell among them and be their God (Exod. 29.45-46), YHWH now dwells among his people in a fuller and more personal way. When Jesus came, he was God's incarnate presence dwelling among his people – the new temple that radiated the Father's glory (Mk 14.58; Jn 1.14, 18). Living water flowed from him to reverse the curse and bring purification from sin (Jn 7.38; Zech. 14.8). After Jesus was glorified, he poured forth the Holy Spirit (Jn 7.39; Acts 2.33). Paul depicts the Holy Spirit dwelling in believers corporately as the temple of God, built upon Jesus the chief cornerstone and growing together in him (Eph. 2.20-22, 'in whom you [ὑμεῖς, 'you all'] also are being built together into a dwelling of God in the Spirit'). He says in Rom. 8.9, 'the Spirit of God dwells in you' (ὑμῖν, 'you all'); in 1 Cor. 3.16-17, 'Do you not know that you are a temple of God, and that the Spirit of God dwells in you?' (ὑμῖν, 'you all'); and in 2 Cor. 6.16, 'For we are the temple of the living God' (quoting Exod. 29.45 and Lev. 26.12). This indwelling presence fulfills the words of the prophets that in the last days, the Branch of David would build YHWH's temple (Zech. 6.12-13) in a more glorious way (Hag. 2.7-9), and YHWH would dwell among them as their God (Jer. 31.1; Ezek. 37.27). Just as the building of Solomon's temple represented the 'culmination of the Exodus'[88] and a step toward restoration of Edenic fellowship, this augmented indwelling presence constitutes a penultimate 'togetherness' of God and his people that anticipates the full communion that John would later describe in its consummate and eschatological form (Rev. 21.3).

Conclusion

Paul's use of the Exodus/New Exodus motif in his structure, hermeneutics, and wording is striking and fundamental. His portrait of humanity enslaved to sin, his description of liberation and redemption through the blood of Christ's Passover sacrifice, his warnings against judgment for disobedience and unbelief, his application of new covenant blessings to the people of God

---

[88] Watts, 'Exodus', p. 482.

through participation in the Messiah, and his representation of believers as sojourners indwelt by the Holy Spirit showcase the enduring and profoundly spiritual significance of what God inaugurated in Israel's history. His writings also illuminate the typological character of earlier Exodus elements and point to surprising fulfillments of established hopes. He identifies the body of believers as the holy and glorious temple, for example, built upon Christ the cornerstone; he also analyzes the inclusion of the Gentiles in the true Israel. In these ways, Paul emphasizes not only seamless continuity with the past and the fulfillment of promise, but also the beauty of God's salvific plan as it draws toward its *telos*. In addition, recognizing that Exodus/New Exodus are essential components of Paul's overarching narrative results in a richer understanding of his use of certain words or concepts (often rooted in the OT) as well as a more satisfying explication of the unity of thought behind seemingly disparate passages.

5

THE EXODUS MOTIF IN HEBREWS AND THE GENERAL EPISTLES

Introduction

Among the non-Pauline Epistles, the Exodus motif figures prominently in Hebrews, 1 Peter, and Jude. As these authors wrote to believers facing difficult situations, they appropriated Exodus/New Exodus storylines, typological elements, and a collage of resonant allusions to encourage their recipients, remind them of their identity and special place in the climax of salvation history, and motivate them to faithful obedience. In addition, the authors of all three Epistles looked back to the example of disobedient Israel and the judgment that befell God's enemies to warn believers of the danger of apostasy.

Hebrews

In the Epistle to the Hebrews, the author juxtaposes the situation of believers with that of their forefathers to showcase the supremacy of God's revelation and promises in Christ. In this 'overlay' schema, he conceives of believers as Exodus sojourners who have been set free and are on the way towards their promised rest and inheritance. The author utilizes multiple points of Exodus/New Exodus comparison and contrast as he urges the wandering people of God to grasp the opportunities and perils of living in 'these last days' (Heb. 1.2).

Hermeneutic

The homily involves a sustained conversation with Scripture.[1] The author analyzes the purpose and effectiveness of OT institutions as well as its whispers and indications that better promises would be available in a new covenant (Heb. 8.6-12). Hebrews employs a multi-faceted typological hermeneutic, based in elements derived from the Exodus. First, the author points out 'preordained connections' within the history of salvation.[2] He asserts that things in the past (e.g. the sacrifices, priesthood, and law/covenant) were imperfect copies and shadows of better realities to come (Heb. 2.11-28; 5.6-13; 9.11-14, 23-26; 10.1-12). This idea of 'perfection', with its inherent continuity and discontinuity, encompasses the preacher's understanding of the relationship between past and present.[3] Second, he adds to this the idea that some of these antitypes were based on heavenly types.[4] This is especially true of the earthly sanctuary or tabernacle, which he declares was 'a copy and shadow' (Heb. 8.5; 9.23) of the 'greater and more perfect tabernacle [in heaven], not made with hands' (Heb. 9.11; cf. 8.2; 9.24). Finally, he discerns that the history of the people of God, in its positive and negative aspects, offers examples for believers in similar circumstances (e.g. Heb. 3.7-19; 8.5; 11.1-40). In this respect, he frames his readers' experience as both a continuation and a repetition of the past.[5] His hermeneutic maintains a temporal

---

[1] For an argument in favor of the homiletical shape of Hebrews, see Thomas G. Long, *Hebrews* (IBC; Louisville, KY: Westminster/John Knox Press, 1997), p. 2.

[2] G.H. Guthrie, 'Old Testament in Hebrews', in Ralph P. Martin and Peter H. Davids (eds.), *Dictionary of the Later New Testament and Its Developments* (Downers Grove, IL: InterVarsity Press, 1997), p. 844.

[3] Long, *Hebrews*, p. 14; Jon C. Laansma, 'Hebrews, Book of', in Kevin J. Vanhoozer *et al.* (eds.), *Dictionary for Theological Interpretation of the Bible* (Grand Rapids: Baker Academic, 2005), p. 278. Piper observes that 'despite their insufficiency, these religious institutions of Exodus foreshadow in their historical actuality the final work of Jesus'. Piper, 'Unchanging Promises', p. 14.

[4] While some scholars, such as Ernst Käsemann, interpret Hebrews through the lens of Greek philosophical categories, I see no reason to do so. The author uses thoroughly Jewish interpretive methods and appeals to biblical sources and narratives to substantiate the arguments. Philosopher Ronald Nash has discredited the notion that NT authors were heavily influenced by Plato and other Hellenistic schools of thought. Ernst Käsemann, *The Wandering People of God: An Investigation of the Letter to the Hebrews* (trans. Roy A. Harrisville and Irving L. Sandberg; Eugene, OR: Wipf & Stock, 2002); cf. Ronald H. Nash, *Christianity & the Hellenistic World* (Bible Study Commentary Series; Grand Rapids: Zondervan, 1984).

[5] Many scholars note how the author positions the readers in the Exodus drama (Watts, 'Exodus', p. 486; D. Mathewson, 'Reading Heb 6:4-6 in Light of the Old

sensitivity that allows him to locate his readers theologically in the time of the wilderness – it is again 'Today', he asserts (Heb. 3.1-15), and the promise of rest still remains for God's people (Heb. 4.7-9; cf. Ps. 95.7, 11).

Here, as does Paul, the author fuses Exodus typology with an Exodus/New Exodus storyline. This section will examine central elements of the Exodus/New Exodus motif in Hebrews according to the previous chapter's 'moments' of Slavery/Exile/Defilement, Redemption/Judgment, Election/Sonship, and Journey.

Slavery/Exile/Defilement

As the author of Hebrews considers the plight of pre-cross humanity, he focuses on three inter-related issues that are epitomized by Israel's situation in Egypt and under the first covenant. First, he depicts humanity as enslaved to the devil, the one who holds 'the power of death', through fear of death (Heb. 2.14-15; cf. 'dead works' in 9.14). He ties this into the Exodus not only with Moses typology (see next section) and language of slavery, fear, and freedom (2.15), but also through an allusion to the help promised to Abraham's 'seed' (σπέρμα) who would be enslaved and oppressed in Egypt (2.16; Gen. 15.13). Second, the author draws on the OT tradition to highlight the persistent dilemma of being outside the promised land and without rest (4.1-11; 11.8-17; 13.10-14). This ties into the exile and separation that resulted from the curse and from later unfaithfulness to the covenant (cf. Heb. 8.9).[6] Those who believe continue to wander as 'aliens and strangers', although they experience restoration in their fellowship with God and a foretaste of eschatological rest (Heb. 4.3; 11.13; 13.10-14). Third, the preacher particularly emphasizes the problem of ritual impurity and defilement.[7] At the Exodus, God called his people to holiness (Exod. 19.6; Lev. 11.44; Deut. 7.6). However,

---

Testament', *WTJ* 61.2 (Fall 1999), pp. 209-25 (223); Laansma, 'Hebrews, Book of', p. 277. However, some such as Matthew Thiessen take this more literally. He argues that 'the author goes beyond a rhetorical or typological use of the Exodus/wilderness period here', radically re-reading Israel's history to show that 'all of Israel's history subsequent to the exodus belongs to the period of the wilderness wanderings' (Matthew Thiessen, 'Hebrews and the End of the Exodus', *NovT* 49.4 (2007), pp. 353-69.

   [6] See previous section on Mt. 11.29.

   [7] For a discussion of the implications of this problem in the ancient world, see David A. deSilva, *Honor, Patronage, Kinship & Purity: Unlocking New Testament Culture* (Downers Grove, IL: InterVarsity Press, 2000), pp. 240-315.

under the old covenant, people lived with a guilty, evil conscience (Heb. 9.9; 10.22). The law provided only a continual reminder of sin (10.3), and the sacrifices were unable to provide cleansing (10.4). Worshipers were separated from their promised inheritance by their transgressions (9.15) and unable to draw near to God; the way into his presence had not yet been disclosed (9.8).

Redemption/Judgment

The Preacher continues to develop the Exodus/New Exodus motif by comparing Jesus and Moses, framing Jesus' work against the background of OT sacrifices and the Isaianic Servant of YHWH, and issuing repeated warnings from Israel's history about the judgment that follows disobedience and unbelief.

Jesus and Moses

First, in several key passages, the author calls attention to parallels between Moses and Jesus. In the fullness of time (Exod. 12.40-41; cf. 'these last days', Heb. 1.2; the 'consummation of the ages', Heb. 9.26), God raised up these deliverers to free his people to serve him (Exod. 4.23; Heb. 9.14; cf. Isa. 61.1; 53.14-15). Through them, God brought redemption and triumphant victory over the enemy (Exod. 15; Heb. 2.14-15; 9.12-15, 26). He placed Moses and Jesus over his household (Num. 12.7; Heb. 3.6),[8] spoke through them (Heb. 1.1-2), and appointed them as covenant mediators (Exodus 19; Heb. 8.6; 9.15; 12.18-24) and advocates for the people (Exod. 32.11-14; Num. 14.13-19; 21.7; Heb. 7.25 cf. Isa. 53.12).[9] Hebrews points out how both leaders stepped down from positions of high honor (Moses 'refused to be called the son of Pharaoh's daughter', Heb. 11.24; Jesus 'was made for a little while lower than the angels', Heb. 2.7-9); they were not ashamed to call God's people 'brothers' (τοὺς ἀδελφοὺς αὐτοῦ, 'his brothers', Exod. 2.11 LXX; cf. Heb. 2.11); and they chose to share in the mistreatment of God's people rather than enjoy their privileges

---

[8] See Peter Enns for a more detailed analysis of οἶκος ('household') and the Moses typology in Hebrews 3. Peter E. Enns, 'Creation and Re-Creation: Psalm 95 and Its Interpretation in Hebrews 3:1–4:13', *WTJ* 55 (October 1993), pp. 269-71. Ironically, the very passage in Numbers 12 that is used to exalt Moses over the grumbling Miriam is quoted to 'accent his inferiority to Christ' (p. 271).

[9] Bruce observes that in Philo, *Who Is Heir of Divine Things?* p. 205, Moses is portrayed as both intermediary and divine ambassador. F.F. Bruce, *Hebrews* (NICNT; Grand Rapids: Eerdmans, rev. Kindle edn, 1990), loc. 5620n8. Some manuscripts have 'shepherds'.

(Heb. 11.25; 2.9-10; 12.2). Furthermore, the author particularly emphasizes how Moses and Jesus looked ahead to their reward and 'set aside the disgrace ascribed by unbelievers and embraced the reproach that accompanies obedience to God' (Heb. 11.26; 12.2).[10] Here, perhaps drawing on Ps. 89.51 or 69.9, the author retrofits Moses through faith into the mold of Christ's obedient suffering ('considering the reproach of Christ greater riches than the treasures of Egypt'). Finally, in Heb. 13.20, the author refers to Jesus as the 'great Shepherd of the sheep' whom God 'brought up from the dead'. Bruce asserts that this title is derived from Isa. 63.11 (LXX), which depicts God as bringing up his people from the sea with the 'shepherd of the sheep' Moses.[11] In this context, the author applies the words to 'Jesus as the second Moses', whose death and resurrection constitute the New Exodus.[12] Through these similarities, the Preacher advances his New Exodus narrative and accentuates the superior position, honor, and example of Christ.

Jesus, Sacrifice, and Servant

Second, the Preacher contemplates how Jesus' death as sacrifice and Servant has made believers holy, atoned for their sin, cleansed their consciences, and enabled them to draw near to God in new covenant relationship (Heb. 8.6-12; 4.16; 7.19; cf. Isa. 43.25; Jer. 31.31-32; 50.20; Mic. 7.18-20).[13] The OT sacrifices (specifically, sin offerings) afforded worshipers provisional forgiveness, fellowship with God from a distance, and symbolic (external) sanctification (Heb. 9.9-15; 12.18-22). Jesus' blood, however, inaugurated the promised new covenant, obtained eternal redemption and forgiveness for transgressions,

---

[10] David A. deSilva, *Bearing Christ's Reproach: The Challenge of Hebrews in an Honor Culture* (North Richland Hills, TX: BIBAL, 1999), p. 53.

[11] Bruce, *Hebrews*, locs. 4358-72; cf. Glasson, *Moses in the Fourth Gospel*, p. 22.

[12] Bruce, *Hebrews*, locs. 4358-72.

[13] In Hebrews, Jesus' death is almost always connected to cleansing and separation from sin and guilt: Jesus offered only one sacrifice, since he had no sin (7.27); the blood of sacrifices was for cleansing and forgiveness (9.23); Jesus was manifested to put away sin by the sacrifice of himself (9.26); Christ was offered to bear the sins of many (9.28); the former sacrifices could not make perfect or cleanse the worshiper forever (10.1); we have been made holy through the offering of Christ's body (10.5); Christ offered one sacrifice for sin (10.12, 14, 26); and Jesus suffered as a sin offering outside the gate (13.10). Faith McGhee, 'Holiness and the Path of Suffering: Lessons for Pentecostals from the Book of Hebrews', in Lee Roy Martin (ed.), *A Future for Holiness: Pentecostal Explorations* (Cleveland, TN: CPT Press, 2013), p. 84 n. 40.

sprinkled the consciences of worshipers, and enabled believers to obtain their promised eternal inheritance (9.12-15; 10.10, 14-18, 29; 12.24; Jer. 31.33-34).

As the Preacher considers Jesus' substitutionary sacrifice, he looks back to a combination of OT sacrifices. First, he recalls the inauguration of the covenant, when Moses sprinkled the book of the law and the people with the blood of calves and goats (Heb. 9.18-22; Exod. 24.6-8). He also mentions the Day of Atonement, on which the High priest offered a bull, a ram, and two goats for his own sins and the sins of the people (Heb. 9.25; Lev. 16.1-28). The bodies of the sacrificial goat and the bull with whose blood the people and altar/mercy seat were sprinkled were burned 'outside the camp' (16.27), and the other goat was sent into exile to bear the people's sins (16.22). In addition, the author makes reference to the red heifer that was sacrificed and burned outside the camp to cleanse the people from sin and impurity (Num. 19; Heb. 9.13). By evoking all of these sacrifices, the author shows how Christ's one, perfect sacrifice effected the new covenant, cleansed and consecrated the worshipers, and removed the pollution of sin from God's presence.[14]

In addition, the author turns to OT texts about Isaiah's Suffering Servant and the Righteous Sufferer of the Psalms to illuminate Christ's sacrifice. He crowns his discussion in ch. 9 with a quotation from Isaiah's fourth Servant Song, indicating in 9.28 that Christ was offered εἰς τὸ πολλῶν ἀνενεγκεῖν ἁμαρτίας, 'to bear the sins of many' (cf. αὐτὸς ἁμαρτίας πολλῶν ἀνήνεγκεν, 'he himself bore the sins of many', Isa. 53.12). The Isaianic Servant presages how Jesus will function as both a sacrifice and a priest: he offers himself as a guilt offering (v. 10) to be crushed, oppressed, afflicted, and cut off for the transgressions of the people to whom the stroke was due (vv. 4-8). His death justifies the many (v. 11) and inaugurates the new covenant (Isa. 42.6).[15] Furthermore, as a priest, he intercedes for the transgressors

---

[14] Barry Clyde Joslin, 'Christ Bore the Sins of Many: Substitution and the Atonement in Hebrews', *The Southern Baptist Journal of Theology* 11.2 (2007), pp. 74-103 (82); deSilva, *Honor, Patronage, Kinship & Purity: Unlocking New Testament Culture*, p. 309.

[15] This ties back into 2.13, when the author introduces a quotation from Isa. 8.17 ('Behold, I and the children whom God has given me'). Isaiah 53.11 further portrays the relationship between the Servant and the people as that of progenitor/offspring: 'he will see his offspring'.

(Isa. 53.12) and 'sprinkles many nations' (Isa. 52.15).[16] In Heb. 10.5-10, the Preacher likewise appropriates Ps. 40.6-8 to demonstrate the provisional, imperfect nature of animal sacrifices and the completion of God's will through Jesus' obedience in offering his body as a new-covenant sacrifice.[17]

Judgment

Third, the author weaves the judgment of disobedient Israel into the background of Hebrews. Like the Israelites in the wilderness, the New Exodus sojourners were in danger of neglecting God's great salvation (2.1-4), hardening their hearts and turning away from God (3.7-19; 6.4-6), not persevering (10.19-39), and refusing to listen to God (12.25).[18] Just as the psalmist cautioned a later generation of Israelites not to follow in their forefathers' unfaithful footsteps (Ps. 95.7-11), the writer to the Hebrews now issues the same warning to his congregation.[19] They are heirs of God's final and perfect word, spoken by God's very Son, confirmed by first-hand witnesses, and testified to with signs and wonders of the Holy Spirit (Heb. 2.3-4; cf. Exod. 7.3).[20] They have been enlightened, tasted the heavenly gift, received the new covenant promise of the Holy Spirit, and tasted the goodness of God's word and proleptic powers of the age to come (Heb. 6.4-5).[21] God has taken them as his sons and guided them with his loving discipline (Heb. 12.5-11). If those who disobeyed the first word were punished for their

---

[16] Bruce, *Hebrews*, p. 32.

[17] George H. Guthrie, 'Hebrews', in G.K. Beale and D.A. Carson (eds.), *Commentary on the New Testament Use of the Old Testament* (Grand Rapids: Baker Academic, Kindle edn, 2007), loc. 35977. Guthrie points out that this Psalm is connected to Jer. 31.31, the key passage that brackets 8.7–10.18. He notes how David's submission to do God's will on behalf of the people typified Christ's obedience.

[18] Simon J. Kistemaker, *Exposition of the Epistle to the Hebrews* (New Testament Commentary; Grand Rapids: Baker Book House, 1984), pp. 18-19.

[19] Bruce suggests that the author may have seen a special significance in the forty years of Num. 14.33/Ps. 95.10, based on evidence of an anticipated end-time probationary period of forty years. If the Epistle was composed shortly before 70 CE, nearly forty years had passed since Jesus' 'exodus' at Jerusalem. 'Hence the urgency of the present appeal to the readers to take heed "so long as it is called 'Today'" (v. 13)'. Bruce, *Hebrews*, locs. 1222-27.

[20] Martin Emmrich discusses how this phrase was bound up with recollection of Israel's redemption from Egypt. Martin Emmrich, 'Pneumatological Concepts in Hebrews' (PhD dissertation, Westminster Theological Seminary, 2001), p. 32; cf. Mathewson, 'Reading Heb 6:4-6', pp. 219-20.

[21] Dave Mathewson astutely points out the Exodus background behind these statements. Mathewson, 'Reading Heb 6:4-6'.

every transgression (Heb. 2.2), the author solemnly queries, 'How will we escape if we neglect so great a salvation?' If those who refused the voice that shook the earth were punished, how much more those who do not heed the voice that will shake both the heavens and the earth (Heb. 12.25-29; Deut. 4.24; Hag. 2.6). They must therefore 'strengthen the hands that are weak and the knees that are feeble' for their New Exodus journey (Heb. 12.12-13; Isa. 35.3).[22]

Election/Sonship

Jesus, the Firstborn Son

The Preacher, like Paul, presupposes the concept of corporate solidarity. However, he works out the sonship of believers and their status as God's chosen people, drawn from the Exodus, in a distinctive manner. The author portrays Jesus in multiple representative roles: Firstborn Son, King/royal Messiah, High Priest, and Forerunner. He introduces Jesus as God's Firstborn early in ch. 1 (vv. 2, 5-6, 8; cf. Exod. 4.22), where the inter-relatedness of the first three roles quickly becomes apparent. The author appeals to a catena of OT texts, including 2 Sam. 7.14 and Pss. 2.7; 8.4-6; 102.5-6; and 110.1, that fuse together these ideas.[23] First, he depicts Jesus the Son as the perfect embodiment of the priestly *rulers* who came before him, including Adam, Melchizedek, and David (e.g. Ps. 45.6 in Heb. 1.8; Ps. 8.4-6 in Heb. 2.5-9; Ps. 2.7 in Heb. 5.5; Melchizedek typology and Ps. 110.1, 4 in Heb. 7; 10.12-13).[24] He uses enthronement language to envision a formal presentation of the Son in heaven to the angels, which coincided with Jesus' sitting down at the right hand of the Majesty (1.3)[25] and inheriting a 'more excellent name' (i.e. the title of Son, 1.4;

---

[22] The author's exhortation to 'make straight paths' evokes not only Proverbs 3 from which the author has been quoting (cf. vv. 6-8) and related Proverbs (e.g. 4.26-26), but New Exodus passages such as Isa. 40.3 and Jer. 31.9.

[23] See section on 'Jesus, the Firstborn' in Chapter 5 for background on representative adoptive sonship of the King and Messiah in Jewish thought.

[24] For a discussion on Adam as a priest serving in an Edenic temple, see Beale, *New Testament Biblical Theology*, loc. 1108.

[25] Käsemann, Ernst, *Wandering People of God*, p. 99. Käsemann negotiates the tension of Jesus' preexistent glory and the bestowal of the title of 'Son' by suggesting that what was hidden in the Godhead 'under[went] eschatological disclosure in the heavenly act of enthronement' on the basis of Jesus' earthly history.

cf. Phil. 2.9-10).[26] His christological reading of Psalm 8 proclaims the Son's dominion over the 'world to come', showing that through Jesus, Adam's appointment as ruler over creation has been perfectly and proleptically fulfilled.[27] Moreover, the Preacher taps into New Exodus expectation of a coming descendant of David, the Branch, who would rule forever in righteousness, build God's temple, and serve as a priest (Gen. 49.10; Isa. 9.5-7; 11.1-5; 16.5; Mic. 5.2; Zech. 3.8; 6.12).[28]

Second, the author offers a sustained reflection on Jesus as High Priest that is unique among NT authors. Ernst Käsemann rightly notes that just as Jesus' Sonship is tied to his rule, his 'installation to the office of high priest clearly corresponds to the bestowal of the title "Son"' in Hebrews (Heb. 1.5-13; 4.14; 5.5-6, 10).[29] Throughout the Epistle, the author highlights Jesus' perfect qualifications for this role, in his essential solidarity with his brothers/children and his qualitative difference. On the one hand, he is *merciful* because he became like his brothers; shared in their flesh and blood; and suffered temptation, weakness, and reproach (2.10-14; 4.15; 5.2; 11.26; 12.2-3; 13.3).[30] On the other hand, he is a *faithful* High Priest before God because he faced suffering and temptation with obedience and holiness (contrasted throughout with Israel's filial disobedience; cf. Num. 14.22; Deut. 6.16). Jesus was thus able to 'taste death for everyone' and make propitiation for the people's sins on the basis of his indestructible life (2.9; 7.16).[31]

---

[26] Guthrie suggests that the inherited name refers not to the title of 'Son', but to the designation of Jesus as heir to David's throne against the background of 2 Samuel 7. Guthrie, 'Hebrews', loc. 34079.

[27] He makes space for this reading by employing βραχύς ('for a little while') temporally to bracket Jesus' time on earth and by infusing οἰκουμένη ('inhabited earth') with an expansive tone to include humans, angelic beings, and the rest of the created order. McGhee, 'Holiness and Suffering', p. 62.

[28] He reinforces this with a reference to Jesus' descent from the tribe of Judah (7.14) and quotations from New Exodus passages (e.g. Jer. 31.31 in Heb. 8.8). Guthrie brings out the Davidic background of Jesus' Sonship/Kingship in Hebrews, noting the use of specific themes (e.g. inheritance) as well as terms such as ὄνομα ('name') and perhaps μεγαλωσύνη ('majesty' or 'greatness') that together point to 2 Samuel 7. Guthrie, 'Hebrews', locs. 34056-79.

[29] Käsemann, Ernst, *Wandering People of God*, p. 98.

[30] The idea and language of testing/temptation in Hebrews (πειράζω, 'to test' or 'to be tempted' [passive], Heb. 2.18; 4.15; and 11.37) is drawn from the wilderness testing. See discussion in Chapter 3 on 'lead us not into temptation'.

[31] For a more detailed analysis of Jesus' perfection through sufferings, see McGhee, 'Holiness and Suffering', pp. 65-85.; David Peterson, *Hebrews and Perfection:*

Third, in light of Jesus' perfect solidarity and perfect obedience, the author further describes him as the Author (ἀρχηγός) and Perfecter (τελειωτής) of faith/salvation (2.10; 12.2) and as a Forerunner or Pioneer (πρόδρομος, 6.20). As the ἀρχηγός and πρόδρομος, Jesus leads from the head and sets the example. He has run the race of faith ahead of his brothers and draws them after himself to glory (2.10).[32] Since he manifested faith to the end, perfect faith appears in him. He is also the author or source of faith and salvation (cf. 5.9; 9.28; 10.20). Believers who are following in his footsteps receive salvation from him (12.2-3). As the τελειωτής or Perfecter of faith, Jesus 'brings faith to its highest attainment, in himself as an example or in others through his high priestly ministry'.[33] This complements both senses of ἀρχηγός; having 'laid the foundation of faith in our hearts', Jesus brings it to completion.[34]

Believers as Sons and Brothers

In Hebrews, believers are brought into God's family through the faithful life and death of the Firstborn Son. There is a 'graced exchange':[35] Jesus shared in their flesh and blood, their weakness and poverty, their temptation, and their punishment, tasting death for everyone (Heb. 2.9). After his vindication, his 'brothers' and 'children' (Ps. 22.22; Isa. 53.10) share in his heavenly calling, his holiness, his exaltation, and his inheritance (Heb. 2.5–3.1; 9.15; 12.10). Through his

---

An Examination of the Concept of Perfection in the 'Epistle to the Hebrews' (Cambridge, England: Cambridge University Press, 1982).

[32] Geerhardus Vos, *The Teaching of the Epistle to the Hebrews* (ed. Johannes G. Vos; Nutley, NJ: Presbyterian & Reformed, 1976), p. 96. deSilva supports the grammatical possibility of taking ἀγαγόντα ('leading') as an adverbial participle that is dependent on ἀρχηγόν ('Pioneer'), 'with which it agrees in gender, number, and case and with which it is linked by predicate position'. David A. deSilva, *Perseverance in Gratitude: A Socio-Rhetorical Commentary on the Epistle 'To the Hebrews'* (Grand Rapids: Eerdmans, 2000), p. 113; cf. Franz Julius Delitzsch, *Commentary on the Epistle to the Hebrews* (Edinburgh: T. & T. Clark, 1872), p. 303. See Chapter 4 for analysis of 'leading' language in connection with the Exodus.

[33] Timothy Friberg, Barbara Friberg, and Neva F. Miller, *Analytical Lexicon to the Greek New Testament* (Baker's Greek New Testament Library; Grand Rapids: Baker, 2000).

[34] Kistemaker, *Exposition of the Epistle to the Hebrews*, p. 368. He cross-references Phil. 1.6, 'He who began a good work in you will perfect it until the day of Christ Jesus'.

[35] Macchia, *Justified in the Spirit*, p. 181. Macchia notes parallels in Jn 1.12-14; 2 Cor. 8.9; and Phil. 2.6-11.

will and his obedience, they are sanctified (Heb. 10.10) and become part of the household of God (Heb. 3.6; Num. 12.7), the 'church of the Firstborn' (ἐκκλησία, Heb. 2.12; 12.23).[36] They live by faith, and by faith, receive life and inherit the new covenant promises (Heb. 10.39–11.40). As part of their sonship, they are to accept suffering as something 'divinely purposeful and personally beneficial' (Heb. 12.4-13).[37] The author has repeatedly held up the paradigms of God's unfaithful son Israel (Hebrews 4) and the faithful Firstborn, Jesus (Heb. 5.8; 12.1-3). Now, he again draws from the story of the Exodus to exhort believers to endure suffering as discipline from the hand their loving Father.[38]

Journey

Finally, the author elucidates how various aspects of the addressees' experience parallel those of the Israelites on their wilderness journey. In particular, he highlights their status as pilgrims, the role of the Holy Spirit in their lives, and the inheritance that lies before them if they persevere to the end. First, the pilgrimage motif in Hebrews is largely patterned after Israel's Exodus journey. The author indicates that this wandering existence is, in fact, intrinsic to their calling.[39] They wander in step with their forefathers like Abraham (11.8-10, 13-16), the prophets, a cloud of faithful witnesses, and Jesus the Pioneer (2.9-18; 11.32-40; 12.1-3).[40] Like those who went before them, they must look

---

[36] The author of Hebrews joins Paul in applying Israel's roles and titles to the Jew-and-Gentile church (e.g. his illustration of them as God's field that must produce a harvest in 6.7-8). See discussion about the people of God in Chapter 3, section on Luke-Acts and n. 152, for the OT background of ἐκκλησία and קהל, 'assembly'.

[37] N. Clayton Croy, *Endurance in Suffering: Hebrews 12:1–13 in Its Rhetorical, Religious, and Philosophical Context* (SNTSMS 98; Cambridge, England: Cambridge University Press, 1998), p. 2.

[38] Proverbs 3 offers a midrashic-type exposition on Deuteronomy 8, which is rehearsing Israel's history and exhorting the people to be faithful to the covenant. Both mention keeping the commandments (Deut. 8.1, 11; Prov. 3.1) in order to have long life and inheritance (Deut. 8.1; Prov. 3.1); walking in YHWH's way and fearing him (Deut. 8.2; Prov. 3.1, 7); and honoring him with wealth and produce (Deut. 8.7-14; Prov. 3.9). In Heb. 12.5-11, the Preacher draws from the capstone of this comparison: 'Thus you are to know in your heart that YHWH your God was disciplining you just as a man disciplines his son' (Deut. 8.5); 'For the LORD reproves him whom he loves, as a father the son in whom he delights' (Prov. 3.12); 'For those whom the Lord loves, he disciplines' (Heb. 12.6).

[39] Käsemann argues that 'the form of existence in time appropriate to the recipient of the revelation can only be that of wandering'. Käsemann, Ernst, *Wandering People of God*, p. 19.

[40] F.A. Chamy terms Jesus the 'sojourner par excellence' (cf. Jn 1.14; 16.28; Mt.

back to their redemption and forward to their inheritance and live the life of faith.

Second, in their wandering, they are given the Holy Spirit's presence. This conforms to Israel's past and fulfills prophetic expectation associated with the New Exodus. Texts such as Neh. 9.20, 30; Isa. 63.11; and Hag. 2.5 indicate that the Holy Spirit guided, instructed, and warned the people at the Exodus.[41] Other Scriptures, such as Ps. 106.33 and Isa. 63.10, reveal that it was the Holy Spirit whom the people grieved in the desert with their rebellion (cf. warning in Heb. 10.29). New covenant writings looked forward to the day when the Holy Spirit would indwell believers and enable them to walk in God's path (Ezek. 36.27; Isa. 32.15; 44.3; Joel 2.28-29; implicit in Jer. 31.33).[42] The recipients of Hebrews, the author proclaims, are living in the 'last days' (Heb. 1.2); through Jesus, God has inaugurated the promised new covenant (Heb. 8.8-13; 9.15; 10.14-17). All of God's people have become partakers not only of the heavenly gift (manna/spiritual provision), but also of the Holy Spirit (Heb. 6.4; cf. Acts 2.1-21), according to Moses' hope (Num. 11.29). The Spirit continues to address them through the Scripture (Heb. 3.7), guiding them to respond to God's voice in obedience (Ps. 95.7-11).[43]

Third, the author continually emphasizes that those who finish the race of faith will inherit what God has promised. This includes the blessings of Abraham (6.11-15); new covenant election, forgiveness, and knowledge of God (8.6); eternal life, salvation, and righteousness (10.36-39); and a 'kingdom which cannot be shaken' (12.28). In particular, the author holds out the interconnected prospects of rest and promised land that YHWH offered to Israel.[44] After living under oppression in a foreign land and wandering in the desert, the people of Israel longed to live peacefully in the land God

---

2.15). F.A. Chamy, 'Royal Priesthood: The New Exodus Framework of 1 Peter 1:1-2:10' (MA dissertation, Trinity Evangelical Divinity School, 2016), pp. 20-21.

[41] This was most likely in a representative way, as YHWH anointed Moses, Joshua, and the elders of Israel (Num. 11.16-25). Mathewson, 'Reading Heb 6:4-6', pp. 217-18; cf. Roger Douglas Cotton, 'The Pentecostal Significance of Numbers 11', *JPT* 10.1 (2001), pp. 3-10 (6).

[42] Psalm 143.10 also connects the Spirit with leading.

[43] Emmrich comments that 'the author's predominant pneumatological concern is to underscore the Spirit's function as guide of the wandering people', just as at the Exodus. Emmrich, 'Pneumatological Concepts in Hebrews', p. iv.

[44] See Chapter 2, n. 49; Chapter 3 section on Mt. 11.28.

swore to give to Abraham's descendants (Gen. 12.7; 13.15; 15.7; Exod. 33.14; Josh. 1.13; 21.44). But they neither fully inhabited the promised land (e.g. Judg. 1.33-36) nor fully enjoyed the promised rest (Heb. 4.8). Later in Israel's exile-fraught history, YHWH imparted to them the hope of both homecoming and New Exodus rest (Isa. 14.3; Jer. 6.16; 31.25; Ezek. 34.15). The Preacher discerns that the sabbath rest of the past and the promised land, like other elements of the old system, were only shadows of the greater and more perfect promises available through Jesus.[45] He first quotes creatively from Ps. 95.7, then links this with God's rest of Gen. 2.2, to advance his argument that God's rest (now rest *given by* God and a resting *with* God) is still available for his people.[46] This rest is a spiritual, eschatological reality, achieved by diligent faith, perhaps proleptically experienced on earth (Heb. 4.3; cf. Mt. 11.28 and NE texts), and consummated upon arrival to the heavenly kingdom (4.1-11).[47] With regard to the land, the author observes that for a time, the people of God wander as exiles 'in deserts and mountains and caves and holes' (11.13, 38), with no lasting earthly city to call home (13.14). Like Abraham, however, they seek the city of God (11.10) – a better, heavenly abode (11.16; 12.22), a 'country of their own' (11.14). They have drawn near to the city of Zion and are 'at the doorstep of God's promised land of rest'.[48]

First Peter

Peter, like the author of Hebrews, depicts believers as New Exodus

---

[45] Here, note the implicit contrast played on the names of Joshua and Jesus: while the first was not able to give God's people rest, the second has made it available. Thiessen suggests that the author intentionally cuts off his treatment of heroes in ch. 11 at Jericho and omits Joshua from the list of exemplars in order to bolster his case further that Israel is still in the time of the exile and that Joshua was incapable of offering the people rest (supplemented by Jesus' example in 12.1-3). Thiessen, 'Hebrews and the End of the Exodus', pp. 365-66.

[46] For a thorough explanation of the quotation from Psalm 95 in Hebrews 4, see Enns, 'Creation and Re-Creation'.

[47] See Guthrie for a more comprehensive discussion on whether this rest is experienced in the present, future, or both. Emmrich argues that it is solely future, whereas Bruce emphasizes that God's rest began when he finished creating heaven and earth. While not fully available yet, it may be experienced here and now by faith. Emmrich, 'Pneumatological Concepts in Hebrews', pp. 29-30; Bruce, *Hebrews*, locs. 1273-1344.

[48] Thiessen, 'Hebrews and the End of the Exodus', p. 369.

sojourners on the way to a heavenly inheritance.[49] He interprets salvation as a recapitulation of God's mighty acts of the past and the fulfillment of Israel's New Exodus hopes.[50] From the opening verses, Peter appropriates Exodus typology to remind believers of their identity as God's holy people, their priestly and missional vocation in the world, and their duty to bring glory to God's name as they endure trials and suffering.[51]

Hermeneutic

First Peter is a letter characterized by 'sustained and profound engagement with Scripture'.[52] It is saturated with OT references, allusions, and images.[53] In particular, First Peter contains the prominent and natural transfer of Israel's titles (e.g. 'a chosen race, a royal priesthood, a holy nation, a people for God's own possession', 2.9) to the mixed community of believers, without any sense of tension: the church is for Peter the continuation of Israel.[54] Peter

---

[49] Marie Boismard comments, «Les chrétiens doivent se considérer au milieu du monde païen comme des étrangers, en marche vers la patrie céleste », ('Christians should see themselves as strangers in the middle of the pagan world, on the way to the heavenly homeland'). Marie E. Boismard, 'Une Liturgie Baptismale Dans La Prima Petri', RB 64.2 (1957), pp. 161-83 (181).

[50] Paul E. Deterding, 'Exodus Motifs in First Peter', Concordia Journal 7.2 (March 1981), pp. 58-65 (74); Chamy, 'Royal Priesthood', p. 147.

[51] Éric W. Zeller, 'Intertextuality in 1 Peter 2:9-12: Peter's Biblical-Theological Summary of the Mission of God's People' (PhD dissertation, Dallas Theological Seminary, 2013), p. 36. Donald Guthrie mentions the OT background of the Epistle and acknowledges that Peter presents believers as the New Israel, but counters arguments in favor of broad, liturgical use of the Exodus motif. Donald Guthrie, New Testament Introduction (Downers Grove, IL: InterVarsity Press, 4th edn, 1990), p. 604.

[52] William L. Schutter, Hermeneutic and Composition in I Peter (WUNT; Tübingen: Mohr Siebeck, 1989), II, p. 43. Per unit of text, it has about the same number of OT references as Hebrews and is only surpassed by Rev. Peter H. Davids, The First Epistle of Peter (NICNT; Grand Rapids: Eerdmans, 1990), p. 24. For a detailed analysis of the quotations and allusions in 1 Peter, see Schutter, I Peter; Benjamin Sargent, Written to Serve: The Use of Scripture in 1 Peter (Library of New Testament Studies 547; London: Bloomsbury T. & T. Clark, 2015); Thomas P. Osborne, 'L'utilisation des citations de l'Ancien Testament dans la première epître de Pierre', Revue Théologique de Louvain 12.1 (1981), pp. 64-77.

[53] Carson comments that 'if one were to extend beyond allusions (however defined) to echoes picking up OT language and themes, scarcely a verse in this epistle would be exempt'. D.A. Carson, 'I Peter', in G.K. Beale and D.A. Carson (eds.), Commentary on the New Testament Use of the Old Testament (Grand Rapids: Baker Academic, Kindle edn, 2007), loc. 37253.

[54] Davids, The First Epistle of Peter, p. 25; Chamy, 'Royal Priesthood', pp. 17-18; Zeller, 'Intertextuality in 1 Peter 2', p. 209; Max-Alaine Chevallier, 'Condition et

discerns that believers are living in the age of Israel's New Exodus hopes fulfilled. This presupposition provides the hermeneutical framework or controlling metaphor for the Epistle.[55] Peter's implicit typology gains grounding and emphasis not only through persistent application, but through strategic, programmatic placement.[56]

Slavery

Peter does not dwell on the past, and the forward-looking New Exodus texts that he echoes anticipate the freedom and redemption that would come about through Christ's work. However, Peter peppers his Epistle with descriptions of believers' lives before their redemption, evoking Israel's slavery in Egypt and her later exiles. His recipients lived in bondage to sin (2.24; cf. 4.3) and were in darkness (2.9; cf. Isa. 9.2; 29.18-19; 42.6-7; 49.9). Moreover, they were 'not a people' and had 'not received mercy' (2.10; Hos. 1.10; 2.23). Finally, they were 'continually straying' (2.25; cf. Isa. 53.6) like sheep without a shepherd.

Redemption/Judgment

As with other NT authors, Peter develops his theology of salvation with overlapping Exodus/New Exodus metaphors.[57] He reminds his audience that they, like Israel long ago, have been freed to serve the living God (1 Pet. 2.16). Through the blood of Jesus, their 'unblemished and spotless' Passover Lamb, they have been redeemed and purchased as God's holy people (1.17-19; 3.18; 2.9; cf. Exod. 12.5).[58] They have also been 'sprinkled' with the blood of Christ (1.2)

---

vocation des chrétiens en diaspora: remarques exégétiques sur sa 1ʳᵉ Épître de Pierre', *RevScRel* 48.4 (1974), pp. 387-400 (398). Contra Sargent, *Written to Serve*; Benjamin Sargent, 'The Narrative Substructure of 1 Peter', *ExpTim* 124.10 (2013), pp. 485-90, who emphasizes discontinuity.

[55] Paul J. Achtemeier, *1 Peter* (Hermeneia: A Critical and Historical Commentary on the Bible; Minneapolis: Augsburg–Fortress, 1996), pp. 69-71. Abson Joseph likewise sees Peter's Exodus-based theological hermeneutic as central to the Epistle. Abson Prédestin Joseph, *A Narratological Reading of 1 Peter* (Library of New Testament Studies; London: Bloomsbury T. & T. Clark, 2012), pp. 55, 59.

[56] Achtemeier notes an *inclusio* in 1.1-2 and 2.9 (the closing verses of the first section), with a repetition of the concepts of election, priesthood, and holiness. Achtemeier, *1 Peter*, p. 73. Because of the presence of ἐκλεκτός/συνεκλεκτός ('chosen'/'chosen with') in 1.1 and 5.13, Schutter suggests an inclusio 'spanning the whole letter'. Schutter, *I Peter*, II, p. 28. Chamy observes the programmatic placement of OT passages in 1 Peter. Chamy, 'Royal Priesthood', p. 4.

[57] Peter maintains a future-oriented, eschatological approach to salvation. He frequently speaks of its future consummation (1.5, 7, 9-10, 13; 2.12; 5.1, 4).

[58] Sargent provides a summary of major scholars' positions on this. Sargent, *Written to Serve*, p. 111. Most see it as a reference to the Passover, although some note

– Jesus has inaugurated the new covenant and consecrated them in their priestly service (Exod. 24.6-8). [59] With the reference to 'sprinkling', through explicit quotation in 2.21-25, and perhaps in 3.18 ('the just for the unjust'), Peter further interprets Jesus' willing sacrifice on behalf of others through the lens of the Isaianic Servant (Isa. 52.15; 53.4-10). He holds up Jesus as a sin offering (v. 24), an example of faithfulness in suffering (vv. 20-21), and a corporate representative (v. 24) who has enabled believers to receive reconciliation, healing, life, and righteousness (vv. 23-24). [60]

First Peter also contains hints of New Exodus judgment along with expectations of salvation, especially in tandem with the Isaianic texts that Peter quotes and alludes to. From 1.22–2.12, Peter weaves in references to and themes from Isaiah 8, 10, and 40 (among others). The entire contexts of these passages fuse together to create a coherent backdrop for Peter's exhortations. [61] The message is clear: YHWH's 'day of visitation' is at hand (2.12; cf. Isa. 10.3; 40.10-11; Lk. 1.68). People's response to YHWH's word (1.25; cf. Isa. 40.6-8) and his chosen Cornerstone (2.6; cf. Isa. 8.14) will result in either reward or punishment (cf. 4.3-7, 17-18).

Election/Sonship

A hallmark of First Peter is the extensive application of Israel's election and vocation to the community of faith. This begins in the very first verse, when Peter addresses believers as ἐκλεκτοῖς παρεπιδήμοις διασπορᾶς ('chosen sojourners of the Diaspora'; cf.

---

more general implications and associations with the Isaianic Servant. The contrast with 'gold and silver' as well as surrounding allusions to the Exodus strengthen the probability that Peter has the Passover in mind. Deterding also mentions the aspect of the Passover lamb's being chosen in advance (Exod. 12.3, 6; cf. 1 Pet. 1.20). Deterding, 'Exodus Motifs in First Peter', p. 58.

[59] Davids, *The First Epistle of Peter*, p. 20; Chamy, 'Royal Priesthood', pp. 23-28; Joseph, *Narratological Reading*, pp. 60-61.

[60] Joseph comments that Peter 'creates a rapprochement between the obedience that Israel once pledged to God, the obedience that Jesus has displayed to God, and the obedience that the author encourages the audience to display'.

[61] Carson, 'I Peter', locs. 37468-69. Peter's language about darkness/light, glorifying God among the nations, and being shepherded by God (1.25; 5.4) also draws on Isaiah and the Exodus. Peter highlights how believers have been given new birth through association with Jesus' resurrection at baptism (1.3; 3.21) and by the word of God (1.22-25; cf. Isa. 40.8). See Chapter 2 for a discussion of new creation as part of the Exodus motif.

2.9; 5.13).[62] Peter indicates that believers have been called/chosen for a divine purpose and are included in the people of God. He continues this trajectory, particularly throughout chs. one and two. First, he utilizes the Father-son terminology that characterized God's relationship with Israel from the Exodus onward ('Father' in 1.2, 3, and esp. 17, with an exhortation to holiness from Lev. 11.44-45; 'obedient children' in 1.14; and 'household of God' in 4.17, cf. Num. 12.7; Heb. 3.2). Second, 1 Pet. 2.1-10 contains a constellation of ideas from several OT texts that use Exodus typology to reinforce believers' identity and the implications of their calling for their relationships with God and others.[63] In 2.5, Peter asserts that his readers are 'living stones', 'being built up as a spiritual house for a holy priesthood, to offer up spiritual sacrifices acceptable to God'. Their status as priests, their spiritual sacrifices, and their formation into God's holy dwelling are participatory: believers must come to Jesus, the precious living Cornerstone, believe in him, and be built up through him (vv. 4-7; cf. Eph. 2.19-22; Ezek. 37.26-27; Zech. 6.12-13; Hag. 2.7-9).[64] Moreover, in 1 Pet. 2.9-10, Peter inserts alternating allusions from Isa. 43.20-21 and Exod. 19.5-6 (cf. Deut. 4.20; 7.6) that locate believers within the familial, national, and eschatological missiology of Israel.[65] The whole nation was consecrated to worship YHWH, follow him in holiness, and orient their lives to his service (Exodus 19). In this vocation, they were to represent him to the peoples: what the priests were to Israel, Israel was to be to the nations. As Eric Zeller observes, however, after Israel's 'failure in national missiology', prophetic anticipation shifted the people's hope to the eschatological work of the Servant of YHWH and the reconstituted remnant.[66] As a result of the Servant's liberating and restorative work, the people would once again be known as YHWH's

---

[62] Jewish communities had used this term to refer to those outside Palestine ever since the exile (cf. Deut. 28.25; Neh. 1.9; Isa. 49.6 LXX). Davids, *The First Epistle of Peter*, p. 46.

[63] Carson, 'I Peter', loc. 37781.

[64] For a discussion on temple/dwelling background and fulfillment, see *A Holy Temple*, in Chapter 4. Douglas Oss insightfully analyzes Peter's use of the 'stone' passages. See Douglas A. Oss, 'The Interpretation of the "Stone" Passages by Peter and Paul: A Comparative Study', *JETS* 32.2 (1989), pp. 181-200.

[65] Zeller, 'Intertextuality in 1 Peter 2', p. ii.

[66] Zeller, p. ii; cf. Michael W. Goheen, *A Light to the Nations: The Missional Church and the Biblical Story* (Grand Rapids: Baker Academic, 2011), pp. 39-40. See Chapter 2 n. 111 for comments about the Servant of YHWH and Israel's calling.

priests (Isa. 61.6; cf. 66.21), would be the means of blessing to all nations, and would proclaim his mighty acts of salvation. That time is now, Peter infers. Finally, in 1 Pet. 2.10, Peter grounds this special status as 'God's possession' (2.9; cf. Tit. 2.14) in God's mercy via New Exodus prophecies from Hos. 1.10 and 2.23. The mercy that YHWH had promised again to Israel is the same mercy that Peter's audience has received (1 Pet. 1.10, 12); this is 'that day' (Hos. 2.21).[67] In these various ways, Peter weaves together Israel's history and hopes to remind Christians of their privileges, mission, and obligations.

Journey

Lastly, Peter frames the status and experiences of God's people in the time between their redemption and salvation in terms drawn from the Exodus. The parallels converge primarily around their wandering, non-resident way of life and the inheritance toward which they are *en route*.[68] First, Peter takes up language from Israel's history to make a theological claim about his readers' status: they are resident aliens, like their spiritual fathers.[69] He calls them 'sojourners' (παρεπιδή-μοις) of the dispersion in 1.1 and 'aliens and sojourners' (παροίκους καὶ παρεπιδήμους) in 2.11 and exhorts them to pass their 'temporary stay' on earth (παροικία) in fear (1.17).[70] These words echo Abraham's words in Gen. 23.4 (πάροικος καὶ παρεπίδημος ἐγώ εἰμι, 'I am a stranger and an alien'), God's words to Abraham about his descendants in Gen. 15.3 (πάροικον ἔσται τὸ σπέρμα σου ἐν γῆ οὐκ ἰδία, 'your offspring

---

[67] Chamy traces 'mercy' language through covenant and New Exodus texts. Chamy, 'Royal Priesthood', p. 34.

[68] Other allusions/parallels include their trials/temptations (πειρασμοῖς, 1 Pet. 1.6; 4.12; cf. Exod. 15.25; 16.4; 20.20), the presence of the 'Spirit of glory' on their journey (1 Pet. 4.14; see Chapter 4, 'New Exodus Blessings'), God's 'mighty hand' (1 Pet. 5.6; cf. Exod. 32.11) that will deliver them and exalt them if they are faithful, and their behavior among the nations (1 Pet. 2.12). Peter further exhorts the community to 'gird up the loins of [their] mind' (1.13): while not an exact match with the Greek text of Exod. 12.12, this is reminiscent of the Israelites' preparations for the Exodus. Deterding, 'Exodus Motifs in First Peter', p. 62; Chamy, 'Royal Priesthood', p. 66.

[69] Achtemeier, *1 Peter*, p. 71; contra John H. Elliott, *A Home for the Homeless: A Social-Scientific Criticism of I Peter, Its Situation and Strategy* (Eugene, OR: Wipf and Stock, 2005), pp. 42-47.

[70] These words both carry the idea of living in a place or among a people that is not one's own, and are translated with words like 'sojourner', 'stranger', 'exile', 'foreigner', and 'alien'. Louw and Nida, *Greek-English Lexicon*.

will be strangers in a land not their own'), and even David's words *after* Israel was dwelling in the promised land (πάροικος ἐγώ εἰμι παρὰ σοὶ καὶ παρεπίδημος καθὼς πάντες οἱ πατέρες μου, 'I am a stranger with you, a foreigner just like all of my fathers', Ps. 38.13 LXX/39.12 MT).[71] Peter insinuates that just as 'at the core of Israel's identity as a nation [was] the memory of their alienness' (Deut. 26.7-9),[72] believers must hold in tension their special election as God's people and their transient, penultimate existence on earth.[73] Second, just as Israel's sojourning was anchored in the promise of a land of her own (Gen. 12.7; 50.24), Peter animates his readers with the hope of a sure and lasting inheritance.[74] Even though they are aliens and strangers on earth, Peter assures them that their new birth into God's family has made them heirs of a living hope, an incorruptible, undefiled, and unfading inheritance (1 Pet. 1.4; 3.9; cf. Paul's logic of 'if a son ... then an heir' in Gal. 4.7).[75] They must suffer disgrace and endure various kinds of trials for a short time – but God himself has prepared something wonderful for them. It is being watched over (τετηρημένην) in heaven and is ready to be revealed at the consummation of their salvation (1 Pet. 1.6-7).

---

[71] Cf. Acts 7.6 and 13.17, of Abraham's offspring living in a foreign land/sojourning in Egypt. As in Hebrews, then, Abraham's wandering status serves as a prototype for the people of God. Chamy, 'Royal Priesthood', pp. 17-18.

[72] Joseph, *Narratological Reading*, p. 74.

[73] Peter's application of this motif, as Max-Alain Chevallier comments, « lui a permis de comprendre la diaspora chrétienne, dans le prolongement de la diaspora juive, non point comme une contingente et déplorable condition, mais comme une nécessaire et lumineuse vocation », ('allowed him to understand the Christian diaspora, as the continuation of the Jewish diaspora, not as an incidental and deplorable condition, but as a necessary and luminous vocation'). Chevallier, 'Condition et vocation des chrétiens en diaspora: remarques exégétiques sur sa 1ʳᵉ Épître de Pierre', p. 398.

[74] According to E.G. Selwyn, the word κληρονομία ('inheritance') that Peter employs in 1.4 often referred to Israel's possession of Canaan in the LXX. E.G. Selwyn, *The First Epistle of St. Peter: The Greek Text with Introduction, Notes and Essays* (Grand Rapids: Baker Book House, 1981), p. 124; cited in Chamy, 'Royal Priesthood', pp. 40-41.

[75] Davids, *The First Epistle of Peter*, p. 52. For a discussion of land in connection with Isaiah's New Exodus promises, see Chamy, 'Royal Priesthood', p. 43; Pao, *Acts and the Isaianic New Exodus*, p. 115.

Jude

Jude, like the OT prophets, appropriates the Exodus/New Exodus motif to remind his readers of the outcome of disobedience and warn them of impending judgment on those who refuse to follow Christ (v. 4).[76] As he condemns false teachers (v. 4) and admonishes his recipients, he notes that prior judgment typifies eschatological judgment. First, he recalls that Jesus destroyed the unbelieving people of Israel whom he had delivered from Egypt (v. 5).[77] In addition, Jude imaginatively depicts the false teachers as perishing in the rebellion of Korah (Jude 11; Numbers 16). He strengthens the parallel by stating that the false teachers not only reject authority (v. 8) like Korah and his followers, but are 'grumblers' (γογγυστής, v. 16; cf. Num. 16.11).[78] Finally, Jude exhorts believers to 'save others, snatching them out of the fire' (ἐκ πυρὸς ἁρπάζοντες, v. 23 LXX). He may be alluding to Amos 4.11, which describes New Exodus judgment befalling Israel for her disobedience (also linked back to Sodom and Gomorrah). YHWH says, 'I overthrew some of you as I overthrew Sodom and Gomorrah. You were like a burning stick snatched from the fire' (ἐξεσπασμένος ἐκ πυρός, NIV).

Conclusion

Hebrews, 1 Peter, and Jude evince widespread utilization of the Exodus motif. Each author has a unique focus, yet draws from this common history to envision the desperate situation of humanity in slavery to sin; the mighty acts of God's redemption in Christ, the Passover Lamb and Suffering Servant; the new covenant and eschatological blessings available to God's people; and the disastrous

---

[76] Second Peter 2.1-22 also warns of judgment on false teachers and prophets, but without explicit references to the Exodus.

[77] As Bruce observes, there is strong textual evidence that the original reading was 'Jesus' and not 'the Lord', perhaps identifying Jesus with the Angel of the Divine Presence (Exod. 23.21) or making reference to the Rock in the wilderness. Bruce, *Hebrews*, loc. 5676 note; Metzger, *Textual Commentary*, p. 725.

[78] Numbers 16.11 LXX employs διαγογγύζετε ('you grumble', cf. Exod. 15.24; Num. 14.2). Other LXX passages about the Exodus use ἐγόγγυσαν ('they grumbled', Num. 17.3; Ps. 105.25; cf. 1 Cor. 10.10) or γογγυσμὸν ('grumblings', Exod. 16.7).

outcome of disobedience. The seamless typology of Hebrews showcases both the continuity of God's actions and the surpassing excellence of the New Exodus salvation. The Preacher especially emphasizes the greater covenant, sacrifice, and High Priest of 'these last days'; the need for endurance and faith; the discipline that believers undergo as God's children; and the heavenly citizenship and rest that await faithful sojourners. Peter likewise encourages believers to embrace the suffering that necessarily accompanies their status as aliens and strangers, following Jesus' footsteps to glory. He invokes their election as the true Israel, members of God's household, holy priests, and a glorious temple to spur them on to holiness and steadfastness. Finally, Jude warns of the judgment that awaits ongoing participants in Korah's rebellion.

6

THE EXODUS MOTIF IN REVELATION

Introduction

In Revelation, John draws from Exodus/New Exodus traditions to envision the eschatological consummation of salvation history. John employs Exodus typology to encourage God's pilgrim people to maintain a heavenly perspective as they journey toward their eternal rest and not conform to the ways of 'those who dwell on earth'. The redemption and judgments prefigured by the Exodus and developed by the prophets provide a literary and theological framework for the Apocalypse and add evocative and emotive force to the apostle's affirmations and warnings. As Revelation concludes the biblical narrative with language and imagery drawn from the beginning books, the continuity, divinely-ordained character, and grand scope of God's plan for creation are made manifest.

Hermeneutic

Revelation is a book communicated in symbols,[1] and John draws these primarily from the OT.[2] In John's tapestry of OT imagery and

---

[1] Revelation 1.1 contains ἐσήμανεν, (translated as 'communicated'), which is a cognate verb to the noun σημεῖον, 'sign'.

[2] Craig S. Keener, *Revelation* (The NIV Application Commentary; Grand Rapids: Zondervan, 2000), p. 21; du Rand and Song, 'The Story of the Red Sea', p. 98; G.K. Beale and David H. Campbell, *Revelation: A Shorter Commentary* (Grand Rapids: Eerdmans, Kindle edn, 2015), p. 17. As many as 278 out of 404 verses in Rev. contain references to the OT, with more than 500 total allusions – surpassing the combined

language, Exodus traditions contribute 'primary colors'.[3] John's appropriation of the Exodus motif is complex and varied, influencing both structure and substance. The book of Exodus (together with Daniel, Ezekiel, and Zechariah) shapes the sequencing and thematic arrangement of major portions of the book (e.g. chs. 8 and 16, where the plagues of Egypt serve as literary prototypes for the bowl and trumpet judgments). Moreover, parallels are evident in narrative plots (e.g. the woman in the wilderness, ch. 12; the victory song by the sea, ch. 15); the climax of focal Exodus themes (e.g. salvation, testing, divine protection); and other typological characterization of people, events, and institutions (e.g. the Lamb who was slain, a kingdom of priests, the dragon, the new Jerusalem, the celebration of the Feast of Tabernacles). Similarly, Revelation indicates (like Hebrews) that earthly worship is patterned on heavenly realities (e.g. the seven lamps in Israel's tabernacle, Exod. 25.37; Zech. 4.2; cf. Rev. 1.12; 4.5; the heavenly ark of the covenant in Rev. 11.19; cf. Exod. 25.10-22).[4] Finally, John points to the fulfillment of prophecy, in which New Exodus texts such as Isa. 65.17 and 66.22 (the 'new heavens and new earth', cf. Rev. 21.1) play a prominent role.[5]

In addition, there is a marked continuity between the Gospel of John and the Apocalypse. John's Gospel portrays Jesus as the Lamb of God, YHWH's tabernacling presence among his people, the New Exodus deliverer, the source of living water and the light of the world, and the Shepherd and King who reigns on David's throne. All of these images reemerge in Revelation as John envisions the dénouement of God's plan.

This chapter will survey the most notable occurrences of the Exodus motif in Revelation, which include slavery/exile, election/

---

allusions of all the other NT books! Beale and Campbell, *Revelation: A Shorter Commentary*, p. 17.

[3] Jay Smith Casey, *Exodus Typology in the Book of Revelation* (PhD dissertation, The Southern Baptist Theological Seminary, 1981), p. ix.

[4] Beale and Campbell comment that 'Israel's earthly temple and its furniture were the microcosmic copy of the archetypal heavenly temple of God'. Beale and Campbell, *Revelation: A Shorter Commentary*, p. 14.

[5] John's hermeneutic often includes surprising twists, such as the universalization of promises and warnings that originally applied to Israel (Exod. 19.6 and Rev. 1.6; 5.10; Zech. 12.10 and Rev. 1.7; Dan. 7.25 and Rev. 12.7; Ezek. 47.12 and Rev. 22.22) as well as ironic or inverted applications such as occurred in the OT prophets. G.K. Beale, *The Book of Revelation: A Commentary on the Greek Text* (NIGNT; Grand Rapids: Eerdmans, paperback edn, 2013), pp. 91, 94.

sonship, and journey elements, but are overwhelmingly related to redemption/salvation and judgment.

Slavery/Exile

John takes up language from Israel's slavery in Egypt and from later exiles to paint a picture of the spiritual situation of believers before their salvation (in slavery to sin, 1.5) as well as the ongoing captivity of the remnant under oppressive worldly rulers.[6] The latter is particularly pervasive in Revelation. First, John suggests this parallel with his descriptions of evil worldly systems and of Christians' suffering. For example, John employs titles like 'Egypt' and 'Babylon' to refer to the 'oppressor of the spiritual children of Jerusalem' (Rev. 11.8; 17.5; cf. Dan. 4.30; Jer. 50.28).[7] The dragon in Rev. 12.9 also appears to be the antitype of Egypt in the war at the Red Sea (cf. Isa. 51.9; 30.7; 27.1; Ps. 74.14; Ezek. 29.3).[8] These indicate John's perception that Christians who remain on earth are subject to mistreatment, tribulation, and persecution according to the models of Israel's past experiences and prophetic visions (e.g. Dan. 7.25; Rev. 17.5-8). They are in exile, awaiting consummation of their redemption, when the kingdom of the world will become the kingdom of Christ (11.15).[9] Just as the Israelites groaned and cried out for deliverance and justice (Exod. 5.8), the martyrs cry out (ἔκραξαν) with a loud voice to their true Master (δεσπότης) on behalf of their brothers (Rev. 6.10; cf. Exod. 2.23; Ps. 79.5-10; Zech. 1.12; also Rev. 19.2 with Deut. 32.43).[10] The radiant

---

[6] Benjamin Wold concludes that allusions to Exodus traditions in Revelation evoke perceptions of exile and return, specifically in connection with the plague septets of Leviticus 26. There, the final seven foretell exile as well as YHWH's later remembrance of his covenant and preserving a remnant. Benjamin G. Wold, 'Revelation's Plague Septets: New Exodus and Exile', in Florentino García Martínez (ed.), *Echoes from the Caves: Qumran and the New Testament* (STDJ 85; Leiden: Brill, 2009), p. 294.

[7] Keener, *Revelation*, p. 369.

[8] Robert H. Mounce, *The Book of Revelation* (NICNT; Grand Rapids: Eerdmans, rev. edn, 1998), p. 232.

[9] Wold, 'Revelation's Plague Septets', p. 296.

[10] For analysis of κράζω ('to cry out') in connection with the Exodus, see Keesmaat, *Paul and His Story*, pp. 77-78.

woman who seems to represent the Church (as the continuation of true Israel) cries out in the travail of childbirth (cf. Rom. 8.22-23, 26), eager for the completion of her suffering.[11] Second, the call to 'come out' of Babylon in order to be holy and to avoid plagues of judgment (Rev. 18.4; cf. Exod. 3.10; 7.5) evokes the context of sojourning and exile. The wording (ἐξέλθατε, 'come out') matches Isa. 52.11 LXX (cf. Isa. 48.20; Jer. 27.8 LXX/50.8 MT; 2 Cor. 6.17), which rehearses Israel's captivity in tandem with redemption first from Egypt, later from Assyria, and ultimately at the time of Israel's future restoration. Finally, just as the Israelites were protected from the last plague in Egypt by marking their houses with the blood of the Passover lamb (Exod. 12.7-13), believers besieged by hostility are sealed with a mark that protects them from Exodus-like plagues and enables them to withstand trials (Rev. 7.2-3). Ezek. 9, which conforms to the shape of the Exodus story (e.g. an angel's marking those who 'sigh and groan' and abstain from abominations, v. 4; other angels' 'smiting' and 'killing' those without the mark, vv. 5-6) most likely lies behind this passage.[12] John's allusions to these Exodus/New Exodus elements not only underscore the similarities between the circumstances of his readers and those of God's people in the past, but also assure the recipients that YHWH will also surely hear their groanings and see their afflictions (Exod. 2.24-25; 3.7-9).

Redemption/Judgment

Redemption/salvation and judgment are two of Revelation's leitmotifs; they reverberate throughout every chapter of John's vision. As John treats these themes, he weaves Exodus and New Exodus typology into the Apocalypse. In particular, he depicts Jesus as a slain

---

[11] Keener discusses groaning and the pains of childbirth in connection with the Exodus. Keener, *Revelation*, p. 218 n. 5; cf. Keener, *Romans*, locs. 3826-29.

[12] Beale, *The Book of Revelation*, p. 409. Torleif Elgvin interprets this sealing in light of priests' being sealed with the name of God in the ancient Near East (cf. Exod. 28.36; Deut. 6.8 and the 'priestly prerogative of every Israelite male in the time of the exile'). Torleif Elgvin, 'Priests on Earth as in Heaven: Jewish Light on the Book of Revelation', in Florentino García Martínez (ed.), *Echoes from the Caves: Qumran and the New Testament* (STDJ 85; Leiden: Brill, 2009), p. 263.

Passover Lamb, conveys parallels in narrative plots, touches on New Exodus shepherding and provision, and warns of plagues and judgments on God's enemies.

The Passover Lamb

First, the Lamb is a prominent figure in the book of Revelation (with around 30 references) in connection with salvation, redemption, and deliverance. As in John's Gospel, the Passover sacrifice provides the primary context for this typology.[13] Two parallel statements about the Lamb particularly point to the underlying Exodus context: John asserts that the Lamb has purchased men for God with his blood (Rev. 5.9; cf. Exod. 15.16) and made them 'a kingdom and priests ... to reign upon the earth' (Rev. 5.10; cf. Exod. 19.5-6) and that Jesus has 'released us from our sins by his blood' and 'made us to be a kingdom and priests' (Rev. 1.5-6). In both passages, the Lamb's death leads to the redemption/deliverance of God's people and enables them to fulfill Israel's priestly vocation. These confirm that John has the Passover lamb in mind.[14] The Lamb's appearance, 'as if having been slaughtered' (ὡς ἐσφαγμένον), could recollect both the slaughtered Passover sacrifice of Exod. 12.6 (σφάξουσιν, 'you shall slaughter', LXX) as well as the Servant-lamb of Isa. 53.7 who was led 'to the slaughter' (ἐπὶ σφαγὴν, LXX).[15]

---

[13] Haugen, 'Consummation of the Exodus', pp. 70-72; Mounce, *Revelation*, p. 132. Keener focuses on the Passover, but mentions general sacrifice. Keener, *Revelation*, p. 187.

[14] Ha Young Son, 'The Background of Exodus 15 in Revelation 15: Focusing on the Song of Moses and the Song of the Lamb' (PhD dissertation, New Orleans Baptist Theological Seminary, 2015), p. 144. In 14.3-4, John again speaks of those who were 'purchased' (14.3, 4) from among men, here as 'first fruits', which Jay Casey argues reflects the Exodus association of the firstborn and first fruits (e.g. Exod. 22.29) and Israel's status as God's firstborn son (Exod. 4.22; 13.15). Casey, 'Exodus Typology in the Book of Revelation', p. 152.

[15] Especially in light of John's heavy intertextual use of Isaiah, the Suffering Servant could provide a secondary background for the Lamb imagery. The honor and strength ascribed to the Lamb in Rev. 5.12-13 parallel the great inheritance and exaltation of the Servant in Isa. 53.12. Moreover, the Servant's work was connected to the people's special status as God's people and their consecration as priests ('sprinkling' in 52.15; their reinstatement as priests in 61.6; 66.21; cf. 1 Pet. 2.9-10). Finally, the Servant typifies the ironic strategy of overcoming through sacrificial submission that the Lamb embodies in Revelation.

Additional Exodus Parallels

In addition to the prominence of the Lamb in John's portrayal of ultimate redemption, other salvation-centered narrative plots and elements evoke the Exodus. The designation ὁ ὢν καὶ ὁ ἦν καὶ ὁ ἐρχόμενος ('the one who is and who was and who is to come', Rev. 1.4, 8; 4.8) recalls God's revelation of his identity ('YHWH' and 'I am who I am') to Moses when God proclaimed his intention to deliver his people (Exod. 3.13-17; cf. Isa. 41.4; 'I am' statements in John's Gospel).[16] Just as the Israelites were spared from the plagues in Egypt (Exod. 8.22; 9.26; 12.13), those who bear God's seal on their foreheads (and who, by implication, do not worship the beast or his image, Rev. 20.4) are protected from the plagues of God's wrath (Rev. 7.3-8; 9.4). The conflict between the woman clothed with the sun and the great red dragon in Revelation 12 is a microcosmic reenactment of the Exodus story: the woman seems to represent the faithful community, and the dragon is the antitype of Pharaoh.[17] Just as Pharaoh (and later Herod) attempted to slay the male offspring of Israel, the dragon seeks to devour the son who is to rule the nations (Rev. 12.4-5; cf. Exod. 1.16) and make war against the rest of the woman's children (Rev. 12.13, 17). The woman flees to the wilderness, where she encounters divine protection and provision (Rev. 12.6; cf. Exod. 16.14-31), including the wings of a great eagle (Rev. 12.14; cf. Exod. 19.4). The woman is saved as the earth swallows up the river from the dragon's mouth (Rev. 12.16; cf. 'the earth swallowed them [the Egyptians]', Exod. 15.12).[18] Just as Pharaoh and his armies drowned in the Red Sea, the dragon and his armies are eventually thrown into the lake of fire (Rev. 20.10).[19]

---

[16] Keener, *Revelation*, p. 69; Mounce, *Revelation*, pp. 45-46.

[17] Beale notes the OT precedent of the sun, moon, and stars in Gen. 37.9 as well as the punishment of the dragon in Isa. 27.1 (identified in the Targum with Egypt, Babylon, and Rome). He interprets the flight into the wilderness as 'a collective allusion primarily both to Israel's exodus from Egypt and the anticipated end-time exodus, which was to occur during Israel's latter-day restoration from captivity' (Isa. 32.15; 35.1; 40.3; 41.18; 43.19-20; 51.3; Jer. 31.2; Ezek. 34.25; Hos. 2.14-17). Beale, *The Book of Revelation*, pp. 625, 643; cf. Wold, 'Revelation's Plague Septets', p. 280.

[18] Keener, *Revelation*, p. 324. Jan Dochhorn ties this to Num. 16.30-33, where the earth swallowed those who participated in Korah's rebellion. Jan Dochhorn, 'Und die Erde tat ihren Mund auf: Ein Exodusmotiv in Apc 12,16', *Zeitschrift für die Neutestamentliche Wissenschaft und die Kunde der älteren Kirche* 88.1-2 (1997), pp. 140-42.

[19] Mathewson argues that 'the sea was no more' (Rev. 21.1) is a further development of the New Exodus motif in Revelation. He contends that the sea exemplifies the affliction, trouble, and powers of evil that threatened God's people. Here, it is 'judged in a new creative act at the climax of God's prophetic revelation'

Moreover, the redeemed sing a song (15.1-4) by the sea of glass that celebrates God's leading his people out of bondage, protecting them from the plagues, and triumphing over his enemies with 'great and marvelous works' (cf. the songs of 5.9-10; 14.3).[20] This is called 'the song of Moses, the bond-servant of God, and the song of the Lamb' (15.3).[21] John's description reinforces the continuity of God's work at the Exodus and in this consummate act of redemption.[22] While the content of the song may incorporate elements from Deut. 31.30–32.43 (as well as Amos 4.13; Ps. 111.3; Jer. 10.7), its primary background reference is Exod. 15.1-18.[23] In addition to echoing themes from Exodus 15 about the glory of God's name and his awesome wonders, the context fulfills the concluding refrain of Moses' song: 'You will bring them and plant them in the mountain of Your inheritance, the place, O YHWH, which You have made for your dwelling, the sanctuary, O Lord, which Your hands have established. YHWH will reign forever and ever' (Exod. 15.17-18).[24] In tandem with this backdrop, Rev. 15.3-4 could portray the realization of New Exodus songs of praise, such as Isa. 12.1-6 ('Give thanks to YHWH; call on his name; make known his excellent deeds among the peoples', 12.4; on the heels of an eschatological vision in ch. 11) and Isa. 42.10 (in the panorama of Isa. 42–43).[25]

---

to demonstrate God's sovereignty and the surety of his people's inheritance. D. Mathewson, 'New Exodus as a Background for "The Sea Was No More" in Revelation 21:1c', *Trinity Journal* 24.2 (2003), pp. 243-58 (257-58).

[20] Some commentators believe that these three passages refer to the same song. Beale and Campbell, *Revelation: A Shorter Commentary*, p. 318. The reference to 'glass' may also have its roots in Jewish tradition, which taught that the Red Sea congealed/crystallized as glass. Beale, *The Book of Revelation*, p. 792.

[21] Beale correctly indicates that the καί ('and') in 15.3 is epexegetical, referring to only one song. Beale, *The Book of Revelation*, p. 792.

[22] Mekilta R. Ishmael 15.1-2 interestingly finds future significance in Moses' declaration, 'I will sing', even using it as proof of the resurrection. Some strands of Jewish tradition expected that Moses would one day sing anew the hymn that he sang with his people on the banks of the Red Sea. cf. Lundberg, *Typologie Baptismale*, p. 140.

[23] Richard Bauckham, *Climax of Prophecy: Studies on the Book of Revelation* (Edinburgh: T. & T. Clark, 2000), p. 299. For a chart detailing thematic parallels, see Son, 'The Background of Exodus 15 in Revelation 15', pp. 56-57.

[24] Just as the song is preceded by Exodus parallels, it is followed by additional Exodus themes (e.g. the erection of the Tabernacle of the Testimony, 15.5; cf. Exodus 40; and the smoke of YHWH's glory filling the temple, 15.8; cf. Exodus 40).

[25] Peter Jung-chu Wu provides a chart comparing common features of Isaiah 40–66 and Exod. 15.1-18 as well as an analysis of 'new song' background of the songs in Revelation. Peter Jung-Chu Wu, 'Worthy Is the Lamb: The New Song in Revelation

New Exodus Shepherding and Provision

Revelation exhibits substantial intertextuality not only with the original Exodus, but also with its recapitulation and development in the prophets. Although the allusions are too numerous to treat individually, two representative components reflect John's portrait of the culmination of the New Exodus metanarrative: the reign of the Branch of David and the prominence of Tabernacles imagery. First, the OT prophets foretold the coming of a descendant of David who would bring salvation, reign in righteousness, shepherd his people, and establish YHWH's presence among them forever.[26] John interacts with these texts throughout Revelation, appropriating both titles and roles to affirm that Jesus is this messianic Shepherd-King. John calls Jesus the 'key of David' who opens and closes doors with ultimate authority, the 'shepherd', the 'root of David', and the 'root and descendant of David and bright morning star' (Rev. 3.7; 5.5; 7.17; 22.16).[27] These echo texts like Isa. 9.1-7 (about the everlasting dominion and righteous reign of the one who will sit on David's throne); Isa. 11.1-5 ('Then a shoot will spring from the stem of Jesse, and a branch from his roots will bear fruit'); Isa. 16.5 ('A throne will be established in lovingkindness, and a judge will sit on it in faithfulness in the tent of David'); Isa. 22.22 ('Then I will set the key of the house of David on his shoulder, when he opens no one will shut, when he shuts no one will open'); Isa. 40.11 ('like a shepherd he will tend his flock'); Jer. 23.5 ('I will raise up for David a righteous Branch; and he will reign as king and act wisely and do justice and righteousness in the land'); Mic. 5.4 ('and he will arise and shepherd his flock in the strength and majesty of YHWH'); and Ezek. 37.24 ('My servant David will be king over them, and they will have one shepherd').[28] The picture of the Lamb's wiping every tear from his people's eyes (7.17) is drawn from an eschatological vision in Isa. 25.8, which depicts a time when

---

5:9–10 in Relation to Its Background' (PhD dissertation, Westminster Theological Seminary, 2005), pp. 52-122; chart pp. 119-20.

[26] John's references to Jesus as one who is 'faithful and true' (Rev. 3.14; 19.11) and to God's 'true and righteous' judgments and acts (15.3-4; 16.5, 7; 19.2) echo a key theme of New Exodus texts (cf. Isa. 9.7; 16.5; Jer. 10.7; 23.5-8).

[27] Numbers 22.16 could lie behind the reference to the 'star'.

[28] Cf. Hos. 3.5; Zech. 3.8; 6.12-13.

YHWH will defeat death, remove his people's reproach, and provide them with long-awaited salvation.

Second, several New Exodus texts anticipate a day when the nations will stream to Zion to worship YHWH with the remnant of Israel (Isa. 60.6-9; 66.18-23; Zech. 14.16-19; cf. Ps. 86.9-10). This is often combined with imagery from the Feast of Tabernacles: God's dwelling with his people, covering them with shade, and providing them with water and light, as in the Exodus.[29] In the New Exodus, YHWH had promised that he would dwell among his people and be their God (Jer. 24.7; 31.33; Ezek. 43.7, 9; Zech. 8.8). The remnant would 'not hunger or thirst, nor will the scorching heat or sun strike them down; for he who has compassion on them will lead them and will guide them to springs of water' (Isa. 49.10). Moreover, YHWH would cover Jerusalem with a cloud by day and fire by night (cf. Exod. 13.21-22) and be to them shade (literally, a 'booth', סכה, cf. Lev. 23.42-43) from the heat (Isa. 4.5-6). As the Jewish people remembered God's provision at the Exodus, especially as they celebrated the Feast of Tabernacles, they looked forward to a time when they would draw water from the well/springs [πηγῶν] of salvation (Isa. 12.3, likely read with Zech. 14.8-9)[30] and see the light of YHWH (Isa. 60.19; cf. Zech. 14.7; Jn 8.12; 9.5; 11.9). Revelation shows the consummation of these hopes. In ch. 7, a great multitude from every tribe and tongue and people and nation join in worship (cf. Rev. 5.9). They hold palm branches (7.9), which allude to the Feast of Tabernacles.[31] The one who sits on the throne 'spreads his tabernacle over' those before his throne (Rev. 7.15). They will never hunger or thirst or have the sun beat down on them (7.16), and the Lamb himself guides them to the springs of living water (ζωῆς πηγὰς ὑδάτων, cf. Jn 4.1-14; Jn 7.37-38). Likewise, in the new creation, God finally dwells among his people (Rev. 21.3); God and the Lamb obviate the need for the tabernacle (Rev. 21.22). They illuminate the city with their glory (Rev. 21.22-27; 22.5; cf. Isa. 24.23; 60.19), and the nations walk by its light (cf. Isa. 60.3, 5; 49.23). A river of the water of life 'flows from the throne of God

---

[29] See Chapter 3, section on the Gospel of John.

[30] Keener, *Gospel of John*, I, p. 1725 n. 215.

[31] Jonathan A. Draper, 'The Heavenly Feast of Tabernacles: Revelation 7:1-17', *JSNT* 19 (October 1983), pp. 133-47 (137); Beale and Campbell, *Revelation: A Shorter Commentary*, p. 156. Others see this as a general victory celebration, but the overall context of the chapter fits better with Tabernacles. See Mounce, *Revelation*, p. 162; Keener, *Revelation*, p. 243.

and of the Lamb' (Rev. 22.1; cf. Ezek. 47.1; Zech. 14.8), and Jesus offers to 'give to the one who thirsts from the spring of the water of life without cost' (Rev. 21.6; cf. Isa. 55.1).

Judgment

The patterns and descriptions of various judgments in Revelation also correspond to God's judgments at the time of the Exodus and in later prophetic warnings. [32] First, the Exodus plagues (Exodus 7–14) especially shape the trumpet and bowl septets (Revelation 8–10; 16). [33] The first trumpet is reminiscent of the plague of hail and fire in Exod. 9.24. The second trumpet and possibly the third recall Egypt's water turned to blood and made undrinkable (Exod. 7.18-19). The bitter waters of Wormwood represent 'the reverse of the miracle of Marah', when bitter waters were made sweet (Exod. 15.25; cf. Jer. 9.15). [34] The fourth trumpet parallels the penultimate plague of darkness in Exod. 10.21, which likely depicted judgment against the highly-revered sun god of Egypt. [35] The locusts of the fifth trumpet recall the plague of locusts in Exod. 10.12. [36] The bowl judgments of Revelation 16, which may reiterate the trumpet judgments, also resemble the plagues of Egypt (the sea's being turned to blood, 16.3-4; frogs, 16.13; boils/sores, 16.2, 11; hail, 16.21; and darkness, 16.10). [37] In the sixth bowl judgment, the River Euphrates is ironically dried up as the Red Sea was, to prepare the way not for God's people, but for agents of destruction (16.12). [38] Just as in Egypt, the plagues punish hardness of

---

[32] For an extended discussion on the reception of Exodus plague traditions in Jewish literature, see David E. Aune, *Revelation 6–16* (WBC 52B; Nashville: Thomas Nelson, 1998), pp. 498-517; L. Gallus, 'The Exodus Motif in Revelation 15–16: Its Background and Nature', *AUSS* 46.1 (2008), pp. 21-43 (35-42).

[33] Wold notes how later biblical and early Jewish literature shortened the ten Exodus plagues to seven (Pss. 78.44-51; 105.28-36; Artap. 3.27-33; Wis. 11–18). Wold, 'Revelation's Plague Septets', p. 280; cf. Aune, *Revelation 6–16*, p. 502. He and others, such as Beale, also see Leviticus 26 in the background here. HaYoung Son offers a more comprehensive comparison of the plagues of Egypt and of Revelation. Son, 'The Background of Exodus 15 in Revelation 15', pp. 117-41.

[34] Mounce, *Revelation*, p. 181.

[35] Keener, *Revelation*, p. 258.

[36] For further discussion, see Iersel, Weiler, and Lefébure, *Exodus–A Lasting Paradigm*, pp. 36-37; Hans-Peter Müller, 'Die Plagen der Apokalypse: Eine formgeschichtliche Untersuchung', *Zeitschrift für die Neutestamentliche Wissenschaft und die Kunde der älteren Kirche* 51.3-4 (1960), pp. 268-78; Casey, 'Exodus Typology in the Book of Revelation', p. 160. Casey examines the influence of other Jewish writings.

[37] Keener, *Revelation*, pp. 392-93; Beale and Campbell, *Revelation: A Shorter Commentary*, pp. 325-27; Bauckham, *Climax of Prophecy*, p. 204.

[38] Casey, 'Exodus Typology in the Book of Revelation', p. 168.

heart, idolatry, and persecution against God's people (who are spared from their effects, cf. Exod. 8.22; 9.4; 10.23).[39] The recipients of these judgments, like Pharaoh, blaspheme God and refuse to repent (Rev. 16.9, 11, 21).[40]

Second, the accounts of the fall of 'Babylon' (Revelation 16–18)[41] and the final victory of God over his enemies are saturated with allusions to passages of prophetic New Exodus judgment.[42] These texts were themselves often patterned on God's mighty judgments in Egypt, which Leviticus 26 and Deuteronomy 32 had established as a paradigm.[43] The fall of Babylon in particular echoes texts like Isa. 13.19-22 (that speaks of Babylon's judgment and desolation); Isa. 21.9 (a vision from the wilderness of Babylon's destruction, cf. Rev. 17.3; 14.8; 18.2); Isa. 34.13-15 (vengeance, brimstone, evil creatures, smoke going up forever, cf. Rev. 19.3); Jeremiah 50–51 (dried up waters, desolation and destruction, trumpets, inhabitation by desert creatures, and final overthrow); Ezekiel 23 (ironically, the fate of Jerusalem at the hand of Babylon, cf. Rev. 17.16); and parts of Daniel.[44] As Babylon and God's enemies drink the cup of divine wrath (Rev. 14.9-10; 16.19; cf. Isa. 51.17; 63.2-6; Jer. 25.15-27), God once again calls his people to 'come out', to be separate from Babylon's sins and be spared her judgments (Rev. 17.4; cf. Jer. 51.6, 'Flee from the midst of Babylon ... do not be destroyed in her punishment'). John also shows how Jesus, the Son of God and righteous Branch of David, enacts swift judgment on the nations (Isa. 11.4; Jer. 23.12), ruling them 'with a rod of iron' (Ps. 2.9; Rev. 2.27; 12.5; 19.15), shattering the wicked like pottery (Isa. 30.14), and treading the winepress of God's wrath

---

[39] Beale and Campbell, *Revelation: A Shorter Commentary*, p. 171.

[40] Watts adds that judgment scenes in Revelation recall the theophany on Mt. Sinai (8.5; 11.19; 16.18-21). Watts, 'Exodus', p. 487.

[41] In Revelation, 'Babylon' represents Rome. Keener, *Revelation*, p. 406. However, as Mounce observes, Babylon the Great is more than first-century Rome: 'every great center of power that has prostituted its wealth and influence restores to life the spirit of ancient Babylon'. Mounce, *Revelation*, p. 321.

[42] Just as with New Exodus promises, many of these judgments were inaugurally fulfilled at an earlier point in history. However, the passages themselves contain eschatological overtones.

[43] Gallus contends that the plagues function as covenant curses (cf. boils for idolatry in Deut. 28.27, 35). Gallus, 'The Exodus Motif in Revelation 15–16: Its Background and Nature', p. 35.

[44] Watts, 'Exodus', p. 487; Mounce, *Revelation*, p. 320; Beale and Campbell, *Revelation: A Shorter Commentary*, pp. 355-83.

(Rev. 19.15; cf. Ps. 2.12).[45] God's triumph is preceded and followed by praise for his 'marvelous works' and 'righteous acts' (Rev. 15.1-4; 19.1-6; cf. Exodus 15), overthrowing those who rise up against him (Exod. 15.7) and avenging the blood of his servants (Deut. 32.43; Rev. 19.2).

Election/Sonship

Revelation, from beginning to end, applies terminology from the election and special calling of Israel to the whole people of God.[46] First, the opening verses proclaim that God has made believers 'a kingdom' and 'priests' (1.6; 5.10; 20.6, cf. Exod. 19.5-6; Isa. 61.6; 1 Pet. 2.9-10). These dual ideas of reigning with Christ and offering cultic service pervade the Apocalypse. Those who overcome as Jesus did share in his authority to rule the nations (Rev. 2.26-27), sit with him on his throne (3.21), and reign upon the earth (5.10; 20.6; 22.5).[47] Furthermore, words from several families connote the idea of *serving* God, both as his bondservants (1.1; 2.19) and especially in cultic worship (λατρεύω, to offer religious service, 7.15; 22.3).[48] Other details could also indicate that John is depicting believers as priests (e.g. receiving the Lord's seal on believers' foreheads, Rev. 7.3; cf. Exod. 28.36-38; Zech. 14.20; the pervasive theme of purification; white robes of 'fine linen', which could point to priestly clothing, Rev. 3.4-5; 6.9-11; 7.9-15; 19.6-8; 22.14; cf. Exod. 28.5; temple symbolism; prayers of the saints offered as incense, Rev. 5.8; 8.3-4; cf. Ps. 141.2; and being called 'first fruits' in 14.4; cf. Num. 3.11-13; 8.14-18).[49] Jesus the

---

[45] Many OT prophetic texts to which John alludes speak of the 'Day of YHWH' that will bring destruction on God's enemies (e.g. Isa. 13.6; Jer. 46.10; Ezek. 30.3; Joel 1–2; Amos 5.17-20; Obad. 1.15-17; Zeph. 1.7-18; Mal. 4.5).

[46] Beale and Campbell, *Revelation: A Shorter Commentary*, pp. 39-40. Note also the universalization of promises and prophecies related to Israel that are applied to the whole believing community and the nations. Beale, *The Book of Revelation*, pp. 91, 94.

[47] Cf. the discussion of the concepts of corporate solidarity and Christ's proleptic fulfillment of humanity's vocation in chapters on Paul's Epistles and Hebrews and the General Epistles.

[48] Louw and Nida, *Greek-English Lexicon*. Serving God day and night is what the priests and Levites did in the temple courts (1 Chron. 9.33; Ps. 134.1; cf. Acts 7.7; Heb. 9.1). Keener, *Revelation*, p. 245.

[49] Elgvin, 'Priests on Earth', pp. 261-75. Elgvin notes, for example, that priests in the ancient Near East were sealed with the name of God on their forehead and that white robes connoted acceptance for priestly service in Second-Temple Judaism (cf. *m. Mid.* 5.5). Beale adds that those who come out of the tribulation function as priests,

Firstborn (1.5) enables believers to serve (like Adam and later Israel) in their intended capacity as rulers over creation and holy priests to God.[50]

Second, John uses various other descriptions that are rooted in Israel's history. He describes the saints as those whom Jesus has purchased with his blood to be his own possession (Rev. 5.9; Exod. 15.16; Ps. 74.2). John also terms believers λαός μου[51] ('my people', Rev. 18.4; cf. Exod. 3.7; Isa. 40.1; 51.16; Jer. 11.4; Hos. 2.23) and κλητοὶ καὶ ἐκλεκτοὶ ('called and chosen', Rev. 17.14; cf. Deut. 28.10; Isa. 41.8-9; 1 Pet. 1.2). He asserts that the believing community constitutes the ἐκκλησία (Rev. 1.4; 22.16; cf. Chapter 3 n. 152), the true Israel, whom he contrasts with the συναγωγὴ τοῦ σατανᾶ ('synagogue of Satan') in 2.9 and 3.9 – those who call themselves Jews, but they are not.[52]

Finally, the Father-Son language that originated at the Exodus emerges in the conceptualization of the renewed creation in 21.7, embedded in a cluster of Exodus allusions: 'I will be his God, and he will be My son' (Exod. 4.22; 2 Sam. 7.14; cf. Rev. 21.3, 'Behold, the tabernacle of God is among men, and He will dwell among them, and they shall be His people, and God Himself will be among them').[53] The words of Prov. 3.12, which speak of YHWH's disciplining those he loves and receives as sons, are found on the lips

---

having their robes sprinkled with the blood of the Lamb (cf. Lev. 8.30; Exod. 19.10). Beale, *The Book of Revelation*, p. 439.

[50] Beale, *New Testament Biblical Theology*, loc. 1108.

[51] As Haugen comments, following Strathmann's research, the usage of this term in the LXX is carefully restricted to Israel as the chosen people of God. Haugen, 'Consummation of the Exodus', p. 85.

[52] Many scholars also believe that the 144,000 (Rev. 7.4-8) refers to the Church, although this raises the question why John would subsequently indicate the presence of a multitude from every nation (7.9). See Casey, 'Exodus Typology in the Book of Revelation', p. 177. Casey comments that the figure stresses the eschatological completeness of the group. In particular, John's characterization of this group as those who are sealed and who follow the Lamb express how 'John has completely christianized the originally Jewish list of the tribes of Israel in the eschaton, to transform it into a picture of the whole Church'. Cf. Mounce, *Revelation*, p. 158; Keener, *Revelation*, p. 231; Beale and Campbell, *Revelation: A Shorter Commentary*, p. 146.

[53] Casey argues for a dependence on Lev. 26.12 (LXX) here in addition to 2 Sam. 7.14, observing that not only the Davidic promises are in view, but those of the Exodus (cf. coalescence of these traditions in 5.5, 9, 12). Casey, 'Exodus Typology in the Book of Revelation', p. 202.

of Jesus as he exhorts the church in Laodicea to be zealous and repent (Rev. 3.19; cf. Heb. 12.6).

As John appropriates Exodus-based motifs and titles in relation to the saints, he intimates that the church is the true Israel, 'the eschatological people of God, the people of the new Exodus'.[54]

Journey

Finally, several inter-related elements in Revelation are analogous to Israel's journey in the wilderness and the inheritance toward which they were called. The themes of sojourning, remaining faithful through temptation, engaging in holy war, dwelling in the city of God/inheritance, and resting particularly draw on the Exodus tradition.[55] First, John underscores the pilgrim status of God's people, who seek the city to come and live by counter-cultural standards, by contrasting them throughout Revelation with 'those who dwell on the earth' (Rev. 3.10; 6.10; 8.13; 11.10; 12.12; 13.9-14; 17.2, 8; cf. Heb. 11.10, 16; 13.14). This terminology is used exclusively of idol-worshipers and indicates their orientation and allegiance: they are at home in the world and find their security in earthly sources.[56] Second, exhortations to remain faithful and persevere in trials and afflictions address specific churches, individuals, and the believing community as a whole (Rev. 1.9; 2.2-3, 10, 19; 3.10; 13.10; 14.12). Revelation 3.10 uses the word πειρασμός ('trial/temptation'), which has strong connections with the Exodus tradition.[57] Just as the people of Israel struggled in the desert to remain loyal to YHWH in the face of temptation and idol-worship and continually had to choose whom they would serve (Josh. 24.15), the saints in the last days undergo trials and persecution and must decide whether to worship the beast

---

[54] Bauckham, *Climax of Prophecy*, p. 327; cf. Dumbrell, *The End of the Beginning*, p. 159.

[55] Other concepts, such as receiving divine provision and nurture (including 'hidden manna' and living water, Rev. 2.17; 7.17), being sheltered from the heat and walking by the light of God's presence (7.16-17; 21.23-24), and beholding the glory of God's presence (as in the temple, along with Sinai-like theophany descriptions like thunder and earthquakes, 21.22; 22.4; 8.5; 11.19) also evoke Israel's journey in the wilderness. Most of these are treated elsewhere in this chapter.

[56] Beale, *The Book of Revelation*, pp. 402-404.

[57] See 'lead us not into temptation' in Chapter 3.

and indulge in idolatrous practices or live as God's holy people.[58] Third, the theme of holy war – of which YHWH's sovereign victory over Pharaoh and the other gods of Egypt provides the fundamental paradigm – pervades the Apocalypse.[59] On the one hand, this ties into the divine warrior motif, as God and the Lamb conquer their enemies and avenge the blood of the saints (Rev. 5.5; 6.10; 11.13-19; 12.7-9; 17.14; 18; 19.11-16; other judgments; cf. Exod. 14.13-14; 15.1-16; 33.2; Josh. 3.10; 24.11-13). On the other hand, like Israel, the saints participate in this 'overcoming' (νικάω, which connotes military conquest) in order to inherit the divine promises (Rev. 2.7, 11, 17, 26; 3.5, 12, 21; 15.2; 21.7; cf. Num. 13.30; Deut. 20.10-20; 1 Jn 2.13-14; 4.4; 5.4) and receive authority to rule over pagan nations (Rev. 2.27).[60] Fourth, some aspects of the inheritance of the saints are grounded in Exodus and New Exodus texts. Themes introduced in other biblical contexts, such as promised land and new creation, became woven together with Exodus/New Exodus, journeyed through the prophets, and reach their climax in the Apocalypse.[61] As Revelation draws to a close, John beholds a 'new heaven and a new earth' (Rev. 21.1; cf. Isa. 65.17) – a place of restoration, healing, life, and joy (Isa. 35.10; 51.11; 65.19; Ezek. 47; cf. Gen. 3.22-24). God offers living water without cost to those who thirst (Rev. 21.6) and dwells among

---

[58] For a discussion on allegiance as a component of John's Exodus typology, see Barbara Ann Isbell, 'The Past Is yet to Come: Exodus Typology in the Apocalypse' (PhD dissertation, Southwestern Baptist Theological Seminary, 2013), pp. 210-27.

[59] Haugen provides an overview of holy war in Revelation against the background of the Exodus. He notes scholars such as Millard Lind and James Plastaras who root this motif in the Exodus rather than the conquest. Haugen, 'Consummation of the Exodus', p. 31. He concludes that 'more extensively than anywhere else in the New Testament, the conflict of the ages is described with war terminology reminiscent of the foundational holy war fought at the Red Sea and of the experience of the OT people of Israel in their wilderness wanderings' (p. 40). Cf. 'The Apocalypse as a Christian War Scroll', in Bauckham, *Climax of Prophecy*, pp. 210-37; 'The Warrior-Messiah' in Mounce, *Revelation*, pp. 350-51.

[60] Beale comments that the promises to those who overcome, while phrased differently, are all versions of the final promise in 21.7: 'He who overcomes shall inherit these things'. Beale and Campbell, *Revelation: A Shorter Commentary*, p. 58.

[61] Casey argues that 'the presentation of the theme of inheritance by the vehicle of Exodus typology is one of the most intricate and extensive motifs in the book of Revelation'. Casey, 'Exodus Typology in the Book of Revelation', p. 171; cf. Gallus, 'The Exodus Motif in Revelation 15–16: Its Background and Nature', p. 26.

his people (Rev. 21.7) in fulfillment of the *telos* (ultimate end) of the Exodus. John also sees 'the holy city, the New Jerusalem' (which combines people, place, and divine presence) 'coming down out of heaven from God' (Rev. 21.2; cf. Isa. 52.1).[62] Those who overcome 'inherit these things' (21.7) and receive a portion in the tree of life and in the holy city (Rev. 22.19; contrast with 21.8). Finally, with the removal of the curse (22.3; cf. Zech. 14.11), the realization of perfect fellowship with God, and entry into the heavenly promised land, God's people are no longer 'aliens and strangers', exiles, or wanderers. They are refreshed (ἀναπαύσονται) from their heavy labors and fully enter into God's rest (Rev. 6.11; 14.12-14; cf. Heb. 4.9-11; contrast 14.11, which says the wicked 'will not rest day or night').

Conclusion

Throughout Revelation, John braids together key Exodus and New Exodus components to represent the eschaton as 'a reinstatement of God's initial purposes and ideals for his creation' and 'the culmination of salvation history'.[63] John forges a link among past, present, and future as key themes such as exile, faithfulness in temptation, judgment on God's enemies, redemption by the blood of a Lamb, and the inclusion of the nations in the true Israel come to fruition via his typological hermeneutic. The reign and shepherding role of the royal Davidic Branch, celebration of the eschatological Feast of Tabernacles, destruction of 'Babylon', and unveiling of a new heaven and new earth indicate that the New Exodus expectations of the prophets have been fulfilled. Most prominently, the purposes of the Exodus are fully realized as God's sons experience ultimate rest, dwell in his presence and see his face, serve him as a kingdom of priests, and inherit what he has promised to the faithful. Revelation brackets the biblical witness with the fusion of a restored Eden and the aspirations of the Exodus, as a loud voice from the throne calls out, 'Behold, the tabernacle of God is among men, and He will dwell among them, and

---

[62] Dumbrell, *The End of the Beginning*, p. 31; Mounce, *Revelation*, p. 382; Beale and Campbell, *Revelation: A Shorter Commentary*, p. 464.
[63] Isbell, 'The Past Is yet to Come', p. 245.

they shall be His people, and God Himself will be among them' (Rev. 21.3; Gen. 1–2; Exod. 6.6-8).

CONCLUSION

Summary

This book has addressed the question, *How do the biblical texts individually and corporately appropriate Exodus/New Exodus components in literary and typological ways to communicate truth about God's redemptive plan for his creation through Christ?*

From early in the Pentateuch, the Exodus emerged as a forward-looking, paradigmatic event. It came to typify YHWH's salvation and judgment, not only on Israel's behalf, but against Israel when she was unfaithful to the covenant. The prophets nurtured the hope of New Exodus activity, first in various stages of return from exile and later, on an eschatological horizon. The motif became intertwined with expectations of the coming prophet like Moses and kingly Branch of David, the inauguration of a new covenant, the rebuilding of a temple filled with YHWH's glory, and even the inclusion of the Gentiles in the people of God.

In the process of analyzing conceptual and verbal indicators of Exodus/New Exodus allusions, parallels in storylines, and typological hermeneutical elements in NT books, it became evident that authors of every genre employed the motif pervasively, deliberately, and distinctively. The Gospels and Acts bridged Israel's past experiences and hopes with the advent of Jesus, whom they present as the long-awaited prophet like Moses and Davidic Messiah. The Gospel-writers highlight how the shape of the story of Jesus' life recapitulates Israel's history in a faithful way. As God's Firstborn Son, he is the true Israel, and those who believe in him constitute the people of God. This particularly ties into Jesus' role as the Isaianic Servant of YHWH, who bears undeserved punishment on his people's behalf and fulfills Israel's missional vocation. In addition, Mark and other authors indicate that

Jesus' coming represents the promised coming of YHWH to Zion, heralding deliverance and portending judgment (Isaiah 40). Jesus leads his people in the wilderness like a shepherd and supplies miraculous bread, living water, light, and rest. His presence is the embodiment of YHWH's glory tabernacling among his people, and what was available through the temple cult is now found in him. As John emphasizes, elements from Israel's Exodus journey and associated feasts pointed ahead to the true realities that Jesus would embody. His death as the Passover Lamb establishes the new covenant, effects eschatological redemption and forgiveness, and leads to the promised outpouring of the Holy Spirit.

In the Epistles and Revelation, we utilized the rubric of slavery/exile, redemption/judgment, election/sonship, and journey to outline the most prominent components of the Exodus motif. Exodus/New Exodus language and imagery comprise an integral part of Paul's symbolic matrix, contributing resonance, intensity, and continuity to his arguments. Paul vividly depicts humanity in bondage to sin, groaning for deliverance. Jesus came, Paul asserts, as both deliverer and sacrifice, to redeem God's people and rescue them from God's wrath. Those who participate by faith in the death and resurrection of Jesus become heirs of Abraham's promise and compose the true Israel. God adopts them as his sons and daughters and sets them apart as a people for his own possession. By the Holy Spirit, God dwells among them, forming them into a holy temple in Christ. They are led by the Spirit, nourished on Christ, and sealed for their future inheritance. Paul also brings into focus how Jesus, as the Servant of YHWH, brings liberation and light to those in darkness, sprinkles many clean, makes a covenant of forgiveness, and is himself peace to those who were far away. Finally, his writings resound with exhortations to heed the past example of Israel and persevere in obedience. Paul quotes and alludes to key Exodus/New Exodus texts (esp. from Psalms and Isaiah) to warn that those who turn away from the truth will experience the covenant curses of hardened hearts and darkened eyes.

In Hebrews, 1 Peter, and Jude, all three authors interpret Israel's example of disobedience through a typological lens, warning of judgment for those who turn away from the truth and harden their hearts. In addition, Hebrews and 1 Peter conceive of believers as Exodus sojourners, 'aliens and strangers', who have been set free and are *en route* to the promised land. Hebrews appropriates explicit

Exodus and New Moses typology to point to better realities that have become available through the work of Jesus, our High Priest. His perfect sacrifice enables believers to draw near to God in worship and experience the cleansing of their consciences. The Preacher exhorts his audience to follow in the footsteps of Jesus, the Firstborn, and accept suffering as discipline from the hand of a loving Father. As believers despise the shame of pagan society, they also join the company of the heroes of faith, who were looking ahead to eternal rest, a country of their own, and an unshakable kingdom. First Peter's application of Israel's status and priestly vocation in the world to the mixed community of believers is noteworthy. Peter calls believers a chosen people, a royal priesthood, and a holy nation for God's own possession. He reinforces this Exodus typology with his references to the blood of the Lamb and his depiction of the Church as a holy temple.

Finally, the motif reaches a climax in John's Apocalypse. It was found to exert influence on both the structure and substance of the book, especially its overarching emphases on salvation and judgment. When John portrays Jesus as the Lamb who was slain and purchased people for God with his blood, the Passover is foremost in his mind. Further contextual signals and parallels, such as the victory song by the sea and references to Israel's consecration as a kingdom of priests (Exod. 19.5-6), support this conclusion. Other narrative plots evince substantial parallels with the Exodus story, and the plague judgments of Revelation recapitulate God's judgments against Egypt. In addition, John's vision is suffused with New Exodus allusions, particularly focused on the reign of the Davidic Branch, the multi-national celebration of the Feast of Tabernacles, and the fall of Babylon. As Revelation draws to a close, the purposes of the Exodus are realized: God's sons and daughters experience rest and fellowship with him in the place he has prepared for them, serving him as his holy people and sharing in Christ's dominion over the new creation.

Implications for Biblical Theology

It is my hope that this study has made a contribution to NT biblical theology on several levels. First, exploring Exodus/New Exodus intertextual allusions, historical correspondences, and structural parallels often sheds light on the background and meaning of specific passages. This research has reinforced my conviction that NT authors appropriated OT language and imagery with purpose and care. They did not haphazardly or randomly insert quotations or phrases to bolster their arguments, running roughshod over the original meanings or contexts. Rather, they discerned an underlying theological resonance between events that bears witness to God's guiding hand in history and were conscious of the broader contexts and narratives behind their selections. The Exodus motif, along with its subsequent New Exodus components, lies at the heart of Israel's redemptive history and is woven into the fabric of Israel's Scriptures. Consequently, approaching interpretation with this framework yields a richer, more authentic theology. In addition to illuminating specific passages, this study has shown the validity and value of examining the broader hermeneutic, storyline, and major themes of NT books in relation to the constitutive elements of the Exodus motif. This results in a greater appreciation for individual authors' typological understanding, unity of focus, and distinctive theological nuances. It can also reveal the interconnectivity and harmony of seemingly discrete passages.

Finally, I believe that the motif is pervasive and fundamental enough to the NT to constitute one legitimate approach for envisaging a NT biblical theology: it encapsulates the overarching storyline of the Bible. Understanding the theological coherence among different texts and events significantly enhances what Richard Clifford has termed the 'divine rhythm' of the Bible, inaugurated in the opening verse of Genesis and maintained until the last book of Revelation.[1] The development of the motif in Scripture exhibits both the basic unity of and the dynamic interchange between the Testaments and expresses the continuity of divine action.

---

[1] Clifford, 'The Exodus in the Christian Bible', p. 360.

APPENDIX

The Exodus as a Historical Event

The Exodus constitutes one of the most controversial historical occurrences in the Bible. Sam Meier aptly appraises this dilemma when he observes, 'The biblical text preserves remarkable memories of second-millennium realities at the same time that it raises major questions on topics where archaeologists disagree with archaeologists, biblical scholars with biblical scholars, historians with historians, and Egyptologists with Egyptologists'.[1] It is far beyond the scope of this study and my expertise to evaluate the situation in detail. However, since the historicity of the Exodus engenders considerable theological implications and is directly related to my topic, it seems prudent to summarize three main stances on the matter and point the interested reader to a few resources.[2]

First, there are scholars who claim that the biblical account possesses neither tangible evidence nor remote plausibility and properly belongs to the realm of fiction. Donald Redford is one proponent of this position.[3] He and most others in this group posit

---

[1] Sam A. Meier, 'History of Israel I: Settlement Period', Bill T. Arnold and H.G.M. Williamson (eds.), *Dictionary of Old Testament Historical Books* (Downers Grove, IL: InterVarsity Press, 2005), p. 425.

[2] Most of the discussions revolve around evidence from Karnak reliefs; Papyrus Leiden 348 (mentions the construction of the pylon of Ramesses and the 'Apiru people who transport stones); the Anastasi Papyri (describe the military strongholds along the way of the Philistines and speak of passage of a group of people coming down from Edom during a drought); the Merneptal Stele (attests to the presence of a Hebrew people in Canaan prior to the 12th c. BCE); the Elephantine Stele (speaks of the pharaoh driving a people out of Egypt around the 12th c. BCE); studies of the law, covenant, ancient portable structures like the Tabernacle, and the Egyptianizing of proper names; and evidence related to early Canaanite settlements.

[3] Donald Redford remarks that dispassionate analysis of the entire event leads to the conclusion that 'it reads much better as folktale – i.e. as myth, rather than history'. Donald B. Redford, 'Observations of the Sojourn of the Bene-Israel', in Ernest S. Frerichs, Leonard H. Lesko, and William G. Dever (eds.), *Exodus: The Egyptian Evidence* (Winona Lake, IN: Eisenbrauns, 1997), p. 69. Other scholars who concur include James Weinstein, William Dever, Thomas Thompson. See Thomas L. Thompson, *The Mythic Past: Biblical Archaeology and the Myth of Israel* (London, England: Jonathan Cape Random House, 1999).

sociological reasons for the invention of the myth and explore Canaanite origins for the Israelites. Second, other scholars concede that the Exodus tradition may contain kernels or traces of historical facts. Rudolf Smend, for example, grants that there could have been a man named Moses with a Midianite wife.[4] Abraham Malamat adds the possibility of a trickling migration of a few hundred people over a long period of time.[5] Ronald Hendel likewise supposes that there was some 'collective memory' of things such as Egyptian oppression and plague as well as traditions about gods and signs and wonders.[6] Egyptologist David Rohl belongs in this category, since he does not believe that the biblical account is wholly historical. However, he accepts a fair portion of the story and puts forward a unique proposal.[7] Rohl offers a provocative redating scheme for Egyptian chronology, concluding that the Sojourn and Exodus belong to the Second Intermediate Period of Egyptian history rather than the New Kingdom (placing the Exodus in 1447 BCE). He suggests that with this new lens, there is evidence for Israel's stay in Egypt's eastern delta that includes houses, ovens, silos, vault tombs, storage cities, graves from plague victims, an Egyptian tomb of Joseph, and a departure of the population *en masse*.

Finally, scholars such as James Hoffmeier and Kenneth Kitchen argue that there is credible indirect evidence to support the biblical account and good reason to conclude that it is factual.[8] Kitchen acknowledges that the external evidence for the Exodus is disparate

---

[4] Rudolf Smend, 'Mose als geschichtliche Gestalt', *HZ* 260 (1995), pp. 1-19.

[5] Abraham Malamat, 'The Exodus: Egyptian Analogies', in Ernest S. Frerichs, Leonard H. Lesko, and William G. Dever (eds.), *Exodus: The Egyptian Evidence* (Winona Lake, IN: Eisenbrauns, 1997). See also the chapter in this volume by Israel Finkelstein.

[6] Ronald S. Hendel, 'The Exodus in Biblical Memory', *JBL* 120.4 (2001), pp. 601-22 (622). Following Egyptologist James Assman, he categorizes the Exodus tradition as 'mneumohistory', in which the historically true and the symbolically true are interwoven so that the past authorizes and encompasses the present (p. 621). Hendel is most concerned with what was symbolically important to the group and how people interpreted events in an existential way.

[7] He comments, for example, that the last plague could not have only affected the firstborns of each household. David M. Rohl, *Pharaohs and Kings: A Biblical Quest* (New York: Three Rivers Press, 1997), p. 11.

[8] See James K. Hoffmeier, *Ancient Israel in Sinai: The Evidence for the Authenticity of the Wilderness Tradition* (New York: Oxford University Press, 2011); James K. Hoffmeier, *Israel in Egypt: The Evidence for the Authenticity of the Exodus Tradition* (New York: Oxford University Press, 1996); K.A. Kitchen, 'Egyptians and Hebrews, from Ra'amses to Jericho', *The Origin of Early Israel* (Beer-Sheva, Israel: Ben-Gurion University of the Negev Press, 1998); K.A. Kitchen, *On the Reliability of the Old Testament* (Grand Rapids: Eerdmans, 2003).

and limited.[9] However, he points to several characteristics of the event that dispose it to not having been recorded or leaving any archaeological evidence, especially the kind that would satisfy inquisitive scientific minds.[10] He and Hoffmeier further examine cultural, geographical, political, and religious background materials from the ancient Near East in the second millennium BCE and determine that while the Exodus and Sinai events are not proven by this evidence, 'their correspondence not just with attested realities (not Sargon-style fantasy) but with known usage of the late second millennium BCE and earlier *does* favor acceptance of their having had a definite historical basis'.[11] I concur with Hoffmeier and Kitchen. In addition, despite the current range of views on the historicity of the Exodus, the authors of the NT give no evidence of doubt that they are referencing actual historical events (e.g. Acts 7.11-44; Heb. 3.16-19; 11.22).

---

[9] Kitchen, *Reliability*, p. 241. 'No Egyptian records specifically mention Israelites working in the East Delta, a Moses who spoke for such a group, or an exodus by a group of this name. Nowhere in Sinai has a body of Late Bronze Age people passing through left explicit traces, still less traces that are labeled as Israelite' (p. 310).

[10] For example, 'It is no use asking the pharaohs to blazon their defeat and loss of a top chariot squadron high on temple walls for all to see'; neither should we expect to find administrative registers authorizing the Hebrews to depart from Egypt, since 99 percent of New Kingdom papyri are lost irrevocably. Furthermore, who would expect to find the mud and reed hovels of slaves from thousands of years ago (when the buildings aren't even above ground level), or traces of a nomadic people in the constantly-shifting Sinai desert (p. 311)? He adds, 'If there never was an escape from Egyptian servitude by any of Israel's ancestors, why on earth invent such a tale about such humiliating origins?' (p. 245).

[11] Kitchen, *Reliability*, p. 312; Hoffmeier, *Ancient Israel in Sinai*, pp. x-xi.

BIBLIOGRAPHY

Abrams, M.H., *A Glossary of Literary Terms* (Beijing: Foreign Language Teaching and Research Press, 7th edn, 2004).

Achtemeier, Paul J., *1 Peter* (Hermeneia: A Critical and Historical Commentary on the Bible; Minneapolis: Augsburg–Fortress, 1996).

Adams, John Wesley, Quentin McGhee, and Roger Douglas Cotton, *Survey of the Old Testament* (Faith & Action; Springfield, MO: Faith & Action Team, 2010).

Albrektson, Bertil, *Studies in the Text and Theology of the Book of Lamentations with a Critical Edition of the Peshitta Text* (Studia Theologica Lundensia; Lund, Sweden: C.W.K. Gleerup, 1963).

Allegro, John M., 'Further Messianic References in Qumran Literature', *JBL* 75.3 (September 1956), pp. 174–87.

Allison, Dale, *The New Moses: A Matthean Typology* (Eugene, OR: Wipf & Stock, 2013).

An, Hannah S., 'The Prophet Like Moses (Deut. 18:15-18) and the Woman at the Well (John 4:7-30) in Light of the Dead Sea Scrolls', *ExpTim* 127.10 (July 2016), pp. 469-78.

Anderson, Bernhard W., 'Exodus Typology in Second Isaiah', in Bernhard W. Anderson and Walter Harrelson (eds.), *Israel's Prophetic Heritage; Essays in Honor of James Muilenburg* (Eugene, OR: Wipf & Stock, 2010).

Arrington, French L., 'Justification by Faith in Romans', in Terry L. Cross and Emerson B. Powery (eds.), *The Spirit and the Mind: Essays in Informed Pentecostalism* (Lanham, MD: University Press of America, 2000).

Ashley, Timothy R., *The Book of Numbers* (NICOT; Grand Rapids: Eerdmans, 1993).

Aune, David E., *Revelation 6–16* (WBC 52B; Nashville: Thomas Nelson, 1998).

Baker, David L., 'Typology and the Christian Use of the Old Testament', *SJT* 29.2 (1976), pp. 137-57.

Balentine, George L., 'Death of Jesus as a New Exodus', *RevExp* 59.1 (January 1962), pp. 27-41.

Barr, James, *The Concept of Biblical Theology: An Old Testament Perspective* (Minneapolis: Augsburg–Fortress, 1999).

Barré, M.L., and J.S. Kselman, 'New Exodus, Covenant, and Restoration in Psalm 23', in Carol L. Meyers and Michael P. O'Connor (eds.), *The Word of the Lord Shall Go Forth: Essays in Honor of David Noel Freedman in Celebration of His 60th Birthday* (Winona Lake, IN: Eisenbrauns, 1983).

Barstad, Hans M., *A Way in the Wilderness: The 'Second Exodus' in the Message of 2 Isaiah* (JSS; Manchester: Manchester University Press, 1989).

Bartholomew, Craig *et al.*, *Out of Egypt: Biblical Theology and Biblical Interpretation* (Grand Rapids: Zondervan, 2006).

Batzig, Nicholas T., 'The Exodus Motif in Luke–Acts', http://feedingonchrist.com/the-exodus-motiff-in-luke-acts/, accessed 14 May 2012.

Bauckham, Richard, *Climax of Prophecy: Studies on the Book of Revelation* (Edinburgh: T. & T. Clark, 2000).

—*The Testimony of the Beloved Disciple: Narrative, History, and Theology in the Gospel of John* (Grand Rapids: Baker Academic, 2007).

Beale, G.K., *A New Testament Biblical Theology: The Unfolding of the Old Testament in the New* (Grand Rapids: Baker Academic, Kindle edn, 2011).

—*The Book of Revelation: A Commentary on the Greek Text* (NIGNT; Grand Rapids: Eerdmans, paperback edn, 2013).

—'The Use of Hosea 11:1 in Matthew 2:15: One More Time', *JETS* 55.4 (December 2012), pp. 697-715.

Beale, G.K., and David H. Campbell, *Revelation: A Shorter Commentary* (Grand Rapids: Eerdmans, Kindle edn, 2015).

Beasley-Murray, George R., *John* (WBC 36; Nashville: Thomas Nelson, 2nd edn, 1999).

—*Baptism in the New Testament* (Grand Rapids: Eerdmans, 1973).

Beaudet, Roland, 'La typologie de l'Exode dans le Second-Isaïe', *Etudes Theologiques: Tricentennaire du Seminaire de Quebec* (Quebec: Les Presses de l'Université Laval, 1963).

Blenkinsopp, Joseph, 'Scope and Depth of the Exodus Tradition in Deutero-Isaiah, 40-55', *Dynamism of Biblical Tradition* (Concilium 20; New York: Paulist Press, 1967).

Blomberg, Craig, 'Matthew', in G.K. Beale and D.A. Carson (eds.), *Commentary on the New Testament Use of the Old Testament* (Grand Rapids: Baker Academic, Kindle edn, 2007).

—'The Unity and Diversity of Scripture', T. Desmond Alexander and Brian S. Rosner (eds.), *New Dictionary of Biblical Theology* (Downers Grove, IL: InterVarsity Press, 2000).

Boismard, Marie E., 'Une Liturgie Baptismale Dans La Prima Petri', *RB* 64.2 (1957), pp. 161-83.

Borgen, Peder, *Bread From Heaven* (NovTSup X; Leiden: Brill, 1965).

Boulton, Matthew Myer, 'Supersession or Subsession? Exodus Typology, the Christian Eucharist and the Jewish Passover Meal', *SJT* 66.1 (February 2013), pp. 18-29.

Bretscher, Paul G., 'Exodus 4:22-23 and the Voice from Heaven', *JBL* 87.3 (September 1968), pp. 301-11.

Bruce, F.F., *Hebrews* (NICNT; Grand Rapids: Eerdmans, rev. Kindle edn, 1990).

—*New Testament Development of Old Testament Themes* (Eugene, OR: Wipf & Stock, 2004).

—*Paul, Apostle of the Heart Set Free* (Grand Rapids: Eerdmans, paperback edn, 2000).

—*The Book of the Acts* (NICNT; Grand Rapids: Eerdmans, rev. edn, 1988).

Brueggemann, Walter, *Reverberations of Faith: A Theological Handbook of Old Testament Themes* (Louisville, KY: Westminster / John Knox Press, 2002).

Buchanan, George Wesley, 'Isaianic Midrash and the Exodus', in Craig A. Evans and James A. Sanders (eds.), *The Function of Scripture in Early Jewish and Christian Tradition* (Sheffield, England: Sheffield Academic Press, 1998).

Burns, Rita, 'The Book of Exodus', *Exodus – A Lasting Paradigm* (Edinburgh: T. & T. Clark, 1987).

Cadbury, Henry J., *The Making of Luke-Acts* (New York: Macmillan, 1927).

Campbell, Antony F., *The Ark Narrative* (SBL Dissertation Series 16; Missoula, MT: Society of Biblical Literature, 1975).

Carson, D.A., 'I Peter', in G.K. Beale and D.A. Carson (eds.), *Commentary on the New Testament Use of the Old Testament* (Grand Rapids: Baker Academic, Kindle edn, 2007).

—*The Gospel According to John* (The Pillar New Testament Commentary; Grand Rapids: Eerdmans, 1991).

Casey, Jay Smith, *Exodus Typology in the Book of Revelation'* (PhD dissertation, The Southern Baptist Theological Seminary, 1981).

Cassuto, Umberto, *A Commentary on the Book of Genesis* (trans. Israel Abrahams; Jerusalem: Magnes Press, 1st English edn, 1964).

Ceresko, Anthony R., 'Psalm 149: Poetry, Themes (Exodus and Conquest), and Social Function', *Biblica* 67.2 (1986), pp. 177-94.

Chamy, F.A., 'Royal Priesthood: The New Exodus Framework of 1 Peter 1:1-2:10' (MA dissertation, Trinity Evangelical Divinity School, 2016).

Chevallier, Max-Alaine, 'Condition et vocation des chrétiens en diaspora: remarques exégétiques sur sa 1ʳᵉ Épître de Pierre', *RevScRel* 48.4 (1974), pp. 387-400.

Childs, Brevard S., *Biblical Theology of the Old and New Testaments: Theological Reflection on the Christian Bible* (Minneapolis: Augsburg–Fortress, 2011).

—*The Book of Exodus: A Critical, Theological Commentary* (OTL; Louisville, KY: Westminster / John Knox Press, Kindle edn, 2004).

Ciampa, Roy E., and Brian S. Rosner, *The First Letter to the Corinthians* (The Pillar New Testament Commentary; Grand Rapids: Eerdmans, 2010).

Clifford, Richard J., 'The Exodus in the Christian Bible: The Case for "Figural" Reading', *TS* 63 (2002), pp. 345-61.

Constant, Pierre, 'Le Psaume 118 et son Emploi Christologique dans Luc et Actes: Une Étude Exégétique, Littéraire et Herméneutique' (PhD dissertation, Trinity Evangelical Divinity School, 2001).

Cotton, Roger Douglas, 'The Pentecostal Significance of Numbers 11', *JPT* 10.1 (2001), pp. 3-10.

Coxon, Paul S., *Exploring the New Exodus in John: A Biblical Theological Investigation of John Chapters 5–10* (Eugene, OR: Resource Publications, 2015).

Craigie, Peter C., *The Book of Deuteronomy* (NICOT; Grand Rapids: Eerdmans, 1976).

Croy, N. Clayton, *Endurance in Suffering: Hebrews 12:1–13 in Its Rhetorical, Religious, and Philosophical Context* (SNTSMS 98; Cambridge, England: Cambridge University Press, 1998).

Cyster, R.F., 'The Lord's Prayer and the Exodus Tradition', *Theology* 64.495 (1961), pp. 377-81.

Dalman, Gustaf, *Jesus-Jeshua: Studies in the Gospels* (trans. Paul Levertoff; London: SPCK, 1929).

Daniélou, Jean, *From Shadows to Reality: Studies in the Biblical Typology of the Fathers* (trans. Wulstan Hibberd; Charleston, SC: CreateSpace Independent Publishing Platform, 2011).

Daube, David, *The Exodus Pattern in the Bible* (All Souls Studies 2; London: Faber & Faber, 1963).

Davids, Peter H., *The First Epistle of Peter* (NICNT; Grand Rapids: Eerdmans, 1990).

Davidson, Richard M., *Typology in Scripture: A Study of Hermeneutical Typos Structures* (Berrien Springs, MI: Andrews University Press, 1981).

Davies, W.D., and Dale C. Allison, *A Critical and Exegetical Commentary on the Gospel According to Saint Matthew: Introduction and Commentary on Matthew I-VII* (ICC; Edinburgh: T. & T. Clark, 1988).

Davis, J., 'Acts 2 and the Old Testament: The Pentecost Event in Light of Sinai, Babel and the Table of Nations', *Criswell Theological Review* 7.1 (2009), pp. 29-48.

Day, Adam Warner, 'Lifted up and Glorified: Isaiah's Servant Language in the Gospel of John' (PhD dissertation, The Southern Baptist Theological Seminary, 2016).

de la Potterie, Ignace, 'Le chrétien conduit par l'Esprit dans son cheminement eschatologique (Rom 8:14)', in Lorenzo De Lorenzi (ed.), *Law of the Spirit in Rom 7 and 8* (Rome: St. Paul's Abbey, 1976).

Delitzsch, Franz Julius, *Commentary on the Epistle to the Hebrews* (2 vols; Edinburgh: T. & T. Clark, 1872).

Dennison Jr., James T., 'The Exodus: Historical Narrative, Prophetic Hope, Gospel Fulfillment', *Presbyterion* 8.2 (September 1982), pp. 1-12.

deSilva, David A., *Bearing Christ's Reproach: The Challenge of Hebrews in an Honor Culture* (North Richland Hills, TX: BIBAL, 1999).

—*Honor, Patronage, Kinship & Purity: Unlocking New Testament Culture* (Downers Grove, IL: InterVarsity Press, 2000).

—*Perseverance in Gratitude: A Socio-Rhetorical Commentary on the Epistle 'To the Hebrews'* (Grand Rapids: Eerdmans, 2000).

Deterding, Paul E., 'Exodus Motifs in First Peter', *Concordia Journal* 7.2 (March 1981), pp. 58-65.

Dexinger, Ferdinand, 'Reflections on the Relationship between Qumran and Samaritan Messianology', in J.H. Charlesworth, H. Lichtenberger, and G.S. Oegema (eds.), *Qumran-Messianism: Studies on the Messianic Expectations in the Dead Sea Scrolls* (Tübingen: Mohr Siebeck, 1998).

Dobbs-Allsopp, F.W., *Lamentations* (Interpretation: A Bible Commentary for Teaching and Preaching; Louisville, KY: Westminster / John Knox Press, 2002).

Dochhorn, Jan, 'Und die Erde tat ihren Mund auf: Ein Exodusmotiv in Apc 12,16', *Zeitschrift für die Neutestamentliche Wissenschaft und die Kunde der älteren Kirche* 88.1-2 (1997), pp. 140-42.

Dohmen, Christoph, 'Exodus: Einem zentralen biblischen Motiv auf der Spur', *BK* 62 (2007), pp. 206-209.

Downing, Christine, 'How Can We Hope and Not Dream: Exodus as Metaphor: A Study of the Biblical Imagination', *JR* 48.1 (January 1968), pp. 35-53.

Dozeman, Thomas B., 'The Wilderness and Salvation History in the Hagar Story', *JBL* 117.1 (1998), pp. 23-43.

Draper, Jonathan A., 'The Heavenly Feast of Tabernacles: Revelation 7:1-17', *JSNT* 19 (October 1983), pp. 133-147.

du Rand, Jan A., and Young M. Song, 'The Story of the Red Sea as a Theological Framework of Interpretation', *Verbum et Ecclesia* 30.2 (2009), pp. 94-98.

Dumbrell, William J., *The End of the Beginning: Revelation 21-22 and the Old Testament* (Eugene, OR: Wipf & Stock, 2001).

Dunn, James D.G., *New Testament Theology: An Introduction* (Nashville: Abingdon Press, 2009).

Ehlen, Arlis John, 'Deliverance at the Sea: Diversity and Unity in a Biblical Theme', *CTM* 44.3 (May 1973), pp. 168-91.

Elgvin, Torleif, 'Priests on Earth as in Heaven: Jewish Light on the Book of Revelation', in Florentino García Martínez (ed.), *Echoes from the Caves: Qumran and the New Testament* (Studies on the Texts of the Desert of Judah 85; Leiden: Brill, 2009).

Elliott, John H., *A Home for the Homeless: A Social-Scientific Criticism of I Peter, Its Situation and Strategy* (Eugene, OR: Wipf and Stock, 2005).

Ellis, E.E., *The Old Testament in Early Christianity* (Grand Rapids: Baker Academic, 1991).

Emmrich, Martin, 'Pneumatological Concepts in Hebrews' (PhD dissertation, Westminster Theological Seminary, 2001).

Enns, Peter E., 'Creation and Re-Creation: Psalm 95 and Its Interpretation in Hebrews 3:1–4:13', *WTJ* 55 (October 1993), pp. 255-80.

Estelle, Bryan D., 'The Exodus Motif in Isaiah', *New Horizons in the Orthodox Presbyterian Church* (January 2008), http://opc.org/nh.html?article_id=534, accessed 12 June 2012.

Evans, Craig A., 'Exodus in the New Testament: Patterns of Revelation and Redemption', in Thomas B. Dozeman, Craig A. Evans, and Lohr, Joel N. (eds.), *The Book of Exodus: Composition, Reception, and Interpretation* (VTSup 164; Boston: Brill, 2014).

—*Mark 8:27-16:20* (WBC; Grand Rapids: Zondervan, 1988).

Evans, Paul S., 'The End of Kings as Presaging an Exodus: The Function of the Jehoiachin Epilogue (2 Kgs 25:27-30) in Light of Parallels with the Joseph Story in Genesis', *McMaster Journal of Theology & Ministry* 16 (January 2014), pp. 65-100.

Fee, Gordon D., *The First Epistle to the Corinthians* (Grand Rapids: Eerdmans, rev. edn, 2014).

Fishbane, Michael, *Biblical Text and Texture: A Literary Reading of Selected Texts* (Oxford: Oneworld Publications, 1998).

—*Text and Texture: Close Readings of Selected Biblical Texts* (New York: Schocken Books, 1979).

Fisher, Fred L., 'New and Greater Exodus: The Exodus Pattern in the New Testament', *Southwestern Journal of Theology* 20.1 (September 1977), pp. 69-79.

Fitzmyer, Joseph A., *The Gospel According to Luke I-IX: A New Translation with Introduction and Commentary* (AB; Garden City, NY: Doubleday, 1982).

Fletcher, Daniel H., *Signs in the Wilderness: Intertextuality and the Testing of Nicodemus* (Eugene, OR: Wipf & Stock, 2014).

Foulkes, Francis, *The Acts of God* (London: Tyndale Press, 1966).

Freedman, William, 'The Literary Motif: A Definition and Evaluation', in M.J. Hoffman and P.D. Murphy (eds.), *Essentials of the Theory of Fiction* (Durham, NC: Duke University Press, 1996).

Fretheim, Terence E., 'The Plagues as Ecological Signs of Historical Disaster', *JBL* 110.3 (September 1991), pp. 385-96.

Frisch, Amos, 'The Exodus Motif in 1 Kings 1–14', *JSOT* 87 (2000), p. 3.

Frye, Northrop, *Anatomy of Criticism: Four Essays* (Princeton, NJ: Princeton University Press, 1957).

Fung, Ronald Y.K., *The Epistle to the Galatians* (NICNT; Grand Rapids: Eerdmans, 1988).

Gadamer, Hans-Georg, *Truth and Method* (New York: Seabury, 1975).

Gallus, L., 'The Exodus Motif in Revelation 15–16: Its Background and Nature', *AUSS* 46.1 (2008), pp. 21-43.

Garsiel, Moshe, *The First Book of Samuel: A Literary Study of Comparative Structures, Analogies and Parallels* (Ramat-Gan, Israel: Revivim, 1985).

Gillingham, Susan, 'The Exodus Tradition and Israelite Psalmody', *Scottish Journal of Theology* 52.1 (1999), pp. 19-46.

Glasson, T.F., *Moses in the Fourth Gospel* (Eugene, OR: Wipf & Stock, 1963).

Goheen, Michael W., *A Light to the Nations: The Missional Church and the Biblical Story* (Grand Rapids: Baker Academic, 2011).

Goldingay, John, *The Theology of the Book of Isaiah* (Downers Grove, IL: IVP Academic, 2014).

Goldsworthy, Graeme, *According to Plan: The Unfolding Revelation of God in the Bible* (Downers Grove, IL: InterVarsity Press, Kindle edn, 1991).

Gottwald, Norman K., *Studies in the Book of Lamentations* (Studies in Biblical Theology; Chicago, IL: A.R. Allenson, 1954).

Green, Joel B., *The Gospel of Luke* (NICNT; Grand Rapids: Eerdmans, 1997).

Greenspahn, Frederick E., 'The Theology of the Framework of Judges', *VT* 36 (1986), pp. 385-96.

Guelich, Robert A., *Mark 1-8:26* (WBC 34A; Grand Rapids: Zondervan, 2015).

Guthrie, Donald, *New Testament Introduction* (Downers Grove, IL: InterVarsity Press, 4th edn, 1990).

Guthrie, George H., *Hebrews* (The NIV Application Commentary; Grand Rapids: Zondervan, 1998).

—'Hebrews', in G.K. Beale and D.A. Carson (eds.), *Commentary on the New Testament Use of the Old Testament* (Grand Rapids: Baker Academic, Kindle edn, 2007).

—'Old Testament in Hebrews', Ralph P. Martin and Peter H. Davids (eds.), *Dictionary of the Later New Testament and Its Developments* (Downers Grove, IL: InterVarsity Press, 1997).

Hahn, Scott, 'Worship in the Word: Toward a Liturgical Hermeneutic', *Letter & Spirit* 1 (2005), pp. 101-36.

Hahn, Scott, *et al.* (eds.), *Canon and Biblical Interpretation* (Scripture and Hermeneutics; Grand Rapids: Zondervan, 2006).

Hasel, Gerhard, *Old Testament Theology: Basic Issues in the Current Debate* (Grand Rapids: Eerdmans, 4th edn, 1991).

Haugen, Philip S., *The Consummation of the Exodus: A Study of the Exodus Motif in the Revelation* (Concordia Seminary, 1985).

Hay, Lewis Scott, 'What Really Happened at the Sea of Reeds', *JBL* 83.4 (December 1964), pp. 397-403.

Hays, Richard B., *Echoes of Scripture in the Letters of Paul* (New Haven: Yale University Press, 1989).

—*Reading Backwards: Figural Christology and the Fourfold Gospel Witness* (Waco, TX: Baylor University Press, Kindle edn, 2014).

Hendel, Ronald S., 'The Exodus in Biblical Memory', *JBL* 120.4 (2001), pp. 601-22.

Hernando, James D., 'Modern Literary Approaches and Biblical Hermeneutics' (Unpublished seminar paper presented at the National Educators' Conference of the Assemblies of God, Minneapolis, 1992).

Hicks, John Mark, 'A Sacramental Journey: A Christian-Theological Reading of Exodus', *Leaven* 21.2 (January 2013), pp. 60-64.

Hobbs, Edward Craig, 'The Gospel of Mark and the Exodus' (PhD dissertation, The University of Chicago, 1958).

Hoffman, Yair, 'A North Israelite Typological Myth and a Judaean Historical Tradition: The Exodus in Hosea and Amos', *VT* 39.2 (April 1989), pp. 169-82.

Hoffmeier, James K., *Ancient Israel in Sinai: The Evidence for the Authenticity of the Wilderness Tradition* (New York: Oxford University Press, 2011).

—*Israel in Egypt: The Evidence for the Authenticity of the Exodus Tradition* (New York: Oxford University Press, 1996).

Holladay, William L., *A Commentary on the Book of the Prophet Jeremiah Chapters 1-25* (Hermeneia: A Critical and Historical Commentary on the Bible; Philadelphia: Fortress Press, 1986).

Holland, Tom, *Contours of Pauline Theology: A Radical New Survey of the Influences on Paul's Biblical Writings* (Geanies House, Scotland: Mentor, 2010).

Holm, Tawny, 'Moses in the Prophets and Writings of the Hebrew Bible', *Illuminating Moses: A History of Reception from Exodus to the Renaissance* (Boston: Brill, 2014).

Howard, J.K., 'Christ Our Passover'': A Study of the Passover-Exodus Theme in 1 Corinthians', *EvQ* 41 (April 1969), pp. 97-108.

Hübner, Hans, *Law in Paul's Thought: A Contribution to the Development of Pauline Theology* (ed. John Riches (ed.), trans. James C.G. Grieg; London: T. & T. Clark, 3rd edn, 2004).

Hui, Timothy K., 'The Purpose of Israel's Annual Feasts', *BSac* 147.598 (1990), pp. 143-54.

Hung, Emmanuel Yun-wing, 'Relationship and Rebirth: A Literary Study of the Exodus Motif in Jeremiah' (PhD dissertation, Westminster Theological Seminary, 2001).

Hunter, Alastair, 'Jonah from the Whale: Exodus Motifs in Jonah 2', in Johannes C. De Moor (ed.), *The Elusive Prophet: The Prophet as a Historical Person, Literary Character, and Anonymous Artist* (Oudtestamentische Studien 45; Atlanta: Society of Biblical Literature, 2005).

Hyde, Clark, 'The Remembrance of the Exodus in the Psalms', *Worship* 62.5 (September 1988), pp. 404-14.

Iersel, Bas van, Antonius Weiler, and Marcus Lefébure (eds.), *Exodus—A Lasting Paradigm* (Concilium: Religion in the Eighties 189; Edinburgh: T. & T. Clark, 1987).

Isbell, Barbara Ann, 'The Past Is yet to Come: Exodus Typology in the Apocalypse' (PhD dissertation, Southwestern Baptist Theological Seminary, 2013).

Isbell, Charles David, *The Function of Exodus Motifs in Biblical Narratives: Theological Didactic Drama* (Studies in the Bible and Early Christianity 52; Lewiston, NY: Edwin Mellen Press, 2002).

Joseph, Abson Prédestin, *A Narratological Reading of 1 Peter* (Library of New Testament Studies; London: Bloomsbury T. & T. Clark, 2012).

Joslin, Barry Clyde, 'Christ Bore the Sins of Many: Substitution and the Atonement in Hebrews', *The Southern Baptist Journal of Theology* 11.2 (2007), pp. 74-103.

Käsemann, Ernst, *The Wandering People of God: An Investigation of the Letter to the Hebrews* (trans. Harrisville, Roy A. and Irving L. Sandberg; Eugene, OR: Wipf & Stock, 2002).

Keener, Craig S., *Revelation* (The NIV Application Commentary; Grand Rapids: Zondervan, 2000).

—*Romans: A New Covenant Commentary* (New Covenant Commentary Series 6; Eugene, OR: Wipf & Stock, Kindle edn, 2009).

—*The Gospel of John: A Commentary* (2 vols; Grand Rapids: Baker Academic, 2003).

Keesmaat, Sylvia C., *Paul and His Story: (Re)Interpreting the Exodus Tradition* (JSNTSup 181; Sheffield: Sheffield Academic Press, 1999).

Keil, Carl Friedrich, and Franz Julius Delitzsch, *Commentary on the Old Testament* (10 vols.; Grand Rapids: Eerdmans, 1988).

Kennedy, R. Joel, 'The Recapitulation of Israel: Use of Israel's History in Matthew 1:1-4:11' (PhD thesis, University of Aberdeen, 2008).

Ki, Dongyoun, 'The Temple, Holy War, and Kingship in Haggai: A Text-Linguistic and Inner-Biblical Study' (PhD dissertation, Trinity Evangelical Divinity School, 2001).

Kistemaker, Simon J., *Acts* (New Testament Commentary; Grand Rapids: Baker Academic, 1991).

—*Exposition of the Epistle to the Hebrews* (New Testament Commentary; Grand Rapids: Baker Book House, 1984).

Kitchen, K.A., 'Egyptians and Hebrews, from Ra'amses to Jericho', *The Origin of Early Israel* (Beer-Sheva, Israel: Ben-Gurion University of the Negev Press, 1998).

—'Exodus, The', in David Noel Freedman *et al.* (eds.), *ABD* (New York: Doubleday, 1992).

—*On the Reliability of the Old Testament* (Grand Rapids: Eerdmans, 2003).

Klein, Ralph W., 'Theology for Exiles: The Kingship of Yahweh', *Dialog* 17.2 (1978), pp. 128-34.

Knowles, Melody D., 'Pilgrimage Imagery in the Returns in Ezra', *JBL* 123.1 (Spring 2004), pp. 57–74.

Köstenberger, Andreas J., 'John', in G.K. Beale and D.A. Carson (eds.), *Commentary on the New Testament Use of the Old Testament* (Grand Rapids: Baker Academic, Kindle edn, 2007).

Kuhn, Thomas, *The Structure of Scientific Revolutions* (Chicago, IL: University of Chicago Press, 1970).

Kurz, William S., *Reading Luke-Acts: Dynamics of Biblical Narrative* (Louisville, KY: Westminster / John Knox Press, 1993).

Laansma, Jon C., 'Hebrews, Book of', in Kevin J. Vanhoozer *et al.* (eds.), *Dictionary for Theological Interpretation of the Bible* (Grand Rapids: Baker Academic, 2005).

Lampe, G.W.H., 'The Reasonableness of Typology', in (by) G.W.H. Lampe and K.J. Woollcombe, *Essays on Typology* (SBT; London: SCM Press, 1957).

Lane, William L., *The Gospel According to Mark* (NICNT; Grand Rapids: Eerdmans, 2nd rev. edn, 1974).

—'Times of Refreshment: A Study of Eschatological Periodization in Judaism and Christianity' (ThD dissertation, Harvard Divinity School, 1962).

Lapide, Pinchas, 'Exodus in the Jewish Tradition', in Bas van Iersel, Anton Weiler, and Marcus Lefébure (eds.), *Exodus: A Lasting Paradigm* (Concilium: Religion in the Eighties 189; Edinburgh: T. & T. Clark, 1987).

Leithart, Peter, 'Passover and the Structure of Joshua 2', *Biblical Horizons* 99 (November 1997), http://www.biblicalhorizons.com/biblical-horizons/no-99-passover-and-the-structure-of-joshua-2/, accessed 25 October 2012.

Leuchter, Mark, 'Samuel: A Prophet like Moses or a Priest like Moses?', in Mignon R. Jacobs and Raymond F. Person Jr. (eds.), *Israelite Prophecy and the Deuteronomistic History: Portrait, Reality, and the Formation of History* (Ancient Israel and Its Literature 14; Atlanta: Society of Biblical Literature, 2013).

Long, Thomas G., *Hebrews* (IBC; Louisville, KY: Westminster / John Knox Press, 1997).

Longman, Tremper, 'Divine Warrior: The New Testament Use of an Old Testament Motif', *WTJ* 44.2 (October 1982), pp. 290-307.

Louw, Johannes E., and Eugene A. Nida (eds.), *Greek-English Lexicon of the New Testament Based on Semantic Domains* (2 vols; New York: United Bible Societies, 2nd edn, 1989).

Lund, Øystein, *Way Metaphors and Way Topics in Isaiah* (Forschungen Zum Alten Testament II 28; Tübingen: Mohr Siebeck, 2007).

Lundberg, Per, *Typologie Baptismale Dans L'Ancienne Église* (Leipzig, Germany: Alfred Lorentz, 1942).

Lundbom, Jack R., *Jeremiah: Prophet Like Moses* (Eugene, OR: Cascade Companions, 2015).

Luzarraga, Jesús, *Las Tradiciones de la Nube en la Biblia y en el Judaismo Primitivo* (Analecta Biblica 54; Rome: Pontifical Biblical Institute Press, 1973).

Macchia, Frank D., *Baptized in the Spirit: A Global Pentecostal Theology* (Grand Rapids: Zondervan, 2006).

—*Justified in the Spirit: Creation, Redemption, and the Triune God* (Pentecostal Manifestos: Grand Rapids: Eerdmans, 2010).

Malamat, Abraham, 'The Exodus: Egyptian Analogies', in Ernest S. Frerichs, Leonard H. Lesko, and William G. Dever (eds.), *Exodus: The Egyptian Evidence* (Winona Lake, IN: Eisenbrauns, 1997).

Mánek, Jindřich, 'New Exodus [of Jesus] in the Books of Luke', *NovT* 2.1 (January 1957), pp. 8-23.

Marshall, I. Howard, 'Acts', in G.K. Beale and D.A. Carson (eds.), *Commentary on the New Testament Use of the Old Testament* (Grand Rapids: Baker Academic, Kindle edn, 2007).

—*Luke: Historian & Theologian* (New Testament Profiles; Downers Grove, IL: InterVarsity Press, 3rd edn, 2001).

—*New Testament Theology: Many Witnesses, One Gospel* (Downers Grove, IL: InterVarsity Press, Kindle edn, 2004).

Martens, Elmer A., *Plot and Purpose in the Old Testament* (Leicester: Inter-Varsity Press, 1981).

Martens, Larry D., 'The Echoes of Moses in Judges: A Study of the Echo Narrative Technique in Exodus 3:1-15, Judges 6:11-21, and Judges 13:1-25' (MA thesis, Providence College and Seminary (Canada), 1995).

Martin, Lee Roy, 'Where Are All His Wonders?": The Exodus Motif in the Book of Judges', *Journal of Biblical & Pneumatological Research* 2 (2010), pp. 87–109.

Mathewson, D., 'New Exodus as a Background for "The Sea Was No More" in Revelation 21:1c', *Trinity Journal* 24.2 (2003), pp. 243-58.

—'Reading Heb 6:4-6 in Light of the Old Testament', *WTJ* 61.2 (Fall 1999), pp. 209-25.

Mauser, Ulrich, *Christ in the Wilderness: The Wilderness Theme in the Second Gospel and Its Basis in the Biblical Tradition* (Studies in Biblical Theology; London: SCM Press, 1963).

McGhee, Faith, 'Holiness and the Path of Suffering: Lessons for Pentecostals from the Book of Hebrews', in Lee Roy Martin (ed.), *A Future for Holiness: Pentecostal Explorations* (Cleveland, TN: CPT Press, 2013).

McGhee, Quentin, Steve Eutsler, and John Wesley Adams, *Gospel of John: The Word Became Flesh* (Faith & Action; Springfield, MO: Faith & Action Team, 2016).

McKeating, Henry, 'Ezekiel the "Prophet Like Moses"', *JSOT* 19.61 (March 1994), pp. 97-109.

McKnight, Edgar V., *Post-Modern Use of the Bible: The Emergence of Reader-Oriented Criticism* (Nashville: Abingdon Press, 1988).

Meeks, Wayne A., *The Prophet King: Moses Traditions and the Johannine Christology* (Leiden: Brill, 1967).

Meier, Sam A., 'History of Israel I: Settlement Period', in Bill T. Arnold and H.G.M. Williamson (eds.), *Dictionary of Old Testament Historical Books* (Downers Grove, IL: InterVarsity Press, 2005).

Metzger, Bruce M., *A Textual Commentary On The Greek New Testament* (Stuttgart: Deutsche Bibelgesellschaft, 2nd edn, 1994).

Michaels, J. Ramsey, *The Gospel of John* (NICNT; Grand Rapids: Eerdmans, 2010).

Miller, David Marvin, 'Seeing the Glory, Hearing the Son: The Function of the Wilderness Theophany Narratives in Luke 9:28-36', *CBQ* 72.3 (July 2010), pp. 498-517.

Moessner, David P., 'Luke 9:1-50: Luke's Preview of the Journey of the Prophet like Moses of Deuteronomy', *JBL* 102.4 (December 1983), pp. 575-605.

Moo, Douglas, *The Epistle to the Romans* (NICNT; Grand Rapids: Eerdmans, 1996).

Moritz, Thorsten, 'Mark, Book of', Kevin J. Vanhoozer *et al.* (eds.), *Dictionary for Theological Interpretation of the Bible* (Grand Rapids: Baker Book House, 2005).

Morris, Leon, *The Gospel According to John* (NICNT; Grand Rapids: Eerdmans, rev. edn, 1995).

Mounce, Robert H., *The Book of Revelation* (NICNT; Grand Rapids: Eerdmans, rev. edn, 1998).

Müller, Hans-Peter, 'Die Plagen der Apokalypse: Eine formgeschichtliche Untersuchung', *Zeitschrift für die Neutestamentliche Wissenschaft und die Kunde der älteren Kirche* 51.3–4 (1960), pp. 268-78.

Myers, Jacob M., *Ezra, Nehemiah* (AB; New Haven: Yale University Press, 1995).

Nash, Ronald H., *Christianity & the Hellenistic World* (Bible Study Commentary Series; Grand Rapids: Zondervan, 1984).

Neusner, Jacob, trans., *The Mishnah: A New Translation* (New Haven: Yale University Press, 1988).

Ninow, Friedbert, *Indicators of Typology Within the Old Testament: The Exodus Motif* (Friedensauer Schriftenreihe; Bern: Peter Lang, 2001).

Nixon, R.E., *Exodus in the New Testament* (London: Tyndale Press, 1963).

Nolland, John, *Luke 1:1-9:20* (WBC 35A; Nashville: Thomas Nelson, 1989).

Ollenburger, Ben C., *Old Testament Theology: Flowering and Future* (Winona Lake, IN: Eisenbrauns, 2004).

Osborne, Thomas P., 'L'utilisation des citations de l'Ancien Testament dans la première epître de Pierre', *Revue Théologique de Louvain* 12.1 (1981), pp. 64-77.

Oss, Douglas A., 'A Note on Paul's Use of Isaiah', *Bulletin for Biblical Research* 2 (1992), pp. 105-12.

—'Paul's Use of Isaiah and Its Place in His Theology with Special Reference to Romans 9–11' (PhD dissertation, Westminster Theological Seminary, 1992).

—'The Interpretation of the "Stone" Passages by Peter and Paul: A Comparative Study', *JETS* 32.2 (1989), pp. 181-200.

Palmer Bonz, Marianne, 'The Best of Times, the Worst of Times: Luke-Acts and Epic Tradition' (ThD dissertation, Harvard Divinity School, 1996).

Pao, David W., *Acts and the Isaianic New Exodus* (WUNT 130; Tübingen: Mohr Siebeck, 2000).

Parry, Robin, 'Prolegomena to Christian Theological Interpretation of Lamentations', in Scott Hahn *et al.* (eds.), *Canon and Biblical Interpretation* (Scripture and Hermeneutics 7; Grand Rapids: Zondervan, Kindle edn, 2006).

Patterson, Richard D., and Michael Travers, 'Contours of the Exodus Motif in Jesus' Earthly Ministry', *WTJ* 66.1 (Spring 2004), pp. 25-47.

Pearce, Matthew Alan, 'The Redemptive Function and Theological Meaning of Matthew's Citation of Hosea 11:1' (PhD dissertation, The Southern Baptist Theological Seminary, 2008).

Peterson, David, *Hebrews and Perfection: An Examination of the Concept of Perfection in the 'Epistle to the Hebrews'* (Cambridge, England: Cambridge University Press, 1982).

Piper, Otto Alfred, 'Unchanging Promises: Exodus in the New Testament', *Int* 11.1 (January 1957), pp. 3-22.

Pitre, Brant, *Jesus and the Last Supper* (Grand Rapids: Eerdmans, Kindle edn, 2015).

—'The Lord's Prayer and the New Exodus', *Letter & Spirit* 2 (2005), pp. 69-96.

Prevallet, Elaine Marie, 'The Use of the Exodus in Interpreting History', *CTM* 37.3 (1966), pp. 131-45.

Prince, Gerald, *A Dictionary of Narratology* (Lincoln, NE: University of Nebraska Press, rev. edn, 2003).

Rad, Gerhard von, 'Typological Interpretation of the Old Testament', *Int* 15.2 (1961), pp. 174-92.

Redford, Donald B., 'Observations of the Sojourn of the Bene-Israel', in Ernest S. Frerichs, Leonard H. Lesko, and William G. Dever (eds.), *Exodus: The Egyptian Evidence* (Winona Lake, IN: Eisenbrauns, 1997).

Rendtorff, Rolf, *The Canonical Hebrew Bible: A Theology of the Old Testament* (trans. David E. Orton; Tools for Biblical Study 7; Leiden: Deo, 2005).

Resseguie, James L., *Narrative Criticism of the New Testament: An Introduction* (Grand Rapids: Baker Academic, 2005).

Reynolds, James Ellis, 'A Comparative Study of the Exodus Motif in the Epistle to the Hebrews' (ThD dissertation, Southwestern Baptist Theological Seminary, 1976).

Rohl, David M., *Pharaohs and Kings: A Biblical Quest* (New York: Three Rivers Press, 1997).

Rosner, Brian S., 'Biblical Theology', in T. Desmond Alexander and Brian S. Rosner (eds.), *New Dictionary of Biblical Theology: Exploring the Unity & Diversity of Scripture* (Downers Grove, IL: InterVarsity Press, 2000).

Rosner, Brian S. *et al.* (eds.), *New Dictionary of Biblical Theology: Exploring the Unity & Diversity of Scripture* (Downers Grove, IL: InterVarsity Press, 2000).

Runions, J. Ernest, 'Exodus Motifs in First Samuel 7 and 8: A Brief Comment', *EvQ* 52 (July 1980), pp. 130-31.

Ryken, Leland, *Words of Delight: A Literary Introduction to the Bible* (Grand Rapids: Baker Book House, 2nd edn, 1992).

Ryken, Leland, James C. Wilhoit, and Tremper Longman III (eds.), 'Exodus, Second Exodus', *Dictionary of Biblical Imagery* (Downers Grove, IL: InterVarsity Press, 1998).

Sailhamer, John, *The Pentateuch As Narrative: A Biblical-Theological Commentary* (Grand Rapids: Zondervan, 1992).

Sanders, E.P., *Paul and Palestinian Judaism* (Philadelphia: Fortress Press, 1977).

Sandys-Wunsch, John, and Laurence Eldredge, 'J.P. Gabler and the Distinction between Biblical and Dogmatic Theology: Translation, Commentary, and Discussion of His Originality', *SJT* 33.2 (1980), pp. 133-58.

Sargent, Benjamin, 'The Narrative Substructure of 1 Peter', *ExpTim* 124.10 (2013), pp. 485-90.

—*Written to Serve: The Use of Scripture in 1 Peter* (Library of New Testament Studies 547; London: Bloomsbury T. & T. Clark, 2015).

Savran, George, '1 and 2 Kings', in Robert Alter and Frank Kermode (eds.), *The Literary Guide to the Bible* (Cambridge, MA: The Belknap Press of Harvard University Press, 1987).

Schutter, William L., *Hermeneutic and Composition in I Peter* (WUNT; Tübingen: Mohr Siebeck, 1989).

Scott, James M., *Adoption as Sons of God: An Exegetical Investigation into the Background in the Pauline Corpus* (WUNT; Tübingen: Mohr Siebeck, 1992).

Seifrid, Mark A., 'Romans', in Andreas J. Köstenberger, G.K. Beale, and D.A. Carson (eds.), *Commentary on the New Testament Use of the Old Testament* (Grand Rapids: Baker Academic, Kindle edn, 2007).

Selwyn, E.G., *The First Epistle of St. Peter: The Greek Text with Introduction, Notes and Essays* (Grand Rapids: Baker Book House, 1981).

Simian-Yofre, Horacio, 'Exodo En Deuteroisaias', *BIB* 61.4 (1980), pp. 530-53.

Smend, Rudolf, 'Mose als geschichtliche Gestalt', *HZ* 260 (1995), pp. 1-19.

Smith, Daniel Lynwood, 'The Uses of "New Exodus" in New Testament Scholarship: Preparing a Way through the Wilderness', *Currents in Biblical Research* 14.2 (February 2016), pp. 207-43.

Snaith, Norman H., and Harry M. Orlinsky, *Studies on the Second Part of the Book of Isaiah* (VTSup 14; Leiden: Brill, 1967).

Son, HaYoung, 'The Background of Exodus 15 in Revelation 15: Focusing on the Song of Moses and the Song of the Lamb' (PhD dissertation, New Orleans Baptist Theological Seminary, 2015).

Stein, Robert H., 'The Benefits of an Author-Oriented Approach to Hermeneutics', *JETS* 44.3 (September 2001), pp. 451-66.

Stendahl, Krister, 'Contemporary Biblical Theology', in George A. Buttrick (ed.), *IDB* (Nashville: Abingdon Press, 1962).

Stevens, B.A., '"Why Must the Son of Man Suffer?" The Divine Warrior in the Gospel of Mark', *BZ* 31.1 (1987), pp. 101-10.

Stock, Augustine, *The Way in the Wilderness: Exodus, Wilderness and Moses Themes in Old Testament and New* (Collegeville, MN: The Liturgical Press, 1969).

Strauss, Mark L., 'The Davidic Messiah in Luke-Acts: The Promise and Its Fulfillment in Lukan Christology' (PhD thesis, University of Aberdeen, UK, 1992).

Stronstad, Roger, *The Charismatic Theology of St. Luke* (Peabody, MA: Hendrickson, 1984).

Stuhlmacher, Peter (ed.), *Das Evangelium Und Die Evangelien* (WUNT 28; Tübingen: Mohr Siebeck, 1983).

Stuhlmueller, Carroll, *Creative Redemption in Deutero-Isaiah* (Analecta Biblica 43; Rome: Pontifical Biblical Institute Press, 1970).

Tate, W. Randolph, *Biblical Interpretation: An Integrated Approach* (Grand Rapids: Baker Academic, 3rd edn, 2014).

—*Interpreting the Bible: A Handbook of Terms and Methods* (Peabody, MA: Hendrickson Publishers, 2006).

Teeple, Howard Merle, *The Mosaic Eschatological Prophet* (Philadelphia: Society of Biblical Literature, 1957).

Thiessen, Matthew, 'Hebrews and the End of the Exodus', *NovT* 49.4 (2007), pp. 353–69.

Throntveit, Mark A., *Ezra–Nehemiah* (Interpretation: A Bible Commentary for Teaching and Preaching; Louisville, KY: Westminster / John Knox, 1992).

Tracy, David, 'Exodus: Theological Reflection', in Bas van Iersel, Anton Weiler, and Marcus Lefébure (eds.), *Exodus: A Lasting Paradigm* (Concilium: Religion in the Eighties 189; Edinburgh: T. & T. Clark, 1987).

Tsan, Tsong-Sheng, 'New Exodus": A Theological Enquiry of the Exodus Motif in Isaiah 19:16-25', *Taiwan Journal of Theology* 32 (2010), pp. 1–22.

Tsevat, M., 'Hagar and the Birth of Ishmael', in *The Meaning of the Book of Job and Other Biblical Studies: Essays on the Literature and Religion of the Hebrew Bible* (New York: KTAV, 1980).

Turner, Max, *Power From on High: The Spirit in Israel's Restoration and Witness in Luke-Acts* (JPTSup 9; Sheffield: Sheffield Academic Press, 1996).

VanDrunen, David, 'Israel's Recapitulation of Adam's Probation under the Law of Moses', *The Westminster Theological Journal* 73.2 (September 2011), pp. 303-24.

Vanhoozer, Kevin J. (ed.), *Dictionary for Theological Interpretation of the Bible* (Grand Rapids: Baker Academic, 2005).

—*The Drama of Doctrine: A Canonical Linguistic Approach to Christian Doctrine* (Louisville, KY: Westminster / John Knox Press, 2005).

Vos, Geerhardus, *Biblical Theology: Old and New Testaments* (Edinburgh: Banner of Truth, rev. edn, 1975).

—*The Teaching of the Epistle to the Hebrews* (ed. Johannes G. Vos; Nutley, NJ: Presbyterian & Reformed, 1976).

Vriezen, Th. C., *An Outline of Old Testament Theology* (Oxford: Basil Blackwell, 2nd edn, 1970).

Wallace, Daniel B., *Greek Grammar Beyond the Basics: An Exegetical Syntax of the New Testament* (Grand Rapids: Zondervan, 1996).

Walsh, Jerome T., 'Elijah', in David Noel Freedman *et al.* (eds.), *ABD* (New York: Doubleday, 1992).

Watson, Francis, *Text and Truth: Redefining Biblical Theology* (Grand Rapids: Eerdmans, 2009).

Watts, R.E., 'Exodus', Brian S. Rosner *et al.* (eds.), *New Dictionary of Biblical Theology: Exploring the Unity & Diversity of Scripture* (Downers Grove, IL: IVP Academic, 2000).

Watts, Rikk E., 'Mark', in G.K. Beale and D.A. Carson (eds.), *Commentary on the New Testament Use of the Old Testament* (Grand Rapids: Baker Academic, Kindle edn, 2007).

—'Consolation or Confrontation: Isaiah 40-55 and the Delay of the New Exodus', *TynBul* 41.1 (May 1990), pp. 31-59.

—*Isaiah's New Exodus in Mark* (Grand Rapids: Baker Academic, 1997).

Webb, William J., *Returning Home: New Covenant and Second Exodus as the Context for 2 Corinthians 6:14-7:1* (Sheffield: Sheffield Academic Press, 1993).

Weinfeld, Moshe, 'Pentecost as Festival of the Giving of the Law', *Immanuel* 8 (1978), pp. 7-18.

Wenham, David, and Steve Walton, *A Guide to the Gospels & Acts* (Exploring the New Testament; Downers Grove, IL: IVP Academic, 2nd edn, 2011).

Wijk-Bos, Johanna W.H. van, *Ezra, Nehemiah, and Esther* (WBC; Louisville, KY: Westminster / John Knox Press, 1998).

Wilder, William Nelson, 'Freed from the Law to Be Led by the Spirit: Echoes of the Exodus Narrative in the Context and Background of Galatians 5:18' (PhD dissertation, Union Theological Seminary in Virginia, 1996).

Wilson, Gerald Henry, *The Editing of the Hebrew Psalter* (SBLSDS 76; Chico, CA: Scholars Press, 1985).

Wold, Benjamin G., 'Revelation's Plague Septets: New Exodus and Exile', in Florentino García Martínez (ed.), *Echoes from the Caves: Qumran and the New Testament* (STDJ 85; Leiden: Brill, 2009).

Wong, Gregory T.K., 'Gideon: A New Moses?', in Robert Rezetko, Timothy L. Lim, and W. Brian Auker (eds.), *Reflection and Refraction: Studies in Biblical Historiography in Honour of A. Graeme Auld* (VTSup; Leiden: Brill, 2007).

Woollcombe, K.J., 'The Biblical Origins and Patristic Development of Typology', in (by) G.W.H. Lampe and K.J. Woollcombe, *Essays on Typology* (SBT; London: SCM Press, 1957).

Woudstra, Marten H., *The Book of Joshua* (NICOT; Grand Rapids: Eerdmans, 1981).

Wright, N.T., *Jesus and the Victory of God* (Christian Origins and the Question of God 2; Philadelphia: Fortress Press, 1997).

—'New Exodus and New Inheritance: The Narrative Structure of Romans 3–8', in *Romans and the People of God: Essays in Honor of Gordon D. Fee on the Occasion of His 65th Birthday* (Grand Rapids: Eerdmans, 1999).

—*Paul: In Fresh Perspective* (Philadelphia: Fortress Press, 2009).

—*The Climax of the Covenant: Christ and the Law in Pauline Theology* (Philadelphia: Fortress Press, 1993).

—'The Lord's Prayer as a Paradigm of Christian Prayer', http://ntwrightpage.com/Wright_Christian_Prayer.htm, accessed 29 January 2014.

—'The New Inheritance According to Paul: The Letter to the Romans Re-Enacts for All Peoples the Israelite Exodus from Egypt to the Promised Land – from Slavery to Freedom', *Bible Review* 14.3 (1998), p. 16-47.

—*The New Testament and the People of God* (Christian Origins and the Question of God; Philadelphia: Fortress Press, 1992).

—*The Resurrection of the Son of God* (Christian Origins and the Question of God 3; Philadelphia: Fortress Press, 2003).

—*What Saint Paul Really Said: Was Paul of Tarsus the Real Founder of Christianity?* (Grand Rapids: Eerdmans, 1997).

Wu, Peter Jung-Chu, 'Worthy Is the Lamb: The New Song in Revelation 5:9–10 in Relation to Its Background' (PhD dissertation, Westminster Theological Seminary, 2005).

Yoder, John Howard, 'Exodus and Exile: The Two Faces of Liberation', *Cross Currents* 23.3 (Fall 1973), pp. 297-309.

Zakovitch, Yair, *'And You Shall Tell Your Son ...': The Concept of the Exodus in the Bible* (Jerusalem: Magnes Press, 1991).

Zeller, Eric W., 'Intertextuality in 1 Peter 2:9-12: Peter's Biblical-Theological Summary of the Mission of God's People' (PhD dissertation, Dallas Theological Seminary, 2013).

Zimmerli, Walther, *Ezechiel* (Biblischer Kommentar Altes Testament VIII; Neukirchen-Vluyn: Neukirchener Verlag, 1979).

INDEX OF AUTHORS

www.ingramcontent.com/pod-product-compliance
Lightning Source LLC
Chambersburg PA
CBHW072138090426
42739CB00013B/3217